Evolution in Reference and Information Services: The Impact of the Internet

Evolution in Reference and Information Services: The Impact of the Internet has been co-published simultaneously as *The Reference Librarian*, Number 74 2001.

<u>The Reference Librarian</u> Monographic "Separates"

Below is a list of "separates," which in serials librarianship means a special issue simultaneously published as a special journal issue or double-issue *and* as a "separate" hardbound monograph. (This is a format which we also call a "DocuSerial.")

"Separates" are published because specialized libraries or professionals may wish to purchase a specific thematic issue by itself in a format which can be separately cataloged and shelved, as opposed to purchasing the journal on an on-going basis. Faculty members may also more easily consider a "separate" for classroom adoption.

"Separates" are carefully classified separately with the major book jobbers so that the journal tie-in can be noted on new book order slips to avoid duplicate purchasing.

You may wish to visit Haworth's Website at . . .

http://www.HaworthPress.com

. . . to search our online catalog for complete tables of contents of these separates and related publications.

You may also call 1-800-HAWORTH (outside US/Canada: 607-722-5857), or Fax 1-800-895-0582 (outside US/Canada: 607-771-0012), or e-mail at:

getinfo@haworthpressinc.com

Evolution in Reference and Information Services: The Impact of the Internet, edited by Di Su, MLS (No. 74, 2001). *Helps you make the most of the changes brought to the profession by the Internet.*

Doing the Work of Reference: Practical Tips for Excelling as a Reference Librarian, edited by Celia Hales Mabry, PhD (No. 72 and 73, 2001). *"An excellent handbook for reference librarians who wish to move from novice to expert. Topical coverage is extensive and is presented by the best guides possible: practicing reference librarians." (Rebecca Watson-Boone, PhD, President, Center for the Study of Information Professionals, Inc.)*

New Technologies and Reference Services, edited by Bill Katz, PhD (No. 71, 2000). *This important book explores developing trends in publishing, information literacy in the reference environment, reference provision in adult basic and community education, searching sessions, outreach programs, locating moving image materials for multimedia development, and much more.*

Reference Services for the Adult Learner: Challenging Issues for the Traditional and Technological Era, edited by Kwasi Sarkodie-Mensah, PhD (No. 69/70, 2000). *Containing research from librarians and adult learners from the United States, Canada, and Australia, this comprehensive guide offers you strategies for teaching adult patrons that will enable them to properly use and easily locate all of the materials in your library.*

Library Outreach, Partnerships, and Distance Education: Reference Librarians at the Gateway, edited by Wendi Arant and Pixey Anne Mosley (No. 67/68, 1999). *Focuses on community outreach in libraries toward a broader public by extending services based on recent developments in information technology.*

From Past-Present to Future-Perfect: A Tribute to Charles A. Bunge and the Challenges of Contemporary Reference Service, edited by Chris D. Ferguson, PhD (No. 66, 1999). *Explore reprints of selected articles by Charles Bunge, bibliographies of his published work, and original articles that draw on Bunge's values and ideas in assessing the present and shaping the future of reference service.*

Reference Services and Media, edited by Martha Merrill, PhD (No. 65, 1999). *Gives you valuable information about various aspects of reference services and media, including changes, planning issues, and the use and impact of new technologies.*

Coming of Age in Reference Services: A Case History of the Washington State University Libraries, edited by Christy Zlatos, MSLS (No. 64, 1999). *A celebration of the perseverance, ingenuity, and talent of the librarians who have served, past and present, at the Holland Library reference desk.*

Document Delivery Services: Contrasting Views, edited by Robin Kinder, MLS (No. 63, 1999). *Reviews the planning and process of implementing document delivery in four university libraries–Miami University, University of Colorado at Denver, University of Montana at Missoula, and Purdue University Libraries.*

The Holocaust: Memories, Research, Reference, edited by Robert Hauptman, PhD, and Susan Hubbs Motin (No. 61/62, 1998). *"A wonderful resource for reference librarians, students, and teachers . . . on how to present this painful, historical event." (Ephraim Kaye, PhD, The International School for Holocaust Studies, Yad Vashem, Jerusalem)*

Electronic Resources: Use and User Behavior, edited by Hemalata Iyer, PhD (No. 60, 1998). *Covers electronic resources and their use in libraries, with emphasis on the Internet and the Geographic Information Systems (GIS).*

Philosophies of Reference Service, edited by Celia Hales Mabry (No. 59, 1997). *"Recommended reading for any manager responsible for managing reference services and hiring reference librarians in any type of library." (Charles R. Anderson, MLS, Associate Director for Public Services, King County Library System, Bellevue, Washington)*

Business Reference Services and Sources: How End Users and Librarians Work Together, edited by Katherine M. Shelfer (No. 58, 1997). *"This is an important collection of papers suitable for all business librarians. . . . Highly recommended!" (Lucy Heckman, MLS, MBA, Business and Economics Reference Librarian, St. John's University, Jamaica, New York)*

Reference Sources on the Internet: Off the Shelf and onto the Web, edited by Karen R. Diaz (No. 57, 1997). *Surf off the library shelves and onto the Internet and cut your research time in half!*

Reference Services for Archives and Manuscripts, edited by Laura B. Cohen (No. 56, 1997). *"Features stimulating and interesting essays on security in archives, ethics in the archival profession, and electronic records." ("The Year's Best Professional Reading" (1998), Library Journal)*

Career Planning and Job Searching in the Information Age, edited by Elizabeth A. Lorenzen, MLS (No. 55, 1996). *"Offers stimulating background for dealing with the issues of technology and service. . . . A reference tool to be looked at often." (The One-Person Library)*

The Roles of Reference Librarians: Today and Tomorrow, edited by Kathleen Low, MLS (No. 54, 1996). *"A great asset to all reference collections. . . . Presents important, valuable information for reference librarians as well as other library users." (Library Times International)*

Reference Services for the Unserved, edited by Fay Zipkowitz, MSLS, DA (No. 53, 1996). *"A useful tool in developing strategies to provide services to all patrons." (Science Books & Films)*

Library Instruction Revisited: Bibliographic Instruction Comes of Age, edited by Lyn Elizabeth M. Martin, MLS (No. 51/52, 1995). *"A powerful collection authored by respected practitioners who have stormed the bibliographic instruction (BI) trenches and, luckily for us, have recounted their successes and shortcomings." (The Journal of Academic Librarianship)*

Library Users and Reference Services, edited by Jo Bell Whitlatch, PhD (No. 49/50, 1995). *"Well-planned, balanced, and informative. . . . Both new and seasoned professionals will find material for service attitude formation and practical advice for the front lines of service." (Anna M. Donnelly, MS, MA, Associate Professor and Reference Librarian, St. John's University Library)*

Social Science Reference Services, edited by Pam Baxter, MLS (No. 48, 1995). *"Offers practical guidance to the reference librarian. . . . A valuable source of information about specific literatures within the social sciences and the skills and techniques needed to provide access to those literatures." (Nancy P. O'Brien, MLS, Head, Education and Social Science Library, and Professor of Library Administration, University of Illinois at Urbana-Champaign)*

Reference Services in the Humanities, edited by Judy Reynolds, MLS (No. 47, 1994). *"A well-chosen collection of situations and challenges encountered by reference librarians in the humanities." (College Research Library News)*

Racial and Ethnic Diversity in Academic Libraries: Multicultural Issues, edited by Deborah A. Curry, MLS, MA, Susan Griswold Blandy, MEd, and Lyn Elizabeth M. Martin, MLS (No. 45/46, 1994). *"The useful techniques and attractive strategies presented here will provide the incentive for fellow professionals in academic libraries around the country to go and do likewise in their own institutions." (David Cohen, Adjunct Professor of Library Science, School of Library and Information Science, Queens College; Director, EMIE (Ethnic Materials Information Exchange); Editor, EMIE Bulletin)*

School Library Reference Services in the 90s: Where We Are, Where We're Heading, edited by Carol Truett, PhD (No. 44, 1994). *"Unique and valuable to the the teacher-librarian as well as students of librarianship. . . . The overall work successfully interweaves the concept of the continuously changing role of the teacher-librarian." (Emergency Librarian)*

Reference Services Planning in the 90s, edited by Gail Z. Eckwright, MLS, and Lori M. Keenan, MLS (No. 43, 1994). *"This monograph is well-researched and definitive, encompassing reference service as practices by library and information scientists. . . . It should be required reading for all professional librarian trainees." (Feliciter)*

Librarians on the Internet: Impact on Reference Services, edited by Robin Kinder, MLS (No. 41/42, 1994). *"Succeeds in demonstrating that the Internet is becoming increasingly a challenging but practical and manageable tool in the reference librarian's ever-expanding armory." (Reference Reviews)*

Reference Service Expertise, edited by Bill Katz (No. 40, 1993). *This important volume presents a wealth of practical ideas for improving the art of reference librarianship.*

Modern Library Technology and Reference Services, edited by Samuel T. Huang, MLS, MS (No. 39, 1993). *"This book packs a surprising amount of information into a relatively few number of pages. . . . This book will answer many questions." (Science Books and Films)*

Assessment and Accountability in Reference Work, edited by Susan Griswold Blandy, Lyn M. Martin, and Mary L. Strife (No. 38, 1992). *"An important collection of well-written, real-world chapters addressing the central questions that surround performance and services in all libraries." (Library Times International)*

The Reference Librarian and Implications of Mediation, edited by M. Keith Ewing, MLS, and Robert Hauptman, MLS (No. 37, 1992). *"An excellent and thorough analysis of reference mediation. . . . Well worth reading by anyone involved in the delivery of reference services." (Fred Batt, MLS, Associate University Librarian for Public Services, California State University, Sacramento)*

Library Services for Career Planning, Job Searching and Employment Opportunities, edited by Byron Anderson, MA, MLS (No. 36, 1992). *"An interesting book which tells professional libraries how to set up career information centers. . . . Clearly valuable reading for anyone establishing a career library." (Career Opportunities News)*

In the Spirit of 1992: Access to Western European Libraries and Literature, edited by Mary M. Huston, PhD, and Maureen Pastine, MLS (No. 35, 1992). *"A valuable and practical [collection] which every subject specialist in the field would do well to consult." (Western European Specialists Section Newsletter)*

Access Services: The Convergence of Reference and Technical Services, edited by Gillian M. McCombs, ALA (No. 34, 1992). *"Deserves a wide readership among both technical and public services librarians. . . . Highly recommended for any librarian interested in how reference and technical services roles may be combined." (Library Resources & Technical Services)*

Opportunities for Reference Services: The Bright Side of Reference Services in the 1990s, edited by Bill Katz (No. 33, 1991). *"A well-deserved look at the brighter side of reference services. . . . Should be read by reference librarians and their administrators in all types of libraries." (Library Times International)*

Government Documents and Reference Services, edited by Robin Kinder, MLS (No. 32, 1991). *Discusses access possibilities and policies with regard to government information, covering such important topics as new and impending legislation, information on most frequently used and requested sources, and grant writing.*

The Reference Library User: Problems and Solutions, edited by Bill Katz (No. 31, 1991). *"Valuable information and tangible suggestions that will help us as a profession look critically at our users and decide how they are best served." (Information Technology and Libraries)*

Continuing Education of Reference Librarians, edited by Bill Katz (No. 30/31, 1990). *"Has something for everyone interested in this field. . . . Library trainers and library school teachers may well find stimulus in some of the programs outlined here." (Library Association Record)*

Weeding and Maintenance of Reference Collections, edited by Sydney J. Pierce, PhD, MLS (No. 29, 1990). *"This volume may spur you on to planned activity before lack of space dictates 'ad hoc' solutions." (New Library World)*

Serials and Reference Services, edited by Robin Kinder, MLS, and Bill Katz (No. 27/28, 1990). *"The concerns and problems discussed are those of serials and reference librarians everywhere. . . . The writing is of a high standard and the book is useful and entertaining. . . . This book can be recommended." (Library Association Record)*

Rothstein on Reference: . . . with some help from friends, edited by Bill Katz and Charles Bunge, PhD, MLS (No. 25/26, 1990). *"An important and stimulating collection of essays on reference librarianship. . . . Highly recommended!" (Richard W. Grefrath, MA, MLS, Reference Librarian, University of Nevada Library)* Dedicated to the work of Sam Rothstein, one of the world's most respected teachers of reference librarians, this special volume features his writings as well as articles written about him and his teachings by other professionals in the field.

Integrating Library Use Skills Into the General Education Curriculum, edited by Maureen Pastine, MLS, and Bill Katz (No. 24, 1989). *"All contributions are written and presented to a high standard with excellent references at the end of each. . . . One of the best summaries I have seen on this topic." (Australian Library Review)*

Expert Systems in Reference Services, edited by Christine Roysdon, MLS, and Howard D. White, PhD, MLS (No. 23, 1989). *"The single most comprehensive work on the subject of expert systems in reference service." (Information Processing and Management)*

Information Brokers and Reference Services, edited by Bill Katz and Robin Kinder, MLS (No. 22, 1989). *"An excellent tool for reference librarians and indispensable for anyone seriously considering their own information-brokering service." (Booklist)*

Information and Referral in Reference Services, edited by Marcia Stucklen Middleton, MLS, and Bill Katz (No. 21, 1988). *Investigates a wide variety of situations and models which fall under the umbrella of information and referral.*

Reference Services and Public Policy, edited by Richard Irving, MLS, and Bill Katz (No. 20, 1988). *Looks at the relationship between public policy and information and reports ways in which libraries respond to the need for public policy information.*

Finance, Budget, and Management for Reference Services, edited by Ruth A. Fraley, MLS, MBA, and Bill Katz (No. 19, 1989). *"Interesting and relevant to the current state of financial needs in reference service. . . . A must for anyone new to or already working in the reference service area." (Riverina Library Review)*

Current Trends in Information: Research and Theory, edited by Bill Katz and Robin Kinder, MLS (No. 18, 1987). *"Practical direction to improve reference services and does so in a variety of ways ranging from humorous and clever metaphoric comparisons to systematic and practical methodological descriptions." (American Reference Books Annual)*

International Aspects of Reference and Information Services, edited by Bill Katz and Ruth A. Fraley, MLS, MBA (No. 17, 1987). *"An informative collection of essays written by eminent librarians, library school staff, and others concerned with the international aspects of information work." (Library Association Record)*

Reference Services Today: From Interview to Burnout, edited by Bill Katz and Ruth A. Fraley, MLS, MBA (No. 16, 1987). *Authorities present important advice to all reference librarians on the improvement of service and the enhancement of the public image of reference services.*

The Publishing and Review of Reference Sources, edited by Bill Katz and Robin Kinder, MLS (No. 15, 1987). *"A good review of current reference reviewing and publishing trends in the United States . . . will be of interest to intending reviewers, reference librarians, and students." (Australasian College Libraries)*

Personnel Issues in Reference Services, edited by Bill Katz and Ruth Fraley, MLS, MBA (No. 14, 1986). *"Chock-full of information that can be applied to most reference settings. Recommended for libraries with active reference departments." (RQ)*

Reference Services in Archives, edited by Lucille Whalen (No. 13, 1986). *"Valuable for the insights it provides on the reference process in archives and as a source of information on the different ways of carrying out that process." (Library and Information Science Annual)*

Conflicts in Reference Services, edited by Bill Katz and Ruth A. Fraley, MLS, MBA (No. 12, 1985). *This collection examines issues pertinent to the reference department.*

Evaluation of Reference Services, edited by Bill Katz and Ruth A. Fraley, MLS, MBA (No. 11, 1985). *"A much-needed overview of the present state of the art vis-à-vis reference service evaluation. . . . Excellent. . . . Will appeal to reference professionals and aspiring students." (RQ)*

Library Instruction and Reference Services, edited by Bill Katz and Ruth A. Fraley, MLS, MBA (No. 10, 1984). *"Well written, clear, and exciting to read. This is an important work recommended for all librarians, particularly those involved in, interested in, or considering bibliographic instruction. . . . A milestone in library literature." (RQ)*

Reference Services and Technical Services: Interactions in Library Practice, edited by Gordon Stevenson and Sally Stevenson (No. 9, 1984). *"New ideas and longstanding problems are handled with humor and sensitivity as practical suggestions and new perspectives are suggested by the authors." (Information Retrieval & Library Automation)*

Reference Services for Children and Young Adults, edited by Bill Katz and Ruth A. Fraley, MLS, MBA (No. 7/8, 1983). *"Offers a well-balanced approach to reference service for children and young adults." (RQ)*

Video to Online: Reference Services in the New Technology, edited by Bill Katz and Ruth A. Fraley, MLS, MBA (No. 5/6, 1983). *"A good reference manual to have on hand. . . . Well-written, concise, provide[s] a wealth of information." (Online)*

Ethics and Reference Services, edited by Bill Katz and Ruth A. Fraley, MLS, MBA (No. 4, 1982). *Library experts discuss the major ethical and legal implications that reference librarians must take into consideration when handling sensitive inquiries about confidential material.*

Reference Services Administration and Management, edited by Bill Katz and Ruth A. Fraley, MLS, MBA (No. 3, 1982). *Librarianship experts discuss the management of the reference function in libraries and information centers, outlining the responsibilities and qualifications of reference heads.*

Reference Services in the 1980s, edited by Bill Katz (No. 1/2, 1982). *Here is a thought-provoking volume on the future of reference services in libraries, with an emphasis on the challenges and needs that have come about as a result of automation.*

Evolution in Reference and Information Services: The Impact of the Internet

Di Su, MLS
Editor

Evolution in Reference and Information Services: The Impact of the Internet has been co-published simultaneously as *The Reference Librarian*, Number 74 2001.

Routledge
Taylor & Francis Group

NEW YORK AND LONDON

First Published by

The Haworth Information Press®, 10 Alice Street, Binghamton, NY 13904-1580 USA

The Haworth Information Press® is an imprint of The Haworth Press, Inc., 10 Alice Street, Binghamton, NY 13904-1580 USA.

Transferred to Digital Printing 2011 by Routledge
711 Third Avenue, New York, NY 10017
2 Park Square, Milton Park, Abingdon, Oxon, OX14 4RN

Evolution in Reference and Information Services: The Impact of the Internet has been co-published simultaneously as *The Reference Librarian*, Number 74 2001.

The development, preparation, and publication of this work has been undertaken with great care. However, the publisher, employees, editors, and agents of The Haworth Press and all imprints of The Haworth Press, Inc., including The Haworth Medical Press® and Pharmaceutical Products Press®, are not responsible for any errors contained herein or for consequences that may ensue from use of materials or information contained in this work. Opinions expressed by the author(s) are not necessarily those of The Haworth Press, Inc.

Cover design by Thomas J. Mayshock Jr.

Library of Congress Cataloging-in-Publication Data

Evolution in reference and information services : the impact of the Internet / Di Su, editor.
    p. cm.
    Co-published simultaneously as The reference librarian, no. 74, 2001.
    Includes bibliographical references and index.
    ISBN 0-7890-1722-9 – ISBN 0-7890-1723-7 (pbk.)
    1. Internet in library reference services. I. Su, Di. II. Reference librarian.

Z711.47 .E96 2001
025.5'24–dc21
                                                2001059402

To the memory of my father, Su Ping

Evolution in Reference
and Information Services:
The Impact of the Internet

CONTENTS

ABOUT THE EDITOR

Di Su, MLS, earned his degree at the University at Albany (SUNY). He is Assistant Professor and Head of Information Literacy at York College Library (CUNY) and holds a research librarian position at PKF PC, an accounting and consulting firm in New York City. He is a member of the Special Libraries Association and the Music Library Association. Di Su has been a contributor to several publications, including the *Scribner Encyclopedia of American Lives*, *Information Outlook*, and *The Reference Librarian*. His research interests include the Internet, business and music.

Preface

Some years ago, if you were told that a library's catalog would be available on a 24/7/365 basis, you might think it was just another fiction. Now we have these OPACs. Perhaps as influential as Johann Gutenberg's invention of movable type printing, which revolutionized the way of information dissemination in ancient time, the Internet can be probably viewed as one of the most significant happenings in the information world in modern time. Library services have been influenced and enhanced by the Internet in many ways, such as methods of information dissemination, scope of information availability, and convenience of information accessibility, just to name a few. The changes made by the Internet have created opportunities for reference librarians. They have also created new challenges for professional competency, such as familiarity with Internet resources and computer literacy. It is not uncommon that one of the professional qualifications in today's reference librarian job description is familiarity with the Internet. A typical reference librarian in this digital age should be one who has been trained or self-trained in using both traditional and electronic resources. He must possess basic knowledge in a wide range of electronic resources and tools, and actively update his knowledge so that he is able to provide services efficiently and assist patrons in a confident way. The ability to utilize Internet resources in reference service is no longer an option.

Aiming at reference librarians in general and electronic services librarians in particular, this thematic volume focuses on the impact of the Internet in reference service and shares some practical issues that are common in our daily work.

The volume is arranged in five sections. Section one serves as an introduction. Joseph E. Straw opens the issue by reviewing the history of electronic reference and background of developments. Teaching information literacy is a part of our job, especially important in an academic library. In section two, Charity B. Hope, Sandra Kajiwara, and Mengxiong Liu describe an increasing role as teachers among librarians. D. Scott Brandt reveals his view of user edu-

[Haworth indexing entry note]: "Preface." Su, Di. Published in *Evolution in Reference and Information Services: The Impact of the Internet* (ed: Di Su) The Haworth Information Press, an imprint of The Haworth Press, Inc., 2001, pp. xvii-xviii. Single or multiple copies of this article are available for a fee from The Haworth Document Delivery Service [1-800-342-9678, 9:00 a.m. - 5:00 p.m. (EST). E-mail address: getinfo@haworthpressinc.com].

xvii

cation from psychological aspects. Jack Styczynski shares his Internet teaching experience at NBC Information Resource Center. Section three includes case studies and strategies related to electronic services. Naomi Lederer presents her survey results on e-mail reference. Susan B. Ardis reveals her survey results on the use of Internet engineering reference in her library. Michael Adams offers ideas and practical guides on how to establish your services through the library's portal site. Section four contains analysis and suggestions on how to evaluate electronic resources. Eric Novotny provides us with various evaluation methods that serve different research purposes. John A. Drobnicki and Richard Asaro present their extensive research on "Historical Fabrications on the Internet." Robert Machalow evaluates some prominent government Web sites. David Garnes and Carolyn Mills give us an overview of health sources on the Internet. Section five involves a new "hat" that at least some of us wear more often, and also a common issue of today: computer technical help from librarians. How do we manage this added responsibility? Tina C. Fu, Kim Bartosz, and Guy LaHaie describe how they implemented "Scholar's Workstations" for patrons to use when the library moved to a new facility. Sheryl Moore tells us how her library manages its computer lab.

I wish to thank the authors of these articles for their valuable contributions. I also wish to thank Dr. Bill Katz for providing this opportunity. It is hoped that readers will find this volume useful and informative.

Di Su

BACKGROUND

From Magicians to Teachers:
The Development
of Electronic Reference in Libraries:
1930-2000

Joseph E. Straw

SUMMARY. Electronic reference is a large part of today's library. Computer technology has clearly been the dominant catalyst for change in library service over the last few decades. Reference service has changed along with the prevailing technology. An exclusive group of searchers serviced electronic information requests during the online searching craze of the 1970s and 1980s. In the library of today, this model of electronic reference is no longer operational. Electronic information is now available to anyone on a computer terminal. In response, all librarians have become familiar with computer technology, and have a new emphasis on teaching and basic information literacy. This article will examine how this came to be, and the technologies that helped make it happen. *[Article copies available for a fee from The Haworth Document Delivery Service: 1-800-342-9678. E-mail address: <getinfo@haworthpressinc.com> Website: <http://www.HaworthPress.com> © 2001 by The Haworth Press, Inc. All rights reserved.]*

Joseph E. Straw is Assistant Professor of Bibliography, University of Akron, Bierce Library, Akron, OH 44325-1709 (E-mail: jstraw@uakron.edu).

[Haworth co-indexing entry note]: "From Magicians to Teachers: The Development of Electronic Reference in Libraries: 1930-2000." Straw, Joseph E. Co-published simultaneously in *The Reference Librarian* (The Haworth Information Press, an imprint of The Haworth Press, Inc.) No. 74, 2001, pp. 1-12; and: *Evolution in Reference and Information Services: The Impact of the Internet* (ed: Di Su) The Haworth Information Press, an imprint of The Haworth Press, Inc., 2001, pp. 1-12. Single or multiple copies of this article are available for a fee from The Haworth Document Delivery Service [1-800-342-9678, 9:00 a.m. - 5:00 p.m. (EST). E-mail address: getinfo@haworthpressinc.com].

KEYWORDS. Library automation, service models, reference philosophy, public service, library history, electronic reference, online searching, CD-ROM reference, reference service, reference history, Internet reference

INTRODUCTION

Technological innovation has played a key role in reference librarianship in the second half of the 20th century. Computer technology has been at the heart of this latest period of innovation in reference work. Clearly, the provision of electronic reference services has changed along with the technology. The first online systems of the 1970s and 1980s required the skills of an exculsive group of searchers and technical librarians. This initiated priesthood of searchers knew the systems and could translate the public's requests into the mysterious language of the machine. These special searchers were able to tap into an almost magical world of information largely on their own. At the beginning of the 21st century, it is clear that this model of electronic reference service has been transformed. In the library of today, all reference librarians must master electronic skills and have a renewed emphasis on instructional services. This article will examine this historical transition and the technologies that helped make it happen. A look into early visions of document retrieval will be combined with the practical technologies of online, CD-ROM, and the Internet to illustrate the evolution of electronic reference service in libraries.

FOUNDATIONS OF A NEW ONLINE WORLD: 1930-1970

The ability to retrieve documents in some form is at the heart of electronic reference. Visions of an automated solution to the problem of getting access to documents were proposed long before they could be practically implemented. Documentalists in Europe during the 1930s saw telecommunications and the emerging technology of television as a way to tap into documents and display them to users.[1] In 1945, the American Vannevar Bush proposed using electronics and light to search a compact storage medium. His imaginary "Memex" machine envisioned using keyboarding and levers to punch in an index code that would retrieve and display pre-recorded documents.[2] Bush even took his idea a step further by expanding the scope of "Memex" to include built in aids

to the process of thinking and memory.[3] It was clear by 1950 that the job of finding information might be aided by machines and technology.

The development of experimental digital computers in the late 1940s made the electronic retrieval of information a practical possibility. Computers would be an ideal medium to address one of the most pressing information problems of this period. The years after the end of World War II saw a massive growth in the amount of scholarly literature. In fields like the sciences, the literature was expanding at nearly expotential levels. Traditional print methods of gathering and searching for information were breaking down. The computational, storage, and searching possibilities of computers were seen as a real solution in controlling the vast explosion of new bibliographic information.[4]

Computers were first applied to the problem of document retrieval in the 1950s. Small bibliographic files were stored on magnetic tapes and run on gigantic mainframe computer systems.[5] Perhaps one of the first serious electronic retrieval applications was the use of numeric databases by the U.S. Census in 1951. Most of these systems, however, remained experimental and could not leave the confines of the laboratory.[6]

In the early 1960s indexing and abstracting services began using computers to automate their production processes. Indexing and abstracting services were able to store and convert vast amounts of bibliographic information to machine readable magnetic tapes. The National Library of Medicine began storing information from its Index Medicus print index to tapes to form the basis for the MEDLARS system in 1960. The Library was able to search this MEDLARS database for the medical community in 1964. By 1969 other indexing and abstracting services were making electronic versions of their products, and providing limited access for their subscribers.[7]

The technologies that were used to build early databases severely restricted their research and commercial viability. Storing information on magnetic tapes made random access to data a virtual impossibility. Retrieval of information depended on clumsy and time consuming batch searching. Information processing was ultimately tied to enormous mainframe computers that often crashed and had limited memory.[8]

Given these restrictions, it is not surprising that these early databases had a very limited impact on most librarians and researchers. Throughout the 1960s, online systems served small elite groups of users. Government scientists, medical researchers, defense contractors, and engineers were the first constituencies for online databases. Despite their limited appeal, a clear alternative to print-based document retrieval had been established by 1970. Luckily a series of developments were occurring that would lead to greatly enhanced access to computer databases.[9]

ONLINE SEARCHING COMES INTO THE LIBRARY: 1970-1985

Technical Background and History

In the early 1970s computer databases began to reach a wider audience. During this period, the capabilities of mainframe computers changed dramatically. At the heart of this change was the development of hard disc storage systems.[10] New technologies like the IBM 3330 disc drive and the IBM 360 computer came into wide use. These developments greatly increased the power, memory, and overall performance of computers.[11]

Disc storage systems also had a profound impact on searching. This technology permitted random access to data, and allowed computers to handle multiple simultaneous users. Disc systems made it possible to use complex indexing schemes to arrange data for more convenient access. New file structures could be set up to describe and search bibliographic fields with more accuracy. The advent of the hard disc made it possible to expand the potential users of bibliographic databases.[12]

While computers themselves were changing, national communications networks were being transformed. The establishment of broadband networks, particularly Tymnet and Telenet in 1975, made communications between computers faster and more reliable. These new national and international communications networks would make it possible to remotely access bibliographic databases.[13]

A multitude of bibliographic databases were available in the early 1970s. Most of them lacked a uniform search protocol or a common operational software. A number of private companies took the lead in using the hard disc and telecommunications to mount multiple databases.[14] A common software and searching protocol would be used to provide access to these "databanks." In 1972 the Lockheed company made available its DIALOG service, and other services like ORBIT, BRS, Lexis-Nexis, and Dow Jones News Service were fast to follow.[15] The development of these services would make online bibliographic searching technically and commercially possible.

Library and Reference Impact

Online commercial services entered the world of libraries in the mid-1970s. Libraries were some of the first subscribers to the new online services. Online searching would rapidly enable libraries to provide a dimension of service that had not been available in the past. Vast stores of bibliographic information could now be accessed and efficiently processed. Research bibliographies could be compiled online with great speed and impressive accuracy. These possibilities were not lost on library users, and soon a boom of requests for online services would be swamping libraries of all types.[16]

Reference librarians were some of the first practical users of online services. They found out quickly that online searching had some difficult and

thorny problems. Many reference librarians were facing unreliable mainframe response times and restrictive use policies. Fee structures imposed by commercial services were often expensive and required careful management of time. The searching protocols were cryptic and demanded considerable training and experience in order to use the services effectively. These logistical and technical problems helped to condition the service models that developed for the use of online searching in the reference setting.[17]

Given such problems, it was clear that library patrons could not be "turned loose" on these systems. Electronic reference would need to be carefully managed by libraries. Access to online information would require the use of trained intermediaries who could control access and closely supervise use. A new profession of "online searcher" was born and quickly assumed a prominent role in the library of the late 1970s and early 1980s.[18]

The producers of commercial online services often trained librarian intermediaries. DIALOG, ORBIT, BRS, and others trained prospective searchers on the idiosyncrasies of their systems. Other searchers learned their trade by the experience of trial and error. When online searching became an accepted practice, many libraries set up separate departments to handle nothing but online service requests. Others delegated online responsibilities to bibliographers or subject specialists that searched in their areas of expertise. Still more libraries designated a certain person or persons as searchers who performed all of the online searching. By 1980 electronic reference had emerged distinct from the print oriented reference desk.[19]

A patron wishing to do an online literature search had to work through a librarian. In working with a librarian, the patron waived much of their participation in the search process. A certain amount of faith was needed for someone to surrender their subject expertise, and perhaps the ultimate success of their project, to the promise of a slick new technology. This surrender of control perhaps adds a kind of magic to the process of online searching. A patron hoping to find something online had to seek the services of a librarian with a knowledge of a unique and powerful computer. The patron's request needed to be translated into a special language that could be understood by the computer. When the language was put into the computer, a strange information alchemy produced something that hopefully would be of relevance and value to the patron.

It is unlikely that online searchers were actual magicians, but they were clearly the masters of electronic reference by the mid-1980s. Their efforts firmly established online searching as a major research tool. They also helped insure the financial success of a number of commercial searching services. Their special skills and knowledge placed them as the people of first resort for those seeking information electronically.

ELECTRONICS COMES TO THE PEOPLE:
CD-ROM IN THE LIBRARY:
1985-1994

Technical Background and History

Just as online searching moved into a position of prominence, a new technology was emerging that would require libraries to revaluate their information retrieval practices. Compact Disc Read Only Memory, or CD-ROM, began to enter the library in the mid-1980s. CD-ROM technology would prove to be a very popular innovation for both patrons and librarians.

What made it possible to use CD-ROM was the appearance of the microcomputer. IBM released the first true microcomputer in 1981, and its accompanying MSDOS operating system opened up personal computing to a new consumer market. Functioning computers that performed a variety of tasks could now be put in the hands of the general public.[20]

Shortly after the appearance of the microcomputer, the Philips and Sony Corporation created the first audio disc in 1982. These discs formed the contemporary medium for storing music. In 1983, Philips and Sony also released a data-bearing disc that could be used with the newly emerging microcomputers. The data bearing discs or CD-ROM, when used in tandem with a microcomputer, would be the way this technology would find its way to the public.[21]

The CD-ROM technology that appeared in libraries had powerful image and storage capabilities. A CD-ROM is a disc that provides an extension of a computer's basic memory. This disc can be read using some kind of optical means. The compact disc itself is 4.72 inches and stores digitized information through a series of pits and grooves located on the surface of the disc. When used with a microcomputer, the disc is run through a CD-ROM drive and a low intensity laser beam reads the data from the pits and grooves. Vast amounts of data can be stored on a CD-ROM, and storage capacity can exceed by many times the information that can be stored on a conventional floppy disc. This massive storage capacity made CD-ROM an attractive medium to house data of all types.[22]

Library and Reference Impact

CD-ROM technology found rapid acceptance in libraries. In 1985 Silver Platter released CD-ROM versions of a number of standard bibliographic databases. It took only a few years before a vast array of CD-ROM databases were flooding the library market. Non-bibliographic material like dictionaries, encyclopedias, directories, and other reference works were also finding their way to CD-ROM. In the late 1980s, CD-ROM versions of standard reference sources were making the options of full-text and graphic images available to library patrons.[23]

CD-ROM was one of the first library technologies that allowed patrons to access computer databases on their own. The library patron benefited from many of the unique features of CD-ROM. Databases on CD-ROM could be searched anytime without incurring the telecommunications and database charges of using an online system. The searching technology was often simpler and more intuitive than those offered by online services. Features like keyword and natural language searching gave patrons the chance to construct their own searches free from mediation. By the late 1980s, a significant end-user culture was growing up around the CD-ROM.[24]

The advent of CD-ROM significantly changed the provisioning of electronic reference service in libraries. Servicing CD-ROM products became a frontline reference desk responsibility. Control of searching was increasingly in the hands of end-users, who expected librarians to be experts in all the software intricacies of the new CD-ROM workstations. Reference staff had to become increasingly familiar with printing, operating systems, and general computer troubleshooting. In order to take advantage of CD-ROM technology, all reference librarians would now have to be exposed to computers and electronic information sources.[25]

The world of online searching in the 1970s and 1980s recognized a distinction between electronic reference and the print orientated reference desk. The expansion of CD-ROM products to include non-bibliographic works blurred the distinction between print and electronic reference. CD-ROM encyclopedias, dictionaries, directories, and other standard reference works freed the patron from dependence on print resources. By the late 1980s, more and more reference questions were being answered electronically.[26]

CD-ROM by no means eliminated traditional online searching, but clearly this medium was under considerable strain. Many libraries that introduced CD-ROM reported a decrease in the number of online searches.[27] Online searchers had to market their skills with the limitations of CD-ROM technology in mind. Patrons frustrated with CD-ROM problems like lack of currency, limited searching capability, and database depth could often be channeled back to the online searching route. The very real problem of end-users using CD-ROM to do poor searches often placed online searching as an expert option that could be used if really knowledgeable and accurate research was needed.

By the early 1990s, an increasingly mixed electronic reference environment had come into being. CD-ROM technology formed a huge end-user community that had wide access to electronic resources. Online searching was a less exclusive club serving a diminishing base of patrons. Electronic sources were hugely popular and highly visible in the library as a whole. For a greater number of reference questions, electronic options were increasingly the place of first resort.

A WORLD OF INFORMATION:
THE INTERNET AND THE LIBRARY OF TODAY:
1993-2000

Technical Background and History

A new networking technology began to take root in libraries at the beginning of the 1990s. This technology linked computers together in a vast super network known as the Internet. The Internet would allow libraries to retrieve an incredible mass of electronic information from computers around the world. The Internet is providing much of the framework for accessing electronic information in many contemporary libraries.

The Internet had its origins in the ARPANET network set up by the Defense Department in 1969. ARPANET linked a number of defense contractor, government, and university computers doing defense related research.[28] The success of this network led the National Science Foundation to form NSFNET, which linked a series of super computer networks for enhanced research use. What kept these networks connected and ultimately led to the Internet was the appearance of a standard Internet Protocol (IP) in 1982. This communication scheme allowed traffic to be routed from one network to another. The IP standard provided for an "open architecture" networking environment. Open architecture environments let networks communicate regardless of their interface or design. The IP design started with only a few computers, but it would eventually allow for the linking of tens of thousands of networks.[29]

The popularity of the first government networks saw the private sector link together a number of different networks to provide access to applications beyond research and education. Commercial networks allowed for a wider access to anything that was legal, and it provided for direct connections for their customers. By 1994, most Internet traffic had been taken over by these commercial networks.[30]

The possibilities of the Internet would be greatly enhanced by the arrival of the World Wide Web (WWW). The WWW is a multi-media hyper linked interface that can access information across the Internet. This technology was designed in 1989 by a group of researchers in Switzerland who conceived of Internet services being delivered with text, sound, pictures, and even animation. The WWW really became a practical possibility with the appearance of the Mosaic browser software in 1993. Invented by Marc Andereesen and Eric Bina at the University of Illinois, Mosaic was the first program to apply a graphical user interface to the problem of retrieving and displaying information from the Internet. Mosaic would evolve into a number of other browsers like Netscape Navigator and Microsoft Internet Explorer that would bring the possibilities of the WWW to the general public. After 1995 the WWW exploded in popularity and is now the dominant interface for getting information over the Internet.[31]

Library and Reference Impact

Libraries were some of the first institutions to take advantage of the Internet's potential. Internet applications like e-mail, WWW, and listservs were rapidly integrated into library operations by the end of the 1990s. Many libraries were able to use things like the WWW as platforms to present locally important electronic resources. Library catalogs, CD-ROM resources, online databases, and open Internet access were often integrated into gateways that permitted libraries to offer electronic services in a more usable streamlined fashion. The library world soon realized it had access to a complete communications technology that gave them the ability to setup different relationships with their patrons. The Internet allows patrons not only to use a powerful retrieval tool, but communicate, package, customize, and perhaps even publish their information to a broader world.[32]

The Internet is transforming the nature of reference work. As all reference librarians are aware, the amount of information available over the Internet is staggering. Internet sources from conventional government documents to unconventional personal information is available for the taking.[33] Control of searching is very much an end-user business, with reference librarians often not knowing what their patrons are doing. In response, all reference librarians must become familiar in navigating both the smooth and rough edges of the Internet. Their Internet knowledge is helping to change the reference desk from a static place to find out what a library might have, into a fluid platform that connects patrons to information anywhere.

Internet technology is changing the way reference librarians communicate with patrons. With more electronic sources available over the Internet, more research is being done virtually. The key linking technology of e-mail is allowing reference transactions to take place outside the walls of the library. E-mail is making it possible for more people to take advantage of library services. By dissolving the walls of the library, reference librarians can now extend their reach to anywhere in the world.[34]

Patrons are using the Internet to tap into a vast array of electronic information, and thus traditional informational requests are declining. It is also clear that many patrons are walking away with information that does not stand up to critical scrutiny. In this kind of setting, it is not surprising that instructional issues are taking on a new importance. Reference librarians are spending more time instructing patrons in the use of technology, and less time trying to track down specific pieces of information. Many patrons are finding they want to learn about Internet fundamentals instead of finding a particular answer over the Internet. Helping patrons to ask better questions, evaluate information, and understand information structures is beginning to define the role of the reference librarian in the Internet environment. Teaching information literacy skills is thus becoming more important for librarians in the information world of to-

day. Increasingly they will find themselves cast as mentors guiding patrons across a complex and varied information landscape.[35]

Despite the vast popularity of the Internet, online searching remains as an electronic option in the library of today. The traditional online searcher is certainly becoming more marginalized as patrons take advantage of multiple electronic reference possibilities. In many libraries, use of traditional commercial services has diminished, and many searchers have seen an erosion in their skills. Online search services are turning away from proprietary telecommunications software, and are moving to WWW based online searching. The use of the WWW for online searching is offering more interfaces and varied opportunities for searching. Online searching still remains as an expert option for patrons that have mastered basic Internet searching and might want a more structured approach for getting information.[36]

The Internet has also diminished the role of CD-ROM in the library. Bibliographic databases are increasingly being delivered through Internet based platforms, and fewer are appearing in CD-ROM format. The growing use of the Internet to integrate locally important electronic resources is decreasing the prominence of the CD-ROM workstation as an option at the reference desk. The increasing demand for text and graphics by patrons makes the Internet a logical medium of choice.[37]

CONCLUSION

The library of today presents patrons with many opportunities for retrieving and using electronic information. The prevalence of electronic reference sources is clearly a product of historical developments. The servicing of online searching, CD-ROM, and the Internet has changed along with these technologies. When online searching first became a possibility, it was the preserve of an exclusive group of privileged searchers. CD-ROM and the Internet opened up electronic reference to a vast community of end-users both inside and outside the library. This democratization of information challenges reference librarians with the task of educating patrons in the skills they will need in navigating through a new information world.

REFERENCES AND NOTES

1. Michael Buckland, "Documentation, Information Science, and Library Science in the U.S.A.," *Information Processing & Management* 32 No. 1 (1996): 63-76.

2. James M. Nyce and Paul Kahn, "Innovation, Pragmaticism, and Technological Continuity: Vannevar Bush's Memex," *Journal of the American Society for Information Science* 40 No. 3 (1989): 214-220.

3. Vannevar Bush, "As We May Think," *Atlantic Monthly* 176 No. 1 (1945): 101-108.

4. M. Lynne Neufeld and Martha Cornog, "Database History: From Dinosaurs to Compact Discs," *Journal of the American Society for Information Science* 37 No. 4 (1986): 183-190.

5. Ibid., 183.

6. Ibid., 183.

7. Ibid., 183.

8. Trudi Bellardo Hahn, "Pioneers of the Online Age," *Information Processing & Management* 32 No. 1 (1996): 33-48.

9. Ibid., 34.

10. Edwin Perry, "Historical Development of Computer Assisted Literature Searching and its Effects on Librarians and their Clients," *Library Software Review* 11 (March/April 1992): 18-24.

11. F.B. Rogers, "Computerized Bibliographic Retrieval Services," *Library Trends* 32 No. 1 (1974): 73-88.

12. Neufield and Cornog, "Database History: From Dinosaurs to Compact Discs," 186.

13. Perry, "The Historical Development of Computer Assisted Literature Searching and its Effects on Librarians and their Clients," 19.

14. Hahn, "Pioneers of the Online Age," 39.

15. Ibid., 40.

16. Stephen E. Arnold and Erik S. Arnold, "Vectors of Change: Electronic Information from 1977 to 2000," *Online* 21 (July/August 1997): 18-22.

17. M.E. Williams, "Online Retrieval: Today and Tomorrow," *Online Review* 2 (December 1978): 353-366.

18. Neufield and Cornog, "Database History: From Dinosaurs to Compact Discs," 186.

19. Hahn, "Pioneers of the Online Age," 43.

20. F. Lenck, "History of the PC," *Computing Now* 9 No. 5 (1991): 12-15, 37.

21. R.J. Moes, "CD-ROM Puzzle: Where do the Pieces Fit?" *Optical Information Systems* 6 No. 6 (1986): 509-511.

22. Kristine Salomon, "The Impact of CD-ROM on Reference Departments," *RQ* 28 (Winter 1988): 203-211.

23. Nancy Melin, "The New Alexandria: CD-ROM in the Library," in *CD-ROM The New Papyrus,* edited by Steve Lambert and Suzanne Ropiequet, 509-516. Redmond, WA: Microsoft Press, 1986.

24. Ibid., 516.

25. Rick Dyson and Carey Kjestine, "User Preference for CD-ROMs: Implications for Library Planners," *CD-ROM Professional* 6 (May 1993): 86-89.

26. Peter Simmons, "CD-ROM: New Papyrus or Passing Fad?" *Microcomputers for Information Management* 6 (December 1989): 293-301.

27. F.W. Lancaster, Cheryl Elszy, Mary Jo Zeter, Laura Metzler, and Yuen-Man Low, "Searching Databases on CD-ROM: Comparisons of the Results of End-User Searching with Results from Two Modes of Searching by Skilled Intermediaries," *RQ* 33 (Spring 1994): 370-386.

28. Vinton G. Cere and Barry M. Leiner, "The Evolution of the Internet as a Global Information System," *International Information & Library Review* 29 (June 1997): 129-151.

29. Ibid., 133.

30. Janet Abbate, *Inventing the Internet*, Cambridge, MA: MIT Press, 1999.

31. John Naughton, *A Brief History of the Future: From Radio Days to Internet Years in a Lifetime*, Woodstock, NY: Overlook Press, 2000.

32. Mark Stover, "Reference Librarians and the Internet: A Qualitative Study," *Reference Services Review* 28 No. 1 (2000): 39-46.

33. Mary Burke, "Internet: The Ultimate Reference Tool," *Internet Research* 7 No. 2 (1997): 101-108.

34. Joseph E. Straw, "A Virtual Understanding: The Reference Interview and Question Negotiation in the Digital Age," *Reference and User Services Quarterly* 39 (Summer 2000): 376-379.

35. Amy Kautzman, "Digital Impact: Reality, the Web, and the Changed Business of Reference," *Searcher* 7 (March 1989): 18-24.

36. Lucinda Conger, "The Old Searcher and the Internet," *Searcher* 7 (November/ December 1999): 44-50.

37. Sheryl Moore, "Weaving the Web: The Impact of the Internet and Other Electronic Technologies on Reference Service," *Louisiana Library Association Bulletin* 60 (Winter, 1998): 114-118.

TEACHING AND TRAINING

The Impact of the Internet:
Increasing the Reference Librarian's Role
as Teacher

Charity B. Hope

Sandra Kajiwara

Mengxiong Liu

SUMMARY. The Internet has brought great changes to reference services in academic libraries. One significant impact has been the growth and evolution of the reference librarian's role as teacher. This article reviews the literature on the librarian's increased teaching role with the emergence of the Internet, discusses the changing student populations who require a librarian's instruction and the skills that students need to achieve information literacy, and reviews how the Internet has affected current

Charity B. Hope is Reference Librarian (E-mail: cbhope@email.sjsu.edu), Sandra Kajiwara is Reference Librarian (E-mail: sandrak@email.sjsu.edu), and Mengxiong Liu is Reference Librarian (E-mail: mliu@email.sjsu.edu), all at Clark Library, San Jose State University, One Washington Square, San Jose, CA 95192-0028.

[Haworth co-indexing entry note]: "The Impact of the Internet: Increasing the Reference Librarian's Role as Teacher." Hope, Charity B., Sandra Kajiwara, and Mengxiong Liu. Co-published simultaneously in *The Reference Librarian* (The Haworth Information Press, an imprint of The Haworth Press, Inc.) No. 74, 2001, pp. 13-36; and: *Evolution in Reference and Information Services: The Impact of the Internet* (ed: Di Su) The Haworth Information Press, an imprint of The Haworth Press, Inc., 2001, pp. 13-36. Single or multiple copies of this article are available for a fee from The Haworth Document Delivery Service [1-800-342-9678, 9:00 a.m. - 5:00 p.m. (EST). E-mail address: getinfo@haworthpressinc.com].

13

teaching strategies including classroom instruction, Web-based instruction, and efforts to integrate information literacy instruction into the curriculum. In addition, it also introduces emerging Internet technologies with their potential impact on teaching and instruction. The authors conclude that the reference librarian's teaching role will further increase with the development of information technologies. *[Article copies available for a fee from The Haworth Document Delivery Service: 1-800-342-9678. E-mail address: <getinfo@haworthpressinc.com> Website: <http://www.HaworthPress.com> © 2001 by The Haworth Press, Inc. All rights reserved.]*

KEYWORDS. Internet, instruction, teaching, World Wide Web, virtual learning, active learning, reference services, information literacy, information competence, reference librarian, Web-based instruction, Internet technologies, interactive learning

INTRODUCTION

The Internet has affected academic libraries in many ways. Perhaps its most significant contribution has been to the growth and evolution of the librarian's role as teacher. More and more of what we do falls into the realm of instruction, and this added emphasis on teaching is due in large part to the Internet's direct impact on our users and the information environment. In addition to the increasing emphasis on the role of teacher, who we teach, what we teach and how we teach have changed in the Internet age.

It is important to note that the expanding relevance of technology, the Internet, and now, the omnipresent World Wide Web to academic research has proceeded hand in hand with changes in the higher education environment, significant curricular reform movements, and changing theories about effective teaching methods in higher education. In other words, there are additional "environmental variables"[1] impacting the role of librarians as teachers. These include:

- Larger enrollments coupled with an increased diversity of the student body.
- Pressure on colleges and universities from students, parents and legislators toward accountability to student needs in the Information Age.
- Increased demand for distance education options.[2]
- Growing recognition among educators that the traditional "Transmission Model" of post-secondary instruction, based on the lecture format, is failing to serve students' needs after graduation. Students can memorize facts, but have trouble applying learned information to unfamiliar problem-solving challenges.[3]

Yet these developments have in turn been fed and influenced by the increasingly important role of networked information in education, society and the workplace. In addition, the innovative application of Web-based technologies may help educators–including librarians–meet the challenge of promoting active learning for more students, with more flexibility to individual needs and a stronger focus on Information Age outcomes. Thus, both through its direct impact on libraries and library users and in its influence on other factors in the higher education environment, the Internet as a change agent for librarians' roles as teachers cannot be overestimated.

GENERAL AGREEMENT: WE ARE TEACHING MORE

In three surveys to Association of Research Libraries (ARL) libraries in the 1990s, Carol Tenopir asked librarians to describe the extent to which electronic resources were used in their libraries, and to reflect upon how this impacted their roles in reference and instruction. In the first of these surveys, distributed in 1991-1992, librarians described a highly automated environment with online catalogs, CD-ROMs, and patron access to mediated online searching. However, as she notes, "the World Wide Web did not exist and patron use of the Internet in the library was still in its infancy."[4] Less than half of the libraries supported direct end-user database searching. In the two follow up surveys, delivered in 1994/1995 and 1997/1998 (the later reflecting, of course, the post-Web environment), several differences in the reference environment emerged. The most telling of these included a significant rise in end-user database searching (over 60% in 1994/1995 and over 80% in 1997/1998) and in-library access by patrons to *non-library* information materials through the Internet (over 70% and over 90%, respectively).[5]

Asked what impact this changing environment had on their roles, librarians–particularly those in the latest survey–pointed to their increasing role as teachers, in formal instruction classes, from the reference desk, and as partners in developing information literacy programs to meet new university curricular requirements. Predictions in the 1991/1992 survey that increasingly user-friendly systems and computer literate students would reduce the need for the librarian's role as a teacher have not come to pass. Instead, librarians are engaged in teaching everything from basic computer skills and the technical details of particular systems, to research strategies, database selection, and the information literacy skills of critical evaluation and synthesis of information. Interestingly, although librarians in the latest survey still look forward to a time when interfaces are simpler and students more computer literate, they no longer see this as leading to a reduction in the instructional role. Instead, they anticipate being free to focus more on helping students with complex concepts

when less basic technical help is needed. Tenopir concludes that "the instructional role of reference librarians will become even more important in the future, with an increased need for formal information literacy instruction, more time required for detailed one-on-one point-of-use instruction, and the challenges of taking high quality instruction to remote users."[6]

A report by Eric Bryant of a June 1999 survey to both academic and public librarians uncovers the same trends. He quotes Allyson Washburn of Dixie College Library in Utah on changing roles at the reference desk: "The main thing we have seen is the explosion of electronic resources that necessitates a lot more personal teaching. While our statistics may not be going up, we are spending a lot more time with each question, explaining how to use the resource and basics such as printing." Another librarian cited in the report, Kathy Winslow of North Carolina Wesleyan College, states, "Multiple formats mean much more emphasis on instruction, especially in electronic resources. Each individual session takes longer since both print and media must be explored."[7]

The growing emphasis on instruction carries through all of the traditional reference duties–reference desk service, individual research consultations, and formal classroom instruction–and has resulted in new reference activities and initiatives as well. Since the mid 1990s, reference desk statistics (the number of patrons served) have gone steadily down, but reference librarians feel as busy as ever, because time spent with each individual user has increased.[8] During the same period, demand for traditional, course-related, one-session library instruction classes has gone up.[9] In addition, a growing number of libraries are developing Web-based instruction modules, often with the goal of covering more content and reaching more students than traditional time- and space-bound methods allow. Librarians are more active and visible in the broader context of higher education as well; both locally and nationally, librarians are working with other educators on campus to integrate information literacy learning outcomes into college and university curricula.

WHO WE TEACH:
HOW HAVE OUR USERS CHANGED IN THE INFORMATION AGE?

In a recent essay, Elizabeth Dupuis notes the importance of grounding library instruction programs in user needs. She writes, "For library instruction to continue to evolve we need to consider the nature of our audience. Who are your students? What do they identify with? What interests them? What type of learning environments do they thrive in?"[10] The answers to these questions have changed with the increasing diversity on college campuses, and with the growth of the World Wide Web as a cultural force.

The "face" of college campuses has changed. In academic libraries we serve diverse user groups–including students of different ages, ethnicities, ed-

ucational backgrounds and computer skill levels. In addition to the "traditional" college student, many mature, working adults are returning to colleges for retraining or skills enhancement. The changing marketplace requires new skills, and workers are obliged to keep up. Adult women are entering the academic community to go back to college and finish a degree interrupted by marriage and family priorities. As the wave of Baby Boomers retire, more and more of them are interested in lifelong learning and enrolling in college classes. With many foreign nationals entering our colleges, English as a Second Language (ESL) students have become a large segment of many colleges, bringing another set of needs and priorities.

Distance learning has created another type of user, the remote user, who has to connect with and use his or her library network from another town, state or even country–or, for that matter, from a dorm room on campus. With access to more and more library resources available through the library Web site, the distinction between a distance learner and an on-campus, remote user grows increasingly blurred.

Even the "traditional" on-campus student aged 18-22 has changed dramatically. Many of these "Generation Y" students have been brought up in a world of computers promising instant information. This is the generation whose parents invested in home computers, multimedia CD-ROMs and educational software (not to mention computer games). For them the Internet is the primary source of information. They may never have been introduced to print indexes, journals, or encyclopedias. They feel more at home in the online environment. These experiences form their expectations and preferences when they arrive on campus–they prefer, and expect, full-text online information resources.

Of course, this description of Generation Y students as tech-savvy and computer literate is only a partial picture; the library also serves students who have attended schools without Internet connections or computers in the classroom or home. And of course, as outlined above, many of our users come from outside this high-tech generation, although they may bring to campus advanced technology skills. Comfort with computers and technology–or the opposite–exists as another layer in the diversity of our users, and another challenge to librarians as teachers. As Harvey Sager points out, "Where we once saw only undergraduates, graduate students, and faculty, we now notice new groups defined by skills, knowledge, and preparedness in using computers and new technology. Emerging information technologies have not caused but have brought into focus the diversity of our user groups and have compelled librarians to consider their unique needs in the delivery of library instruction."[11]

Whether our students are computer literate or not, they differ from their counterparts from the pre-Internet era most significantly in one key regard–their expectations. As one librarian commented in Tenopir's survey, "The biggest change is increased user expectations. More and more users expect to be able

to find everything online, full text."[12] Indeed, the less experienced Internet searchers may have even higher expectations: They expect–through their untested internalization of the media hype surrounding the World Wide Web–that finding information will be easy and fast. Although students' expectations are in accordance with librarians' goals for offering easy, fast, online access to relevant information to library users,[13] these expectations are often unrealistic in the current hybrid information environment of diverse information media and fragmented organizational schemes. Unfortunately, many of our interactions with students occur at the moment when this point has been driven home; a student, perhaps after hours of frustrated searching, may seek help at the reference desk.

Unpromising as this instructional moment may be–the student may be frustrated by his or her own failed efforts, and impatient with the librarian's need to start from the beginning–it is more worrisome to consider how often it does *not* occur. Pressed for time, students perhaps naturally value convenience over quality. Thus, a search outcome that they judge to be "good enough," in that it results in several full-text sources that seem to have some relation to the problem at hand, may satisfy them. Computerized keyword searching will almost always yield *something*. The fact that the first few items in a set of results may not be the most relevant and most authoritative information for their research topic may appear less important than the time involved. Of course, students are right in setting a high premium on their time. "Good enough" may be just that, and–to the extent that the information sources that they select allow them to successfully complete their assignments–students are certainly justified in making their own decisions about what constitutes value in information. However, with an incomplete understanding of the diverse information environment and a strong preference for online sources, students often don't realize that some pieces of information are found much faster in "traditional" sources of information–i.e., books–or by using the telephone. Even today's library school students make this mistake.[14] More disturbingly, these easily satisfied library users may not be making deliberate, selective choices about content value and the value of time expended at all. They may not recognize that better sources of information might be available to them. With a seemingly successful search, and ignorant of the fact that better–or at least *different*–options exist, why would a student ask for help?

Other factors may also limit our students' willingness to ask for assistance. As many writers have observed, a salient characteristic of today's students is the degree to which they want and expect to work independently. Encouraging and empowering students to become independent learners is also one of the key goals of the information literacy movement in libraries, discussed later in this essay. However, as Ron Heckart suggests, students working in our increasingly computerized research environments might also feel that they are

supposed to solve their problems independently instead of asking a person for help: "If machine help proves to be one aspect of a future in which students work mostly at computers, mostly in isolation, a broad perspective seems essential. One potential problem such a perspective might bring into focus is user disinclination to seek human help if it is retained in some form as a last resort option. The availability of such help might reassure the librarian, but the inference that the user might draw is that, normally, one ought to succeed with machine help and that turning to human help is evidence of ineptitude."[15]

WHAT WE TEACH: THE INFORMATION AGE COMPETENCIES

Do students have the skills that they need to thrive in the information age research environment? The first step to answering this question is to determine what those skills are. Library instructors have long struggled with the tension between teaching searching mechanics and research concepts, and the Internet environment has brought plenty of both. On the mechanics side, navigating networked electronic resources depends on basic and not-so-basic computer skills–typing, using the mouse, saving, printing, using email, negotiating multiple windows, etc. Conducting effective searches requires the utilization of specialized search syntax, a basic understanding of how computer search engines work, and the mastery of certain key concepts–Boolean operators, relevancy searching, and more. Also required are fairly advanced database and Web navigation skills: "scanning" full-text for content and matching keywords, recognizing common navigational elements (for example, that navigation menus are often found on the left side of a Web page), and–importantly–understanding site boundaries and relationships between linked documents.

The sheer number and variety of resources in the networked information environment has added considerably to the content that librarians must be prepared to teach. As Brendan Rapple states, "With the advent of the electronic library, librarians must now teach not only. . . home resources, but also point to the existence of and means to access, the vast aggregate of global material. They must indicate local, national and international catalogues, an immense world of government and business resources, local and distant CD-ROM bibliographic databases, an abundance of full-text databases, the increasingly important realm of electronic journals, and up-to-the-minute news of local and world events on the Internet."[16] Rapple goes on to include the use of email, listservs and online newsgroups on the list of essential skills that students must learn, and librarians must be prepared to teach. Indeed, the list is endless if one considers the ever expanding content of the Internet.

Moreover, as Harvey Sager writes, "If new technologies have given us new skills to teach, they have also made clear how fleeting the useful shelf life of

many of these skills might be."[17] As he points out, it was in recognition of the short-lived usefulness of tool-based teaching in the electronic environment that the Bibliographic Instruction Section of ACRL in 1987 revised its *Model Statement of Objectives for Academic Bibliographic Instruction*: "The role of BI is not only to provide students with the specific skills necessary to complete assignments, but to prepare individuals to make effective life-long use of information. . . . By describing processes rather than tools, it is hoped that the Statement will remain effective long after the present new technology becomes old."[18] Thus, Sager writes, did the challenges of the new technological environment help to "literally rewrite" the goals of library instruction, and bring forth a new teaching framework, information literacy.[19]

Although the idea of information literacy was articulated in the late 1980s, it is with the growth of the World Wide Web in libraries in the mid-1990s that most librarians began to recognize the essential nature of these skills. With the explosion of materials available electronically, and with the lack of quality control on the Web, library users need strong evaluation skills to counter information overload and to navigate an electronic information landscape as rich in misinformation as in fact. Although as Barbara MacAdam argues, students are by nature critical and willing to challenge authority through their lifelong exposure to mass media and advertising,[20] this "everyday life" cynicism may not translate into a more critical evaluation of formal information sources. Students still seem too ready to believe what they read. In the Internet environment, without quality control, their naïveté can have disastrous consequences on the quality of their research-based assignments.

The evaluation of information quality, of course, is only one of the high-level cognitive skills that most librarians now recognize are needed for "information consumers" to be information literate; users must be able to "recognize when information is needed and have the ability to locate, evaluate, and use effectively the needed information."[21] Our goal as reference librarians in teaching students the information literacy skills that they need in an electronic information environment extends beyond the college years; we hope to enable young people to become independent, life-long learners, capable of thoughtful, active participation in their education, in the workplace, and in public life.

Evidence from the classroom, however, provides a clear indication that many students are far from information literate. A number of teaching faculty and college administrators have observed a growing "find it and stick it together" phenomenon in student papers; rather than synthesizing information to support a coherent and thoughtful argument, students cut and paste together chunks of preset paragraphs and quotes.[22] As a result, papers are jumbled, often lacking an articulated thesis, and sometimes (knowingly or unknowingly) plagiarized. Problems in the quality of student research and writing existed before the Internet. However, the ease with which a student can copy electronic text,

and the expectation of finding "instant information" online, may detract from a student's ability and willingness to use that information effectively–through critical evaluation and synthesis–and ethically, with full credit given to the source. Helping students to become information literate is therefore even more critical in the Internet environment. As David Rothenberg writes, his responsibility as an educator is to "teach students how to read, to take time with language and ideas, to work through arguments, to synthesize disparate sources to come up with original thought. [He must help his students] understand how to assess sources to determine their credibility, as well as to trust their own ideas more than snippets of thought that materialize on a screen."[23] Most teaching librarians would add that it is their responsibility–working in partnership with department faculty–to help students learn these concepts as well.

In addition to the *finding, evaluating,* and *using* information abilities, information literate people are those who have created a cognitive map for information space(s). Within this *world of information* (or place, or terrain, or landscape–the metaphor emerges again and again), the empowered information seeker proceeds with purposeful, deliberate movement. David Carr describes the independent, information literate learner at work, moving through and reshaping this world: "In this landscape the learner would be shown in motion: examining and interpreting information through a personal lens, or a private exploratory system; devising and revising telling images as new information appears; breaking through, overcoming obstacles to new information; finding an almost aesthetic appreciation for the rich net of connections; marking the meanings and uses of mistakes; experiencing dullness and confusion; staring in boredom; quitting for awhile; perhaps reorganizing the whole field into new patterns as an effect of one moment's insight."[24]

Of course, this has its flip side in the disempowered information seeker who moves randomly through a mysterious, incomprehensible information space, following links without being sure where they lead, hoping to stumble across what he or she needs. Unfortunately, the experience of librarians reveals that many college students lack a conceptual map of information space. Shackelford, Thompson, and James describe a familiar scenario in academic libraries: "Students may sit down at workstations with the remains of searches on the screens and not know what databases they are immersed in. When their searches do not yield the expected results, students may simply move to other computers, never questioning what went wrong."[25]

To be information literate, users must have a "cognitive grip" on the size, scope, and shape of the information world.[26] Students need to understand that when they open a database (including a public Web search engine) they are entering and exploring a specific information space with a particular, limited scope. They need to learn to look for the scope of the resources that are available to them, and they need to understand the differences between Web-based

databases and the public Web. They need to learn to select the resources that will most likely contain the type of information that they want. Comprehending the scope of information spaces on the Internet is particularly difficult, because of the flattening effect of the computer screen. It is ironic but true that the Internet, arguably the most richly complex and multidimensional information source of all time, is subject to what Charles Bunge called the "peep hole effect" of computerized information, whereby only a small portion of the source and its structure can be seen at one time.[27]

The challenge that the networked information environment poses–the number of high and low level skills required by students to interact with it effectively, and their current lack of these skills–cannot be answered by artificially limiting students' information options, although this is certainly the strategy of some. In some instances, teaching faculty–and even librarians–actively dissuade students from using the Internet for their research, because of the potential for students to encounter "poor quality" information, or because they fear that students will misuse electronic information sources. However, as more and more valuable content migrates to the Web, including materials not published elsewhere, this position becomes untenable. In addition, the distinction between "library information resources" and "Internet resources" is weak, and weakening, as more and more of our collections and services go online. A better strategy, and certainly a more appropriate strategy given the educational mission of colleges and universities, is to teach students to negotiate the complex world of information, not to protect them from it.

USER NEEDS: MECHANICS AND CONCEPTS

To the questions–Should we teach mechanics or concepts? Manual skills or mental framework? Information skills or information literacy?–most librarians favor the conceptual, mental, literate side. These are the more important, cognitive abilities that enable lifelong learning. However, as the earlier discussion makes clear, successful information seeking in the Internet environment requires both technical skills and conceptual abilities, and most librarians are currently trying to teach both, because our users need both.

Writing in 1995, Harvey Sager included both mechanical and conceptual skills in his outline of librarian teaching responsibilities, although, true to the longstanding pedagogical priorities of library instructors, he preferenced the latter as more important: "What we teach should always be based on user needs. Do we teach technology? Yes, we must. Do we teach the use of specific sources? Yes, we must. Do we teach process? Yes. Context? Yes. . . . However, it is not as important that students remember the details of searching a particular database as it is that they develop the longer-term skills of being able

to identify the scope of a database; the appropriateness of content for their discipline, field, and topic; and to develop information skills around sound research principles, methodologies, and concepts."[28]

Some writers have suggested that within the last few years, librarians have been freer to emphasize the concepts over mechanics in instruction. Elizabeth Dupuis argues that library instruction in networked resources has "evolved" from its focus on the technical "how-to" toward an emphasis on more fundamental research concepts in the later half of the 1990s: "Perhaps as a combination of students' growing comfort with the Internet and the shear number of resources available, libraries reverted to teaching broadly applicable skills rather than specific steps to use resources. Helping students learn transferable, information literacy skills became a common goal."[29]

However, the vision of library instruction captured by other writers leads one to suspect that, for many, the above passage may describe an ideal, rather than a realized evolution. As one librarian noted in a recent article by Carol Tenopir, "We are in a transitional time, with both old and new skills competing for limited instructional opportunities."[30] Helping students to achieve information literacy is a shared goal, but in reality, we focus on less lofty learning objectives at least some of the time.

HOW WE TEACH: THE IMPACT OF THE INTERNET AND INFORMATION TECHNOLOGY

Active Learning in Library Classrooms

In the essay, "From Transmission to Research: Librarians at the Heart of the Campus," James Wilkinson summarizes the emerging pedagogy of the "Research Model" of education, within the family of "resource-based learning," "active learning," "problem-based teaching," "case-based learning," and others. Unlike the traditional "Transmission Model" of teaching, in which knowledge is passed down—usually through lectures—from teacher/expert to student/novice, students within the Research Model paradigm learn through asking questions, forming hypotheses, and gathering and synthesizing information to test their ideas and come to a conclusion. Teachers in this model are guides and coaches, and students learn by doing. Advocates of the Research Model, and other active learning variants, argue that students are better able to understand and retain information that they have wrestled with through active inquiry. Learning is more personalized to the interests and abilities of individual students. In addition, students learn the process of problem solving as well as the content of a given subject area. As Wilkinson writes, "The research

model assumes that content is not an end in itself, but a means to a greater end, which is learning how to learn."[31]

Wilkinson points out that information technology (IT) is not necessarily "in harmony" with the new pedagogy, but that in fact, because computer-assisted instruction is often inflexible and predictable, it often mimics the Transmission Model.[32] His remarks serve as a useful warning; as discussed in the next section, it is important to utilize sound pedagogical practices when designing "virtual" learning environments, and there may be limits to the effectiveness of automated instruction. And, of course, active learning methods in which students learn by doing, discussing, writing and reflecting have been applied successfully in libraries without the use of technological tools.[33] However, in libraries, information technology–in the form of networked, hands-on computer classrooms with access to library databases on the Internet–has greatly increased the feasibility of active learning methods. For librarians, technology has been a significant force helping "the sage on the stage [become] the guide on the side."[34]

Librarians have always known the value of actively engaging with information, but ironically, we have historically been among the worst culprits of the top-down, lecture-driven, one-size-fits-all, Transmission Mode teaching. There are reasons for this, of course. Librarians feel pressure to cover all of the information that students will need for successful research in the limited instructional opportunities available to them–usually course-related, one-shot sessions of 50 minutes to just over an hour. This has traditionally meant a content-packed lecture or "canned" demonstration, with little time left over for questions and answers. However, this seems to be changing. Although limited quantitative data is available on the extent to which academic libraries in the United States are incorporating active learning methods into instruction, evidence of a growing trend is provided by a recognized increase in the number of computer classrooms in libraries and the results of recent research conducted in other North American libraries.

Although they do not give specific figures, Linda Shirato and Joseph Badics' report on a 1995 Library Orientation Exchange (LOEX) survey on trends in library instruction cites an increased use of hands-on computer training from earlier LOEX surveys. Likewise, although the lecture as a mode of instruction is still the heaviest used (by 94% of the respondents), some libraries reported using the lecture *in combination* with hands-on experience. More definitive evidence of libraries' embrace of active learning concepts can be seen in the survey from librarians' articulation of pedagogical ideals, if not practices. Asked what instructional methods they considered most effective, librarians listed hands-on searching, individual instruction, short lectures in combination with hands-on practice, and active learning methods, generally.

These are easily contrasted with the more generic or passive modes of instruction identified by librarians as least effective: lectures, tours, print handouts, and workbooks. As more teaching librarians have access now to hands-on computer labs than when the survey was conducted in 1995, it is reasonable to assume that more of them have been able to put their pedagogical ideals into practice.[35]

A recent study conducted in Canadian academic libraries yields more precise data on the increase of active learning strategies in library instruction. In 2000, 63.9% of respondents reported utilizing hands-on instruction in computer labs as a mode of learning, a significant increase over the 43.2% librarians using hands-on methods in a similar 1995 survey. The lecture or demonstration as a mode of instruction, on the other hand, while still common, appeared to be on the decrease–72.2% in 1995 had dropped to 66.3% in 2000.[36]

The Canadian survey asked librarians to evaluate the degree to which information technology had changed the nature of instruction. Of the 81.7% of respondents that claimed IT had influenced modes of instruction "quite a bit" or "a great deal," most pointed out this evolution from instructor-led demonstrations to hands on instruction. Perhaps as a result of this change, 72.1% of respondents reported their belief that technology had improved instruction. Respondents stated that technology had made instruction more effective, dynamic, spontaneous, interesting, participative, individualized, relevant to student interests, flexible to different learning styles, and better able to reach more students. This latter point clearly refers to Web-based instructional efforts, discussed in the next section.[37]

Less positive perceptions of the impact of information technology also emerged. One respondent voiced her concern that "with [the] focus on technology, there is less time to devote [to] talking about strategy, [the] nature of information sources, etc."[38] It is not clear from the context of this observation whether the respondent was referring to the tension discussed earlier in this essay between teaching technical skills at the expense of research concepts, or whether he or she was observing that the addition of hands-on searching by students reduced the time available to the librarian for covering content. This latter point is certainly true. Unless additional instructional time is made available, librarians may indeed find that they need to cover less content. Implementing active learning methods takes time–both preparation time and classroom time. The payoff, advocates of active learning strategies argue, is in the student's deeper integration of the concepts that are covered.

In addition, active learning methods may be particularly important for the "content" that librarians want students to learn. Information literacy is less a body of knowledge than a *process* and a set of abilities. Even one of the less

complex components of information literacy, effective database searching, requires that students learn by doing. Searching electronic resources is a recursive process–initial search strategies need to be adjusted and refined through the evaluation of intermediate results. To successfully learn this, students need not only a strong conceptual understanding but also practice. As Patricia Breivik notes, "Information literacy cannot be taught by librarians and faculty, it must be learned by students through experiences shaped by librarians and faculty."[39]

Web-Based Instruction

At the same time that the Internet has helped teaching librarians to bring hands-on, active learning into library classrooms, it has also provided an opportunity to move beyond the limitations of classroom instruction. Though effective for some purposes, face-to-face instruction in the form that most librarians have known it–in brief encounters at the reference desk, short "one-shot" instruction sessions, library-offered credit classes, and one-on-one research consultations–has been rightly criticized as not allowing enough time for significant impact on student learning, not being flexible enough to meet students' varied educational backgrounds or learning styles, or simply not reaching enough students. The acceptance of information literacy objectives beyond assignment-driven information searching skills has created a heightened awareness of these difficulties; the new content requires more time to teach and depends more on individualized student learning variables. Our more ambitious goal–information literacy as a learning outcome for all students–is less forgiving of the hit or miss methods that may have worked, albeit imperfectly, in the past. Likewise, our growing recognition that we need to provide for the information literacy needs of distance learners, and for all students who do not come into the library, has challenged us to develop instructional models that are less time-bound, more flexible and modular, and more accessible remotely–to allow students to learn at the level, pace, time and *place* that they prefer. Finally, in this era of more and more demand for library and information literacy instruction, librarians are looking for instructional models that are less demanding of a librarian's time than face-to-face instruction.

To these ends, a growing number of libraries have developed or are developing instructional Web sites in the form of self-paced, interactive tutorials, with the goal of helping students to master both basic research skills and the more elusive conceptual skills of evaluation and "effective use." Like traditional face-to-face library instruction, Web-based library instruction is usually not offered as a semester-long course. Rather, it usually "consists of modules that can be used to complement and supplement the one-shot library

instruction."[40] A body of best practices for the design of online instruction is developing; appropriately, librarians are bringing to Web-based instruction the principle of student-centered, active learning discussed in the previous section.

In a recent article, Nancy Dewald draws from noted learning theorists and Web-instruction researchers, including Skinner, Piaget, Knowles, McManus, and others, to posit pedagogical guidelines for library Web-based instruction. A strong emphasis on active learning principles immerges from her discussion, in which she outlines three key considerations for good design–achieving learner motivation, organizing module content, and building in high levels of interactivity. Although she discusses these three design considerations separately, Dewald acknowledges that these areas frequently overlap. Thoughtful organization, for example, encourages learner motivation, as discussed later. And a focus on interactivity is central to all other design considerations in the online instructional environment, as it is the mechanism by which learners actively engage with instructional content.[41]

Motivation, that force which encourages learners to enter into and progress through instructional modules, is a necessary foundation for successful Web-based instruction. Sound Web-based instructional design, Dewald outlines, includes both extrinsic motivation (motivation based outside the learner) and, importantly, intrinsic motivation (stemming from the learner's interest and *self*-motivation). Of these, extrinsic motivation is perhaps the easiest to accomplish. Immediate and frequent feedback as the learner progresses through practice exercises, for example, provides external motivation in the form of positive reinforcement and encouragement. If the Web modules or exercises are required, that can also serve as an obvious source of external, extrinsic motivation. The more elusive intrinsic motivation–the individual motivation of the learner–must be accomplished by, as Dewald notes, building an instructional space in which the student is "actively involved in learning."[42] By engaging the learner in active inquiry, by asking students to wrestle with and apply new knowledge through problem solving exercises, the designer of online instruction modules will capture a student's interest and build a learner's intrinsic motivation.

The organization of library instruction modules can also play a role in sparking a learner's interest and motivation, and in meeting the varying abilities and learning needs of our diverse students. Dewald outlines the benefits of building "guided yet user-definable paths" into online instruction, in which learners can either move step-by-step through the lesson in the order determined by the librarian-designer or, by linking to sections of the content in order of interest, choose a more individualized "learning path." The instructional space that allows for this flexibility accommodates learners with different abil-

ities and learning strategies, and keeps the learners interest by allowing them to "customize the instruction."[43]

Interactivity, in the form of active-learning exercises or in learner-defined pathways, thus engages and interests students. Interactive elements also, of course, enable enhanced learning by allowing students to practice and apply skills in new contexts. One well-known example of highly interactive Web-based library instruction is the Texas Information Literacy Tutorial (TILT), developed by librarians at the University of Texas at Austin.[44] TILT includes student-customized content to engage learners (for example, illustrative examples drawn from the student's identified area of interest), "live" database searching practice, interactive activities and games, and built-in skills assessment, in the form of (usually multiple choice) exercises and quizzes to measure learning outcomes. In the *SiteVision* section of TILT, in which students are asked to evaluate Web sites for use in a college research paper, the developers used interactive forms to capture student input. Student evaluations of Web sites are then posted to a shared online bulletin board of student responses, so that learners can compare their choices with those of their peers and of the librarians. In a recent article, TILT developers Clara Fowler and Elizabeth Dupuis note the importance of these interactive elements to helping a student integrate, apply, and retain the concepts that they learn: "As students learn concepts and skills in the tutorial, the interactions require students to incorporate what they learn in the context of a research problem. Students first reinforce learned concepts through recall and later are encouraged to think divergently when evaluating information. . . . Incorporating problem-based learning increases the relevance and long-term retention of the information."[45]

Most librarians have designed Web-based modules to complement, rather than replace, classroom instruction. Integrating TILT into the University of Texas library instruction program as a prerequisite to face-to-face sessions has allowed librarians in the classroom to focus on high-level, information literacy concepts and challenging learning activities: "We no longer have to exclude teaching certain concepts in library sessions to teach basic skills in the allotted time."[46] However, Fowler and Dupuis point out that some department faculty have chosen to assign the Web-modules without an accompanying library session for basic Freshman courses, freeing up librarian time to focus on more advanced sessions. The authors also note a more disturbing indicator that online instruction is sometimes seen as a substitute for in-person instruction, rather than its counterpart; to their surprise, some library administrators hoping that they could use TILT and hire fewer librarians contacted them.

It is important to note that despite the promise of Web-based instruction to help students learn a foundation of information competencies, there are limitations to this "canned" or automated instruction. Marvin Wiggins suggests that although these tools are useful and effective for teaching rules and basic skills,

they are usually not flexible enough to help students learn truly complex "how or why" issues that require give and take–such as choosing a topic, or interpreting and synthesizing information to come to conclusions. The challenge is to put the human (librarian) where he or she is needed, while relying on automated instructive tools where they can work. The most effective instructional program, he argues, utilizes both automated and in-person instruction: "The marriage of these two methods of learning (first, of facts of an established body of knowledge to be learned, and a research strategy that works; and second, the interface with an inquiring mind and student application of the meaning of information found) will enrich instruction. The librarian's role becomes one of opening the door beyond structured programs."[47]

As we look to Web-based instruction to serve our distance learners, we need to keep in mind the importance of making this "interface with an inquiring mind" available for follow-up and give and take. Librarian-student interaction need not be face-to-face, however; though currently underutilized, the Internet as a communications medium could also serve instructional goals, through email, synchronous chat, or discussion lists.

Moving into the Curriculum

George Allen argues that librarians need to help students learn the artistry of acquiring information, rather than simply teaching them the techniques of information seeking: "The artistry required here is not only skill in selecting where first we should look and by what method, but also the ability to determine what answers are relevant and what ones beside the point. This artistry must then find expression in its determination of whether the relevant answers are confirming or disconfirming, and if the latter how a negative result might serve to improve upon the sort of question asked or the way by which it is asked."[48]

Artistry, in other words, is a matter of *judgement,* rather than technique; and judgement, he argues, is not a teachable skill that can be transmitted from professors or librarians to students in a classroom. Thus, traditional library instruction that focuses on teaching students data gathering techniques–even when augmented by the active learning methods described earlier–is not enough. Rather, he suggests, librarians have a more essential role to play as creators of and participants in "contexts for learning," in which students first learn a few searching techniques, then make choices about when, where, and how to apply those techniques. Then, with teacher-librarians as mentors and critics, students learn the strengths and weaknesses of those choices; and move on to another assignment, in which they make more choices, and again are offered feedback on those choices. Such feedback from a librarian to a student might include, "What were the tools they used needlessly or forgot to use?

What sorts of data did they think likely to be worth gathering, that they surely should have had the foresight to know would not be? Conversely, what data that they didn't include should they have anticipated the need for? How did they go about deciding what to keep and with what to dispense, when to narrow their inquiry and when to broaden it, and how might they have been more sure-footed or efficient or effective?"[49] From this cycle, students in dialogue with librarians learn from their choices to make better choices; they learn good judgement, or artistry.

To accomplish this goal, librarians will have to move beyond their traditional instructional roles. As Allan points out, "The usual educational division of labor, confining the librarians to the retrieval of the resources and the course instructor to the pedagogical use of those resources, just won't work. If what happens is to be genuine learning rather than merely teaching, librarians are going to have to be in the classroom and instructors in the library, working as a team, with students, not just on their behalf."[50] Brendan Rapple agrees that librarians must, and will, take on new teaching roles: "Not only will librarians help faculty and students do research, they will also help faculty develop new pedagogical methods for the electronic age. Many will become much more active in curriculum design, in devising and evaluating assignments, in team teaching, and in teaching for-credit courses."[51] Writing in 1998 and 2000, respectively, Patricia Breivik and Kimberly Donnelly argue that librarians need to move outside the library to work with administrators and department faculty in crafting comprehensive campus strategies for helping students learn information literacy–"formal, concrete, sequenced programs"[52] in which "subject-specific efforts build upon a foundation of research skills mastered as part of general education or core curriculum offerings."[53]

To achieve this role of full partner and collaborator in the teaching and learning enterprise, librarians will have to overcome some longstanding barriers–one of these is the difficulty many librarians have encountered in building strong partnerships with department faculty to create effective, integrated library instruction programs. As Evan Farber and Larry Hardesty have noted, building these relationships is far from easy, perhaps due to a faculty culture that resists change. Or, as Larry Hardesty suggests, the educational role of librarians may be something that doesn't occur to them: "They simply have not thought about the library."[54] That the challenge of getting teaching faculty to work with librarians remains a constant decades after it was first discussed is disheartening, yet both writers see reason to hope, and ground that optimism–first and foremost–in the impact of the Internet. Technology, Hardesty argues, "will facilitate an expanded involvement of librarians in the educational process."[55] Farber concurs: "The teaching faculty is increasingly aware of the educational challenge the Internet poses, and also aware that they do not have the time or expertise to keep up with the continual changes and improve-

ments. They know that while they can provide some guidance in helping students find and evaluate information, they'll have to depend on librarians to really do the job."[56]

Building integrated information literacy instruction programs will take time, effort, money, and a whole-hearted library and campus commitment. However, as Hannelore Rader notes, this is the "optimal time" for these initiatives, as there is a growing recognition that college curricula need to change to "educate individuals for high performance and achievement in the twenty-first century's information environment."[57] Information technology, Harvey Sager writes, is the librarian's ally in our effort to expand our role in defining the nature of this change: "New information technology is a force that breaks down barriers between faculty and librarians and helps us gain recognition and status within the educational community. This can be an ally in creating a climate of collaboration for achieving broader educational goals."[58]

LOOKING FORWARD: THE POTENTIAL IMPACT OF EMERGING INTERNET TECHNOLOGIES

The current information environment is not an ideal learning environment–it is fragmented, disorganized, and needlessly complex. Part of this, of course, stems from the inevitable complexity of an environment in which information is produced in so many forms, by so many creators, and for so many purposes. But there are mundane, unnecessary complexities as well–and these can get in the way of librarians helping students to master higher-level, information literacy skills. Encountering difficulty in the research process is not always a useful learning experience. Consider, what steps do you describe in explaining to a group of students the process for tracking down the full-text of an article?

1. Sometimes, the full-text is online. If not . . .
2. Check the *library catalog*. If you don't find it in the catalog . . .
3. Check the database of electronic journal holdings (if you have one). If the journal is not listed there . . .
4. Use InterLibrary Loan. If you don't have time to wait . . .
5. Visit another local library. (Search the library catalog for the library that you want, etc.)

Other examples of mundane research difficulties abound: How complex is your library's authentication process for remote access to online resources? How does your library Web site rate in terms of usability and accessibility? How many different database search interfaces do novice users encounter? Of course, persistence in the face of difficulties is a necessary life skill, but most

people can only retain so many details, and this sort of low-level procedural information can eat up an educational encounter. What more could students be learning if these mundane, everyday research needs could be more intuitive? If the basics are easier, reference librarians will have more time to teach, and students more patience to learn, information literacy skills. If we want to help students learn to conceptualize and negotiate the truly complex information environment, and to evaluate and synthesize the diverse information sources that they find, we need to simplify that which *can be* simplified, and remove whatever unnecessary complications we can. We need to improve the information environment for student learning. Just as the Internet has transformed the shape of, and objectives for library instruction, the thoughtful application of current and emerging Web-based technologies may help to improve the learning environment. To make this happen, teaching librarians need to be more aggressive in seeking out and advocating for products and systems that help us meet our instructional objectives, and we need to be more active in improving the design of our existing tools. Patricia Breivik argues that librarians need to "influence the design of library systems and products (e.g., software, printed material) in order to make them more user friendly, thus, producing savings of staff time. Librarians' ultimate goal in this regard must be to have as few different user interfaces to information sources as possible and to have those that do exist be as intuitive as possible. Their time needs to be spent not in teaching the use of technology, online systems and complex reference tools but rather in how to evaluate, organize and effectively use information."[59]

Even if we cannot always deliver user-friendly search interfaces to commercial databases, the tools that we develop onsite (library Web pages, for example) should have *proven* high levels of usability. And we should continue to search for technological (and non-technological) solutions that will reduce the unnecessary complications in the information environment. Common interface solutions are an example, and equally promising is SFX, an emerging technology that promises to provide pre-Internet levels of integration and structure to the fragmented information environment. Using the OpenURL standard framework, an SFX server provides locally customized, dynamic links between related records in a given library's multiple databases, and between those records and related library services. For example, an article citation in *ERIC* could link to the full-text in *InfoTrac* (or another database, depending on the library's subscriptions) and to the local library catalog, and to an InterLibrary Loan or document delivery form. The various possibilities for full-text retrieval that took five minutes to explain is suddenly made manifest with a set of links. When you consider how this technology could also be harnessed to link together article citations and a periodical record in *Ulrich's* (identifying the journal as peer-reviewed, or not), or an author entry in *Who's Who* (providing evidence of the authority of the author), the power of SFX as a tool for improving student learning, even of high-level concepts, becomes clear.[60]

Systems librarians and library administrators–who often lack direct, daily contact with library users–may not always recognize the potential of new technologies to transform and improve the learning environment. As advocates for student learning, it is the responsibility of teaching librarians to bring these tools to their attention, and to articulate their potential value.

CONCLUSION

The impact of the Internet on libraries and librarians has been transformational, and nowhere is this truer than in the reference librarian's role as teacher. As Harvey Sager writes, "In nearly all of these instructional areas and objectives [–from traditional library instruction to the creation of 'learning environments that foster critical thinking skills and information literacy'–] new and emerging technologies have provided opportunities, challenges, and impetus. It would not be an exaggeration to say that technology has validated BI as an essential library mission, and revolutionized the 'what,' the 'way,' and the 'why' we think about, write about, and deliver bibliographic instruction to our diverse user populations."[61] More work needs to be done to reach the goals for student learning brought about by the information literacy movement, but we have new resources to help us in meeting these goals.

What do we have that will help us? We have an unprecedented level of support for and acknowledgment of our teaching role on high levels from administrators and curriculum committees. We have new openings with faculty who are unsure how to solve on their own the challenge posed by students' low level of information literacy and research skills. We have students who want for themselves what we want for them–independence and self-reliance in seeking and choosing information. We have a theoretical and practical teaching framework developed and enhanced over the last decade–information literacy. And though our traditional roles as information providers, gatherers, organizers and gateways have eroded over the past decade, in our role as teachers we have a growing confidence in the continuing usefulness, relevancy and value of our potential contributions to student learning in the age of the Internet.

REFERENCES

1. Elizabeth A. Dupuis, "The Creative Evolution of Library Instruction," *Rsr: Reference Services Review* 27, no. 3 (1999): 289.

2. The first three "agents" outlined in Dupuis, 289.

3. James Wilkinson, "From Transmission to Research: Librarians at the Heart of the Campus," in *Future Teaching Roles for Academic Librarians,* ed. Alice Harrison Bahr (Binghamton, NY: The Haworth Press, Inc., 2000), 25-40.

4. Carol Tenopir, "Electronic Reference and Reference Librarians: A Look Through the 1990s," *Rsr: Reference Services Review* 27, no. 3 (1999): 276.

5. Tenopir, "Electronic Reference and Reference Librarians: A Look Through the 1990s," 276-279.

6. Tenopir, "Electronic Reference and Reference Librarians: A Look Through the 1990s," 279.

7. Eric Bryant, "Triumph of the Web," *Library Journal* 124, no. 19 (1999): 4; Bryant, 6.

8. Carol Tenopir, "Reference Use Statistics," *Library Journal* 123, no. 8 (1998): 32, 34.

9. Dupuis, 287-90.

10. Dupuis, 290.

11. Harvey Sager, "Implications for Bibliographic Instruction," in *The Impact of Emerging Technologies on Reference Service and Bibliographic Instruction*, ed. Gary M. Pitkin (Westport, CT: Greenwood Press, 1995), 53.

12. Carol Tenopir, "The Impact of Digital Reference on Librarians and Library Users," *Online* 22, no. 6 (Nov 1998): 84.

13. The relationship between students' expectations of and librarians' goals for increased online access to information has attracted critical attention from at least one scholar, who holds libraries partially responsible for what he sees as an increasing tendency for students to cut and paste "snippets of thought" into their papers, rather than evaluating, synthesizing, and integrating ideas. David Rothenberg writes, "When college libraries are diverting funds from books to computer technology that will be obsolete in two years at most, they send a clear message to students: Don't read, just connect." See David Rothenberg, "How the Web Destroys the Quality of Students' Research Papers," *Chronicle of Higher Education,* par. 10 [online] (15 August 1997 [cited 2 February 2001]); available from World Wide Web @ http://www.chronicle.com/che-data/articles.dir/art-43.dir/issue-49.dir/49a04401.htm.

14. Mary Ellen Bates, "The Newly Minted MLS: What Do We Need to Know Today," *Searcher* 6, no. 5 (May 1998): 31.

15. Ron J. Heckart, "Machine Help and Human Help in the Emerging Digital Library," *College & Research Libraries* 59, no. 3 (May 1998): 257.

16. Brendan A. Rapple, "The Librarian As Teacher in the Networked Environment," *College Teaching* 45, no. 3 (summer 1997): 114.

17. Sager, 56.

18. ACRL/Bibliographic Instruction Section Task Force on Model Statement of Objectives, *Model Statement of Objectives for Academic Bibliographic Instruction* (1987): 256-261, quoted in Sager, 56.

19. Sager, 56.

20. Barbara MacAdam, "From the Other Side of the River: Re-Conceptualizing the Educational Mission of Libraries," in *Future Teaching Roles for Academic Librarians,* ed. Alice Harrison Bahr (Binghamton, NY: The Haworth Press, Inc., 2000), 85.

21. American Library Association, *Presidential Committee on Information Literacy: Final Report* [online] (Chicago: American Library Association, 1989 [cited 2 February 2001]); available from the World Wide Web @ http://www.ala.org/acrl/nili/ilit1st.html.

22. Wendy R. Leibowitz, "Technology Transforms Writing and the Teaching of Writing," *Chronicle of Higher Education* [online] (26 November 1999 [cited 2 February 2001]); available from World Wide Web @ http://www.chronicle.com/weekly/v46/i14/14a06701.htm; Lorie Roth, "Educating the Cut-and-Paste Generation," *Li-*

brary Journal 124, no. 18 (1 November 1999): 42-44; David Rothenberg, "How the Web Destroys the Quality of Students' Research Papers," *Chronicle of Higher Education* [online] (15 August 1997 [cited 2 February 2001]); available from World Wide Web @ http://www.chronicle.com/che-data/articles.dir/art-43.dir/issue-49.dir/49a04401.htm.

23. Rothenberg, par. 12.

24. David W. Carr, "The Situation of the Adult Learner in the Library," in *Librarians as Learners, Librarians as Teachers: The Diffusion of Internet Expertise in the Academic Library,* ed. Patricia O'Brien Libutti (Chicago: Association of College and Research Libraries, 1999), 23.

25. Jean Shackelford, Dot S. Thompson and May Beth James, "Teaching Strategy and Assignment Design: Assessing the Quality and Validity of Information via the Web," *Social Science Computer Review* 17, no. 2 (summer 1999): 200.

26. Linda Shirato, "LOEX and Library Instruction," *Rsr: Reference Services Review* 27, no. 3 (1999): 215.

27. Charles A. Bunge, "Reference Services," in *ALA World Encyclopedia of Library and Information Services* (Chicago: American Library Association, 1980), 468-474.

28. Sager, 54.

29. Dupuis, 289.

30. Tenopir, "Electronic Reference and Reference Librarians: A Look Through the 1990s," 278.

31. Wilkinson, 36.

32. Wilkinson, 34.

33. For numerous examples of proven active learning exercises in library instruction see Tracy Bicknell-Holmes and Paul Seth Hoffman, "Elicit, Engage, Experience and Explore: Discovery Learning in Library Instruction," *Rsr: Reference Services Review* 28, no. 4 (2000): 313-322.

34. Janine Schmidt and Gulcin Cribb, "Leading Life-Long Learning: The Library's Role" (paper presented at the annual meeting of the International Association of Technological University Libraries (IATUL), Chania, Greece, May 1999): par. 12 [online] [cited 2 February 2001]; available from World Wide Web @ http://educate.lib.chalmers.se/IATUL/proceedcontents/chanpap/cribb.html.

35. Linda Shirato and Joseph Badics, "Library Instruction in the 1990s: A Comparison with Trends in Two Earlier LOEX Surveys," *Research Strategies* 15, no. 4 (1997): 223-237.

36. Heidi Julien, "Information Literacy Instruction in Canadian Academic Libraries: Longitudinal Trends and International Comparisons," *College & Research Libraries* 61, no. 6 (November 2000): 510-523.

37. Julien, 510-523.

38. Julien, 520.

39. Patricia S. Breivik, "Take II–Information Literacy: Revolution in Education," *Rsr: Reference Services Review* 27, no. 3 (1999): 272.

40. Nancy H. Dewald, "Web-based Library Instruction: What Is Good Pedagogy?" *Information Technology and Libraries* 18, no. 1 (March 1999): 26.

41. Dewald, 26-31.

42. Dewald, 28.

43. Dewald, 29.

44. Digital Information Literacy Office, "Texas Information Literacy Tutorial (TILT)" [tutorial online] (Austin, Texas: University of Texas at Austin, 1999-2000 [cited 2 February 2001]); available from the World Wide Web @ http://tilt.lib.utsystem.edu.

45. Clara S. Fowler and Elizabeth A. Dupuis, "What Have We Done: TILT's Impact on our Instruction Program," *Rsr: Reference Services Review* 28, no. 4 (2000): 344.

46. Fowler and Dupuis, 345.

47. Marvin E. Wiggins, "Instructional Design and Student Learning," *Rsr: Reference Services Review* 27, no. 3 (1999): 227.

48. George Allen, "The Art of Learning with Difficulty," in *Future Teaching Roles for Academic Librarians,* ed. Alice Harrison Bahr (Binghamton, NY: The Haworth Press, Inc., 2000), 10.

49. Allen, 15.

50. Allen, 16.

51. Rapple, 114.

52. Kimberly M. Donnelly, "Building the Learning Library: Where Do We Start," in *Future Teaching Roles for Academic Librarians,* ed. Alice Harrison Bahr (Binghamton, NY: The Haworth Press, Inc., 2000), 60.

53. Patricia Breivik, *Student Learning in the Information* Age (Phoenix, Arizona: The Oryx Press, 1998), 43.

54. Larry Hardesty, "Reflections on 25 Years of Library Instruction: Have We Made Progress?" *Rsr: Reference Services Review* 27, no. 3 (1999): 244.

55. Hardesty, 245.

56. Evan Farber, "Faculty-librarian Cooperation: A Personal Retrospective," *Rsr: Reference Services Review* 27, no. 3 (1999): 233.

57. Hannelore Rader, "The Learning Environment–Then, Now and Later," *Rsr: Reference Services Review* 27, no. 3 (1999): 221.

58. Sager, 52.

59. Breivik, "Take II–Information Literacy: Revolution in Education," 273.

60. For more information on SFX and the OpenURL framework, see Herbert Van de Sompel and Oren Beit-Arie, "Open Linking in the Scholarly Information Environment Using the OpenURL Framework," in *D-Lib Magazine* [online journal] (vol. 7, no. 3, March 2001 [cited 15 March 2001]); available from the World Wide Web @ http://www.dlib.org/dlib/march01/vandesompel/03vandesompel.html.

61. Sager, 51.

Reference, Mental Models
and Teaching Technology

D. Scott Brandt

SUMMARY. It would be easy to say that technology is complicating things for reference, but things are more complicated than that. Technology should be a system for solving problems, but for many people, both librarians and users, it *is* the problem. But in some ways it hides an even older problem–understanding things from the user's point-of-view. Contemporary cognitive and educational theories note that we are not paying enough attention to the user/learner, that we do not understand the mental models of those who use libraries, library systems and reference. As more technology is used and complicates systems for users, we should focus more on what users bring to the reference/learning interaction. *[Article copies available for a fee from The Haworth Document Delivery Service: 1-800-342-9678. E-mail address: <getinfo@haworthpressinc.com> Website: <http://www.HaworthPress.com> © 2001 by The Haworth Press, Inc. All rights reserved.]*

KEYWORDS. Reference, learning, mental model, teaching, analogies, system model, constructivism, Internet, technology

If we agree that teaching, in various manifestations, is an important part of reference, then we need to determine how we can best facilitate learning expe-

D. Scott Brandt is Associate Professor and Technology Training Librarian, Purdue University Libraries, 1530 Stewart Center, Room 279, West Lafayette, IN 47907-1530 (E-mail: techman@purdue.edu).

[Haworth co-indexing entry note]: "Reference, Mental Models and Teaching Technology." Brandt, D. Scott. Co-published simultaneously in *The Reference Librarian* (The Haworth Information Press, an imprint of The Haworth Press, Inc.) No. 74, 2001, pp. 37-47; and: *Evolution in Reference and Information Services: The Impact of the Internet* (ed: Di Su) The Haworth Information Press, an imprint of The Haworth Press, Inc., 2001, pp. 37-47. Single or multiple copies of this article are available for a fee from The Haworth Document Delivery Service [1-800-342-9678, 9:00 a.m. - 5:00 p.m. (EST). E-mail address: getinfo@haworthpressinc.com].

riences. Others have described the need to include information seeking skills and information literacy components in reference. Previously the author has argued that teaching information technology skills in the context of teaching about the software and hardware make up what we call teaching, or training, the Internet.[1] Simple training does not work, however, unless conceptual understanding is added to help learners acquire new knowledge and alter their mental models. Users do not need to be experts like librarians–they need better understanding of what they do and how they can do it differently.

HOW THE INTERNET IMPACTS REFERENCE

What does reference mean in the new millennium? The focus in reference services has changed over the last ten years, due in large part to information technology, which is best identified with the Internet and related applications. For the longest time, the emphasis was on knowing the bibliographic tools which could best suit customers, clients and patrons. Early on, Katz declaimed that reference is more than "simply answering questions."[2] He makes a strong case for defining reference as a service utilizing tools and resources–of which a layperson (non-librarian) usually is unaware–to answer questions. In the past 20 years those resources have become increasingly digital, supported online with software tools ranging from simple web pages (e.g., "webliographies") to sophisticated indexes and search engines (e.g., encyclopedias).

The application of technology to such services seems a natural progression. For a while there was an emphasis on taking advantage of technology by moving traditional reference resources in digital form to the Internet for easier access by librarians.[3] Once reference sources were made available online for librarian use, it would only be a matter of time before they could be accessed by end users as well. This sets up an interesting question, "Do end users use references resources the same way librarians do?" While it's ridiculous to say that resources are for librarians only, it is well known that as part of their job they study, understand and use them more than end users. Likely, resources are accessed by end users only when users are referred to them or stumble upon them. Reference, by definition then, seems to imply user and reference librarian interaction.

Some would argue that librarian-user interaction hasn't changed much over the last 20 years. Tyckoson's recent reflection on changes in reference since the mid-1980s points out several of the trends in the past couple of years. Foremost is that technological improvements, especially expert systems, have not progressed to the point of being easy to use and widespread. Resources modeled after AskJeeves use a fairly simple data engine to serve up facts such as units of measure, but have a long way to go to actually interpret complex ques-

tions, let alone provide answers to them. Thus, virtual reference still requires librarian interactions–email or video conferencing is not that much different than telephone service. Tyckoson argues that reference still follows a basic traditional model, although technology has put a new face on it. He notes that technology rich solutions, such as knowledge cartography and consumer analysis, have in fact been performed to various degrees by librarians for years preceding the advent of the personal computer.[4]

One thing librarians have begun to focus on is the role of information literacy throughout library activities. Recently more emphasis has been put on teaching as an important component of reference service. In many ways, information literacy and reference are two sides of the same coin–one aims at teaching to groups, the other aims for one-on-one. Both of them fulfill the goal of the library profession to create an environment "conducive to discovery and self-learning."[5] The aspect of teaching as a role for librarians is manifested in many ways. Obviously, there is the expert guide who can interpret queries and assist with finding information. There is the role of instructor who provides subject-based seminars on using specific resources. There is the role of teacher, promulgating information literacy. There is also a role as trainer, helping others use information technology to achieve their goals. All of these hats must be worn by all librarians, to some extent, unless they can escape into specialization. Technology, to a large degree, has forced these roles on them–whether or not they accept this as an opportunity is up to the individual librarian. Janes suggests several possibilities for online or digital reference which are considered radical by some. Among them are moving beyond FAQs to reusable objects (i.e., information broken up into component parts for reuse in different situations), applying data mining techniques to reference data, and linking directly to reference data or librarians in the online catalog.[6] Proponents warn that we should not use technology to facilitate activities simply because it's available.

Pragmatists tend to look at the outcomes or goals which technology can help us achieve. For a while it seemed the focus on technology was on how it could be used to better facilitate traditional services in reference. In some ways, the Internet was seen primarily as a delivery medium to allow remote access by users to resources and expert librarians. However, as it became clear that the Internet could be used for other services or services in a new way, other models for reference have begun to take shape. Early services such as Yahoo!, Amazon and AskJeeves in the commercial sector have led the way for developments such as MyLibrary and the LC's Digital Reference Initiative in the library world. Coffman, however, argues that we have not gone far enough in learning from the commercial sector.[7] He has suggested that online catalogs could learn a thing or two about user friendliness from Amazon, and that libraries should emulate corporations which have handled hundreds of times more

questions through customer service and help desks. In fact, Coffman suggests a model for reference based on various aspects of corporate call centers.

REPRESENTATIONAL AND SYSTEM MODELS

Both Tyckoson and Coffman discuss models of service–the "access engineer" and the call center. A traditional representational model of reference is one in which a reference librarian is visited by a patron, a need is expressed and interpreted, and the librarian identifies appropriate resources to the patron and helps her or him use them. There are many variations of models of reference, including a tiered system, roving reference, scheduled appointments, etc. Tyckoson argues that librarians have kept up with technology by incorporating at appropriate points within the general model. For instance, rather than literally visit the librarian, patrons can use technology such as email or web forms to make contact. This is a user passive model, in which the patron requests that the librarian do much of the work for her or him. Coffman argues that the model could be changed further to accommodate patron needs better. He, and others, insist that technology could be used to do some of the expert work of the librarian. This could be termed a user active model, in which the user accesses a knowledge base to facilitate solving her or his need. Both of these models are approaches to dealing with situations involving reference. Basically, they are abstract or general approaches, and could thus be termed representational models.

Representational models are very useful because they allow us to describe approaches to work in general terms that can be understood by others and applied to a variety of settings. The user active model, for instance, could be applied to corporate, academic, and public libraries. Each setting would involve different applications of the general model, but the basic model would provide the framework from which to work. The user active model implies not only action, but implies learning. Students who are required to use an online catalog once as part of a "hunt exercise," for instance, are not very active learners. There is a big difference between simple doing, and learning.

The resources and tools used by librarians and end users can often be expressed as representational models so that they can be shared and understood by others. Often, these are called system models, since they describe the general or abstract workings of a system. An example of a system model that librarians should be very familiar with is the online catalog. In basic terms, the online catalog is a database, or set of tables, which uses data control rules to ensure accuracy and consistency of information and provides pointers to the sources described by bibliographic information. The system can be described by how it is structured (tables), organized (rules) or used (interface). For in-

stance, the rules could be subject cataloging, name authority, etc., and the pointers could be LC or Dewey call numbers or even URLs. The interface would include both the navigation (usually graphical windows-based with drop-down options, etc.) and the system features (such as combining sets with Boolean operators, limiting results, etc.).

The importance of understanding the system model is borne out in a few studies.[8] The basic premise is twofold: (1) the better a user understands the system model, the better the user knows the system, and (2) the better the user can use the system, the better she or he can achieve information goals. In other words, librarians have expert knowledge of online catalogs, indexes, and other online resources which allows them to be expert users. Documenting and sharing new models of reference is key in the new millennium. It seems to follow, that if we can somehow pass this expert knowledge on to others, then they would be expert users as well. However, acquiring such a depth of knowledge is the goal of a library and information science student, not a patron, client or customer. End users interact with systems for different reasons, usually simply as a medium for getting to a result. They do not think about how well the system is structured and its various nuances unless they can help lead to easier and faster results.

It seems clear that there is a role in reference for facilitating learning, but how much, and how? Rader argues that the impact of technology on reference service makes it necessary for librarians to offer technology training and assistance in addition to resource expertise and information seeking instruction. She describes the need for information literacy in one-on-one sessions, but she defines literacy quite broadly.[9] This includes help with questions about technology as well as networking problems. This is echoed by Rockman and Watstein, who insist that librarians must include the role of trainer, and specifically technology trainer, among the many hats they wear. But rather than take on the enormous task of turning users into experts, it has been argued that librarians should simply aim to shape or alter users' mental models of information technology so users can become better, not perfect, retrievers of information.

MENTAL MODELS

A mental model is different than a representational model. Mitchell and Dewdney describe the mental model as "a working model of the system that individuals construct in their mind to facilitate interaction," but it is easy to misinterpret the two as synonymous. The mental model is much more complex than a representational or system model. The terms representational, system, conceptual and design model often are used interchangeably and denote that

the model describes the general aspects of a particular system. In contrast, the mental model is a broader understanding which is used to comprehend the system as a model in the first place. The mental model is a cognitive condition–it is a complicated set of knowledge and beliefs which is used both as a source of referent understanding and as a tool for problem solving. It is not always as accurate as a system model, and is often incomplete, though it can be modified through continued interaction with a system. People can use mental models incorrectly, unscientifically, superstitiously or parsimoniously because they are deeply ingrained, comfortable and often have deep emotional attachment.[10]

Psychologists emphasize that a mental model is much more complicated than a representational model. It is not just a knowledge base or tool, it includes active processing and organizing of, as well as creating inter-connections between, knowledge. Mayer states that internal cognitive processes–selection, organization and integration–are engaged and constructed during learning to shape mental models.[11] The recent focus of cognitive theory is on the learner, what mental models she or he brings to the learning process, and how to help learners alter their mental models so that they can construct, not simply absorb, knowledge.

Take, for instance, what is generally described as the layman's mental model of the solar system. Having been told early on that planets have orbits and revolve around the sun, we build a set of knowledge about those orbits and their general behavior. Our system model might be a diagram of concentric rings representing orbits around a sun. With that knowledge we can understand how moons or satellites orbit planets. Depending on how much we know, we might be able to draw on our mental models of planets and gravity to understand or solve problems related to the falling orbit of a space station. Or we can associate that mental model with the structure of atoms, and the basic model of how electrons orbit around a nucleus. An astronomer or aerospace engineer might scoff at this simplistic mental model, but it is how the layman understands. In order to learn differently, learners must be willing and able to alter, add to or reshape their mental models. In order to teach, librarians must understand users' mental models.

Educational theorists warn that mental models are not only complex, they are literally indescribable. Neither the individual or an objective clinician can actually articulate what a person's mental model is. Rather, a person may be able to articulate her or his working mental model–and this is often described in terms of representational or systems models.[12] For instance, when asked to describe her mental model of a computer, a student may say that it is like an electronic filing cabinet which can connect to other electronic filing cabinets over the Internet. This roughly alludes to how she conceptualizes the computer, but it does not provide insight into how that model will be used when she

works on a computer and encounters problems or needs to anticipate results, or how it will be used to help construct new knowledge.

What is the end user's or novice's mental model of reference, or information querying? We know that the expert librarian's model is centered around the research process. But what about end users?

STUDIES IN MENTAL MODELS

Several investigations have been made into the mental models of information users. While not all of them provide direct insight into users' mental models, most of them reveal aspects of mental models, users' external representations of their mental models, and various methodologies for exploring or analyzing them.

Studies in human-machine interaction have focused on cognitive aspects of searching in an attempt to better develop an understanding of users' mental models to then better design system interfaces. The intent is to build interfaces that relate more directly to a user's mental model, is thus more "intuitive" and easier to use. In this type of research, scientists attempt to match the system model with the users' external representation of their mental model.[13] Another study attempted to identify characteristics of mental models related to searching.[14] Their results indicate that aspects of mental models can be interpreted in manifestations of search behavior. They suggest that further analysis of users can be performed by relating search strategies and searching tactics, and that ultimately these will help fill in the pieces of pictures of mental models for searching. Staggers and Norcio provide an excellent description of mental models as they relate to applications such as systems design and use.[15]

However, more research is needed on why people have difficulty with beginning the search process–that is, why do they have problems articulating their reference questions? Do they have a system model for the organization of reference resources? What mental models do they use to solve information problems in a networked and information rich environment?

In areas directly related to libraries, researchers have explored the relationship between mental models, information seeking and retrieval.[16] One group classified aspects of the participants' mental models in relationship to search strategies. They found evidence that searchers use mental models to varying degrees but were unable to conclude how they change their models over time and across various tasks or systems. One study predicted that students who were given a conceptual model of an online catalog would be able to alter their mental models and use them when it came to solving complex tasks.[17] An interesting aspect of this research is that the undergraduate students distinguished between performing tasks and describing aspects of the system–the author speculates that multiple mental models were involved. Teenage stu-

dents will use other mental models to try to make up for a lack of knowledge, understanding or skill in another area.[18] Unfortunately, those other mental models are likely to be somewhat shallow and underdeveloped, contributing in the Pitts study to constrained learning and less success in achieving desired information seeking outcomes. Turkle argues that students sometimes rely on mental models of computing which are built from learning how to play on computers, not on critical thinking. She notes that students resort to trial-and-error methods based on fast hand-eye coordination that produce results but only simulate learning.[19]

RECONSTRUCTING FUTURE REFERENCE SERVICE

Information technology is complex and pervasive. Many people have a hard time interpreting interfaces and have difficulty navigating as well as identifying or manipulating the elements in the browser which lead to results. In reference, as in other forms of instruction, it can be difficult to determine what to teach about the Internet or information technology and how to do it. Understanding users' mental models is only half the problem–teaching them is the other. Too often the urge is to gauge how far the user is from being an expert, and then try to make one. There are two problems with this premise. First, users may not need to be experts, they may only need some help reshaping their mental models. Second, the approach to helping users alter their thinking should be based on their models, not the models of expert librarians.

Understanding that learners construct their knowledge using their mental models is fundamental to what educational theory calls constructivism. It states that students use their mental models to interpret information, build new knowledge, and add to or create new mental models.[20] Traditional teaching based on lecturing assumes little about the learner and her or his mental model. Just because an interaction is one-on-one doesn't mean that it is by default better. If a reference librarian is talking to a student and describing things in terms of the librarian's mental model, the student may have little to which she or he can attach the information. Imagine, for instance, a NASCAR driver trying to teach a 15-year-old how to drive. In its simplest form, this problem is described as speaking in jargon–using terms that other people do not understand. But of greater consequence is that the learner uses a different mental model to try to comprehend what the librarian is trying to teach. As noted in the Pitts study, novices will try to compensate when their own models are not in tune with that of the learning.

Vygotsky, considered one of the most influential theorists in language development of the past few decades, insists that knowledge acquisition happens when the target of learning is pushed just beyond the learner's current thresh-

old of understanding (mental model). He coined the term "zone of proximal development" to characterize that part of learning which stretches the learner:

> [T]his . . . is what we call the zone of proximal development. It is the distance between the actual developmental level as determined by independent problem solving and the level of potential development as determined through problem solving under adult guidance or in collaboration with more capable peers.[21]

In other words, he believes that with facilitation, a learner uses what she or he already knows to learn something new. Constructivists argue that if that something new is closely related to what they already know and in a form they can relate to, the learning will be more easily and deeply integrated by the learner.

How do we apply constructivist approaches to teaching the Internet as part of reference? First, we take into account the user's mental models. Rather than ask if someone has used an online index before, ask about something that may be more common and for which they already have a mental model. For instance, remind them of the categories in the yellow pages of the phone book. Tell them to think of a given resource like an electronic version of the yellow pages. Ask if they can think of categories for their topic. Then, playing off of their mental model, relate yellow page categories to subject headings and controlled vocabulary. In this way someone could use her or his mental model of searching in the phone book to relate to searching in an index.

Similar approaches apply to other aspects of Internet technology. Users may not have strong mental models of how Web pages work. However, they do have mental models which relate to using televisions, telephones, ATMs and other technology. Thus, websites could be related to tv channels, and web pages that do not load could be relate to busy telephone signals or wrong numbers. Once you identify a model you can relate to, then you can aim for that zone of proximal development to alter or reshape their mental models. Additional research into mental models of novice information technology users is forthcoming.[22]

Whether the general model of reference changes in the millennium, the Internet and information technology will be key factors. If the model remains traditional, technology will continue to be a means of delivery for contacting librarians or accessing reference resources such as pathfinders, bibliographies, etc. When incorporating some teaching or training into the one-on-one, reference librarians need to think about where the user is coming from and how they look at searching. If it changes dramatically, it will be to take further advantage of verbots, artificial intelligence, expert systems and the like. It is likely that under the latter scenario, reference librarians will be the ones to help adapt the

technology or provide the content. In either model, they need to think about the user's mental model. They cannot continue to provide services, or build new resources, based on their own mental models.

REFERENCES

1. Brandt, D. Scott. "What Does 'Teaching the Internet' Mean?" *Computers in Libraries,* 15: 8 (September 1995): 34-35.

2. Katz, William A. *Introduction to Reference Work.* Volume 1. 6th. ed. New York: McGraw-Hill, 1992.

3. Force, Ron. "Planning Online Reference Services for the 90s." *The Reference Librarian,* 43 (1994): 107-115.

4. Tyckoson, David A. "What's right with reference." *American Libraries,* 30:5 (May 1999): 57-63.

5. Rockman, Ilene F. & Watstein, Sarah B. "Reference Librarians/Educators: Vision of the Future." *Reference Librarian,* 66 (1999): 45-59.

6. Janes, Joe. "Why Reference Is About To Change Forever (But Not Completely)," University of Washington, Seattle. Reference in the New Millennium: The Evolving Role of the Information Professional. The VRD 1999 Annual Digital Reference Conference. Harvard Graduate School of Education. Cambridge, MA. October 14, 1999. *http://www.vrd.org/conferences/VRD99/indexnf.html.*

7. Coffman, Steve. "Reference as Others Do It." *American Libraries,* 30: 5 (May 1999): 54-56.

8. Gillian Michell and Patricia Dewdney. "Mental Models Theory–Application for Library and Information Science." *Journal of Education for Library and Information Science,* 39: 4 (Fall 1998): 275-281.

9. Rader, Hannelore B. "Information literacy in the reference environment: Preparing for the future." *The Reference Librarian,* 71 (2000): 25-33.

10. Norman, D. "Some observations on mental models," in D. Gentner and Al Stevens, eds. *Mental Models.* Lawrence Erlbaum, Hillsdale, NJ, 1987, 7-14.

11. Mayer, Richard E. "Cognition and Instruction: Their Historic meeting with educational psychology." *Journal of Educational Psychology,* 84: 4 (1992): 405-412.

12. Hueyching Janice Jih, and Thomas Charles Reeves. "Mental models: A research focus for interactive learning systems." *Educational Technology and Research Development,* 40: 3 (1992): 39-53.

13. Navarro-Prieto, Raquel & Scaife, Mike, & Rogers, Yvonne. "Cognitive strategies in web searching." 5th Human Factors & the Web. Gaithersberg, MD, June 3, 1999. *http://zing.ncsl.nist.gov/hfweb/proceedings/nararro-prieto/index.html.*

14. Choo, Chun Wei & Detlor, Brian & Turnbull, Don. "Information seeking on the Web: An integrated model of browsing and searching." First Monday 5: 2 (February 2000). *http://www.firstmonday.org/issues/issue5_2/choo/index.html.*

15. Staggers, Nancy, and A. F. Norcio. "Mental models: Concepts for human-computers interaction research." *International Journal of Man-Machine Studies,* 38 (April 1993): 587-605.

16. Savage, Pamela et al. "An investigation of mental models and information seeking behavior in a novel task." Poster session presented at SIGIR '97. Philadelphia, PA, July 27-31, 1997. *http://www.scils.Rutgers.edu/tipster3/sigir97.html.*

17. Borgman, Christine L. "The user's mental model of an information retrieval system: An experiment on a prototype online catalog." *International Journal of Human-Computer Systems,* 51 (1999): 435-452.

18. Pitts, Judy. "Mental Models of Information." *School Library Media Quarterly,* 23 (Spring 1995): 177-184.

19. Turkle, Sherry. "Seeing through computers: Education in a culture of simulation." *American Prospect,* no. 31 (March-April 1997): 76-82.

20. Tobin, K., and Tippins, D. "Constructivism as a referent for teaching and learning." K. Tobin, ed. *The Practice of Constructivism in Science Education.* AAAS Press, Washington, D.C., 1993, 3-21.

21. Vygotsky, L. S. *Mind in Society.* Cambridge, MA: Harvard University Press, 1978.

22. Uden, Lorna and D. Scott Brandt. "Learning with technology: A preliminary study." *Online Information Review,* 24: 4 (2000): 334-337.

17. Borgman, Christine. "The user's mental model of an information retrieval system: An experiment on a prototype online catalog." International Journal of Human-Computer Studies, 51 (1999): 435-452.

18. Zhu, Bob. Mental Models of Information. pp. 2-5 (Wu, David), Palo Alto, CA: 25 Spring, 1999, 277-316.

19. Tinsley, Harry. "Seeing through complexities: Education in academic libraries." American Libraries, no. 31 (March-April 1997): 76-82.

20. Dobson, Cindy, and Virginia P. Ondrusek. "A collaborative plan for teaching and learning." In Thomas G. Kirk, ed. Continuing Education for Librarians. Westport, CT: ..., 1999. 4-27.

21. Wygopski, L. S. Mind in Society. Cambridge, MA: Harvard University Press, 1978.

22. Yelon, Laura, and D. Scott Brandt. "Learning with technology: A participatory study." Online Information Review, 24 (12/2001): 311-337.

The Evolution of Internet Training in a Corporate Library

Jack Styczynski

SUMMARY. In the last six years, training corporate employees how to use the Internet for business purposes has changed dramatically. The emphasis has shifted primarily to the World Wide Web, and more on how to use it most effectively, rather than on just the basics of how to use it from square one. This article describes how Internet training sessions given by librarians at the National Broadcasting Company have evolved since 1995, and details the lessons of today, while looking toward the ones of tomorrow. *[Article copies available for a fee from The Haworth Document Delivery Service: 1-800-342-9678. E-mail address: <getinfo@haworthpressinc.com> Website: <http://www.HaworthPress.com> © 2001 by The Haworth Press, Inc. All rights reserved.]*

KEYWORDS. Internet, World Wide Web, teaching, training, bibliographic instruction, corporate library, news library

INTRODUCTION

As the person who was originally hired in May 1995 to teach employees at the National Broadcasting Company how to use the Internet, I've seen a great

Jack Styczynski is Research Librarian, NBC Information Resource Center, 30 Rockefeller Plaza, Room 2661-E, New York, NY 10112 (E-mail: Jack.Styczynski@nbc.com).

[Haworth co-indexing entry note]: "The Evolution of Internet Training in a Corporate Library." Styczynski, Jack. Co-published simultaneously in *The Reference Librarian* (The Haworth Information Press, an imprint of The Haworth Press, Inc.) No. 74, 2001, pp. 49-53; and: *Evolution in Reference and Information Services: The Impact of the Internet* (ed: Di Su) The Haworth Information Press, an imprint of The Haworth Press, Inc., 2001, pp. 49-53. Single or multiple copies of this article are available for a fee from The Haworth Document Delivery Service [1-800-342-9678, 9:00 a.m. - 5:00 p.m. (EST). E-mail address: getinfo@haworthpressinc.com].

change in the focus of training sessions over the past six years. When I began, the mission was to give complete novices some understanding of the Internet, what it could do for them, how they could get access to it, and how to navigate it in the most basic fashion. Training was actually done on a DOS-based browser at that time, and it was very rudimentary. Essentially outdated utilities such as Gopher and Telnet were still significant, and that was evident in the day's literature on how to teach the Internet.[1] Soon, as graphical browsers and the World Wide Web became dominant, the focus changed. In most cases, NBC employees were still Internet novices, but the emphasis shifted to teaching them how to use the Web *only*. Even e-mail and discussion forums–still used today, but once the staple of many an Internet lesson[2]–had seen their impact greatly diminished as similar offerings morphed onto the Web. The Web had become by far the most useful utility, and access was easily available. Yet as recently as November 1998, Internet training literature still rightfully included topics as basic as "Introducing Terminology and Important Concepts."[3] Today, most people already know the lingo and how to "surf" the Web when they come into a lesson, so librarians in the NBC Information Resource Center have essentially moved past teaching such basics, and have evolved to teaching employees which Web sites will help them most, and how to find them quickly. In other words, the focus is less on how to use the Internet, and more on how to use it *efficiently*.

The introduction to my training sessions has changed dramatically since the early days. Back then, I often began with a 15-minute lecture, which included a brief history of the Internet, an explanation of the difference between a "provider" (such as America Online) and a "browser" (such as Netscape), and another explanation of how utilities such as Gopher, Telnet, FTP, Usenet News, and the World Wide Web differed (and how they were all *parts* of the Internet as a whole). Many of the basics I taught then remain true now, but are far less significant, and have thus been eliminated from the lessons of today. I do still make it clear that there is more to the Internet than just the Web, and that the two terms are not synonymous, but I don't go into much detail.

AT THE NATIONAL BROADCASTING COMPANY

It should be mentioned that the vast majority of NBC employees who seek Internet training are in the deadline-driven News Division. Rarely can they arrange their schedules to allow for large group lessons, or to spend more than an hour or two in training. Typically, two or three people are able to attend a 90-minute lesson. Everyone gets a computer, and is able to see what I am doing on mine as well. I find such groups to be ideal, because lessons can still be tai-

lored to individuals, while at the same time allowing for questions from others that a single trainee may not have thought to ask. These days, most NBC employees have already used the Internet quite a bit, so to make the best use of the available time, I generally dispense with any "lecture." You don't want trainees to leave your lesson suffering from information overload anyway. After telling them that the Web can give them access to proprietary fee-based databases such as Nexis and Dow Jones, and asking what sites they have already used and what type of information they need for their jobs, we move right into the "hands on" portion of the lesson.

It should also be mentioned that this "hands on" portion of any Internet lesson at NBC *does not* include training on the aforementioned fee-based databases. Training for those is done in completely separate sessions, often taught by someone from the database companies themselves. In fact, our recently developed subject-specific Internet lessons place an emphasis on the fact that there are free alternatives for some of the information available in these fee-based databases. Of course, we stress *reliable* alternatives, which has always been an important point in our lessons. Many Web sites are reliable, and many Web sites are not, and we tell trainees that it will be up to them to determine which is which.

FINDING AND EVALUATING WEB SITES

For the "less experienced" Internet users who still come to our library for general Web lessons, one way we help them determine reliability is by teaching the concept of domains, which allow you to both find and evaluate sites. This is usually the first part of the "hands on" portion of any general lesson we give. Web domains are formulaic, and as many trainers will tell you, can often be correctly guessed for a given entity.[4] The domain for the FBI Web page is *www.fbi.gov,* and the domain for the New York Times Web page is *www.nytimes.com.* And as much as you can trust the FBI for a list of the nation's Top 10 Most Wanted Criminals, or the New York Times for the latest news from Gotham, you can trust their useful Web sites too. Web site domains typically begin with a "www." Those letters are then followed by the name (or its abbreviated version) of an entity, and an applicable domain suffix. Common domain suffixes are ".com" for commercial concerns, ".org" for non-profit organizations, ".gov" for government agencies, and ".edu" for educational institutions.[5] There are others as well, such as ".net" and various country codes, and as users begin to discover them all, they tend to get better at correctly guessing an entity's Web domain. This is easily the quickest and *most efficient* way of finding information on the Web. It's also a great way to *evaluate reliability,* because if a domain includes an entity you recognize followed by the appropriate suffix, it's prob-

ably legitimate. (One example of an *inappropriate* suffix is in the domain *www.whitehouse.com*, which is a pornographic site, rather than *www.whitehouse.gov*, which is the site of our government's executive branch.)

Of course, correctly guessing domains is not always possible, nor is it always the most appropriate way of finding information on the World Wide Web. For example, many times a user wants to find numerous sites about a given *subject*, rather than just the site of a given *entity*. So in our general lessons, we also teach trainees how to use keyword search engines and subject catalogs.[6] Even experienced Web users rarely know the difference between them, and once they do, they become better searchers. In fact, the only similarity between the two is that they both allow you to find information by keyword. But the search engines allow you to search for a keyword *anywhere* on a *computer-indexed* Web page, and list results in order of *relevancy*, which a computer formula determines by evaluating things such as keyword placement and frequency. Conversely, a subject catalog is maintained by *people*, and keywords may be searched only in the *titles* and *brief descriptions* that they index and list under appropriate subject headings. The significance to this is that search engines tend to be better updated, more complete, and preferable for searches on *narrow* topics, while subject catalogs tend to be more intuitive, and preferable for searches on *broad* topics. It's also important to let trainees know that no search engine nor subject catalog indexes anywhere near the entirety (or even the majority) of the Web, so becoming familiar with several is a good practice, so that if one doesn't find what you seek, you can try others. And that most of the popular search engines allow for more advanced phrase or Boolean searching as well. Each is a little different in that regard, but most provide fairly easy-to-understand advanced search instructions. There have been quite a few favored search engines since I first began giving Internet lessons, but *www.google.com* seems to be a hot one these days. As for subject catalogs, *www.yahoo.com* has remained the most popular from the moment I started my training sessions, right up through now. But being indexed in either hardly guarantees a site's reliability. Evaluating the domain of any pages retrieved will usually still be the best way to determine that, although exceptions may occur when schools or normally reliable businesses host personal home pages.

SPECIFICALLY RECOMMENDED SITES

Most NBC employees are also interested in learning about more specific subject-oriented Internet resources. News folks in particular usually want to know the best sites for reference, news (of course), business, government, and politics. General lessons targeted to less-experienced Web users normally conclude by going over a few of the most useful and reliable, such

as *www.anywho.com*, *www.mapquest.com*, *www.newspaperlinks.com*, and *fullcoverage.yahoo.com*. I've listed these and several others on an annotated page of Internet essentials that I use as a basis for my general lessons, as well my own research. That page can currently be found at *members.nbci.com/hotsheet*.

For anyone who wants to get even deeper into subject-specific sites, our library has developed a more comprehensive Intranet page that lists reliable resources from a wider variety of categories, and an accompanying annotated "Journalist's Guide to Internet Resources" in Microsoft Word format to appease those who prefer having a printed listing of useful sites. All trainees are made aware of both resources. And as mentioned previously, we are also now offering follow-up subject-specific Internet lessons, which detail free alternatives for some of the information available in fee-based databases. Some of the sites in those lessons include *us.imdb.com*, *thomas.loc.gov*, *www.infoplease.com*, *www.britannica.com*, *www.biography.com*, and *www.bartleby.com*. When trainees come across a site during *any* lesson that they think they might use in the future, they are encouraged to save it in their browser list of "favorites," so that they won't have to remember and type the site's address every time they want to visit. Many already know how to do this, but if not, they are shown.

CONCLUSION

Thinking back a mere six years, the Internet seems like a totally different animal than the one I first began training people how to use. I knew it well then, but almost everything I teach now has been learned since. The job of librarians will be to stay on top of all the changes, so that they can effectively train the users of the future. In the year 2007, I'm sure this article on Internet training will be as outdated as the ones from the mid-1990s are now. Amazing.

NOTES

1. Marshall, Lucy et al. "Training for the Internet in a Corporate Environment," *Computers in Libraries* 14 (November/December 1994): 60-64.
2. Greenfield, Louise et al. "A Model for Teaching the Internet: Preparation and Practice," *Computers in Libraries* 16 (March 1996): 22-25.
3. Cibbarelli, Pamela R. "Guidelines for Successfully Teaching the Internet," *Information Outlook* 2 (November 1998): 19-22.
4. McDermott, Irene E. "Internet Instruction: Spreading the Web," *Searcher* 8 (July/August 2000): 72-76.
5. Sandy, John H. "Choosing a Great Domain Name," *Information Outlook* 4 (November 2000): 16-22.
6. Fonseca, Tony and King, Monica. "Incorporating the Internet into Traditional Library Instruction," *Computers in Libraries* 20 (February 2000): 38-42.

ELECTRONIC SERVICES

E-Mail Reference:
Who, When, Where, and What Is Asked

Naomi Lederer

SUMMARY. This article begins by summarizing national findings of e-mail reference services in academic and public libraries. It next describes types of e-mail reference services as well as commonalities, differences, appearance of the question form, audience, and turnaround time for selected Colorado libraries. The article then focuses on giving a detailed overview and analysis of two years of Colorado State University's e-mail reference experiences. The number, type of question, who/where the questions come from, and to whom the questions are sent are examined. The unexpected uses of the service are identified. Lastly, broader issues to do with e-mail reference services are discussed. This article is based on a presentation given at the Internet Librarian 2000 conference. *[Article copies available for a fee from The Haworth Document Delivery Service: 1-800-342-9678. E-mail address: <getinfo@haworthpressinc.com> Website: <http://www.HaworthPress.com> © 2001 by The Haworth Press, Inc. All rights reserved.]*

Naomi Lederer is Reference Librarian and Assistant Professor, English, Speech, and Communications & Technical Journalism, Colorado State University, 150 Morgan Library, Fort Collins, CO 80523-1019.

[Haworth co-indexing entry note]: "E-Mail Reference: Who, When, Where, and What Is Asked." Lederer, Naomi. Co-published simultaneously in *The Reference Librarian* (The Haworth Information Press, an imprint of The Haworth Press, Inc.) No. 74, 2001, pp. 55-73; and: *Evolution in Reference and Information Services: The Impact of the Internet* (ed: Di Su) The Haworth Information Press, an imprint of The Haworth Press, Inc., 2001, pp. 55-73. Single or multiple copies of this article are available for a fee from The Haworth Document Delivery Service [1-800-342-9678, 9:00 a.m. - 5:00 p.m. (EST). E-mail address: getinfo@haworthpressinc.com].

KEYWORDS. E-mail reference, academic, public, libraries, questions, types, categories, users

E-mail reference is a service that has probably been around as long as librarians have had e-mail. Researchers with a question can ask their questions no matter what time of day it is. The time frame for a reply varies–if sent to a specific person, the reply must wait until that person reads the message and replies to it. In recent years there has been an increasing amount of formalization of this type of service; instead of sending the message to one person, a service address is created so that multiple librarians can access it and no one person needs to be responsible for it. With the advent of the World Wide Web, there are increasing numbers of "ask an expert" (or even a librarian) services that even casual Web users will come across. This article covers the e-mail reference services of libraries, national academic and public libraries, Colorado libraries, and gives a close examination of an academic library in Colorado. The analysis should be useful for librarians at other academic institutions and may serve as a comparison.

NATIONAL E-MAIL REFERENCE SURVEY: LIBRARIES WITH DIGITAL REFERENCE

A May 1999 survey of 150 academic libraries (chosen from a possible 931) discovered that 45% of the libraries had some kind of e-mail reference service (67 of the 146 academic libraries with Web sites). Half of these services were linked from the library's home page.[1] Association of Research Libraries (ARL) members have embraced e-mail reference in even greater numbers than academic libraries in general. Of the 110 libraries examined in February 1999, 102 (over 92%) had e-mail reference services.[2] In contrast, a March/April 2000 survey of public libraries found that of the 352 examined (81% or 293 had Web sites) only 12.8% weighted overall (that is, 64) had e-mail reference services. Of these, 56% were linked from the library home page.[3] It thereby appears that academic libraries have embraced e-mail reference service in greater numbers than public libraries.

The existence and types of policies created for academic versus public libraries also vary. Academic libraries more frequently mentioned turnaround times for answers to questions, which users were permitted to use the service, and the types of questions that were appropriate for the service. Public schools were more likely to have a service policy on questions; private schools were more likely to have a technological barrier. Technological barriers included "requiring users to enter bar code numbers, e-mail addresses, or passwords to use the service."[4] In the public library world, the largest libraries were more likely to have some kind of policy regarding the service (39% versus 10%).[5]

FOCUS ON COLORADO: SELECTED LIBRARIES, JUNE/JULY 2000

The examination of Colorado libraries looked at both academic and public libraries. Academic libraries were identified at colleges, universities, state colleges, state junior colleges, community colleges, and libraries that serve a combination of these types of post secondary educational institutions. The type of school was taken from the name of the school. Public libraries were identified as belonging to a larger (population over 100,000) or smaller (population less than 100,000) community. There were twenty-three academic and twelve public libraries with Web pages. Three of the libraries were at colleges; ten at universities; ten at state, junior or community colleges (SJCC)–grouped together here; two in larger communities; and ten in smaller communities.

Categories of e-mail reference service were determined as:

- Yes, had service and had form to fill out (e-mail reference with form)
- Yes, had service, but with basic e-mail link only (basic e-mail)
- No e-mail reference service at all (no e-mail reference)
- An e-mail address to make an appointment with a librarian (e-mail for appointment)
- E-mail address for director and staff were listed (e-mail addresses of staff)
- E-mail reference is specifically for distant students (distant student e-mail reference)

Of the thirty-five libraries with a Web page (eight additional libraries did not appear to have a Web page):

- 8 had e-mail reference with a form
    1 college, 4 university, 1 SJCC, 2 smaller communities
- 8 had basic e-mail reference
    2 college, 4 university, 1 SJCC, 1 smaller community
- 8 had no e-mail reference
    2 SJCC, 2 larger communities, 4 smaller communities
- 2 had e-mail for appointment
    both SJCC
- 6 had e-mail addresses of staff
    1 university, 2 SJCC, 3 smaller communities
- 3 had distant student e-mail reference
    1 university, 2 SJCC

In summary, in Colorado there were 16 libraries with e-mail reference, 16 libraries without e-mail reference, and 3 libraries with e-mail reference specifically for distant students. At the time of the survey, the smallest city in Colo-

rado with a library Web page (it had no e-mail reference) was Gunnison, with a population of 5,438. The smallest city with e-mail reference was Sterling, population 11,543. However, it is interesting to note that the listed e-mail reference address was not hotlinked on the Web page. The city with the largest population without an apparent e-mail reference service was Denver, population 532,066.[6]

E-MAIL REFERENCE SERVICES

The names for e-mail reference services in Colorado vary. Names included: "Ask a Librarian," "Virtual Reference Desk," and "E-mail Reference." Other services didn't have a name, per se, just a basic "mailto" link. Most of these basic links had no directions attached to them, although one library did say to include a name and e-mail address in the message. The general lack of direction is puzzling because there is a need for a name or at least an e-mail address; the reply option is not going to work when the user sends the question from a public access computer terminal.

The services offered by e-mail reference focused on brief ready-reference, research guidance, short factual questions, and providing citations for information sources. Some services indicated that the questioner may be asked to come to the library for additional help. Limitations included: no legal advice, no in-depth reference, and no questions related to circulation or loan concerns. Turnaround time for the services varied–the largest difference in time for academic libraries was based on whether or not classes are in session. Time frames were: next time librarian on duty, 24 hours, one working day (or weekday) during semesters, and 48 hours.

Indications as to who is allowed to use the service varied as well. Permitted questioners were affiliates (in academic communities this meant students, faculty, and staff), non-affiliates with questions related to the local community or library, current members of a community (presumably citizens of a city), and no limit mentioned. One of the libraries surveyed, the University of Wyoming, has a fee-based reference service for non-affiliates. The service, UWIN PLUS <http://www-lib:uwyo.edu/ELS/UWin/default.htm>, is linked from their Ask a Librarian page <http://www-lib:uwyo.edu/Dservs/Ref/ref-frm.htm>. (The University of Wyoming is, and has been, considered part of "Colorado" by libraries, so the author did not hesitate to include it in the survey.)

When the library had a form for the questions, pre-questions (that is, information asked about the questioner, not related to the question itself) included:

- name,
- e-mail address,
- student grade level (found on public library sites),

- phone number–with area code,
- where you live–city/state,
- status/affiliation,
- won't need information after, and
- subject area of question.

The space for the question itself was prefaced by:

- Question;
- Your question/Your question(s);
- Type in your reference question (please be detailed and specific);
- What is your reference question? Please be detailed and specific;
- Enter your question here;
- Please tell us your question. Please type your question into the area below. To help us answer your question accurately, please be as specific as possible. If you have already done some research, let us know where and the result;
- Your inquiry. Type your question below, and be as complete and specific as possible. Provide us with as much detail as you think is helpful. Telling us why you want the information is very helpful (but not necessary).

The submission button found on the forms had various terms on them:

- Submit Query
- Send your question
- Submit Question
- Send E-mail
- Submit

One "Submit" button had next to it "Click the 'Submit' button when done. NOTE: If you are having problems with the above form, you may also e-mail your inquiry to: [address]."[7]

In the author's opinion, the best layout for an Ask a Librarian service was found at the Denison Memorial Library, University of Colorado Health Sciences Center, Denver <http://www.uchsc.edu/library/askalibrarian.html>. The page had very few words on it, and had a well-thought out FAQ/How do I? feature. The FAQs were attached to a drop down menu that had very popular questions along with "more freq. asked questions." Going to the questions, there are clear answers, one with an online catalog screen snapshot to help users understand how to tell whether the library owns a particular journal. Non-affiliates, who cannot use the service to ask questions, can read the FAQs and answers.

COLORADO STATE UNIVERSITY LIBRARY DETAILS

Colorado State University's Library, a member of the Association of Research Libraries, formally launched its e-mail reference service in August 1998. (Direct e-mail reference service had been available for a long time–and still is–directly to subject specialists.) The service is called "Ask a Librarian" <http://lib.colostate.edu/reference/emailref.html> and for the first year was available from the Libraries' home page. The reply e-mail address is emailref@manta.colostate.edu. On August 16, 1999, a new library home page design was revealed; currently to get to the service one must select "Services and Workshops" and find Ask a Librarian on the list (it is listed first on the alphabetical list). This removal of Ask a Librarian from the library home page has directly impacted the number of questions asked. As will be discussed later in this article, the number of questions asked dropped dramatically.

Ask a Librarian officially serves members of the Colorado State University (CSU) community. Members are defined as affiliates–students, faculty, and staff. In addition, the service is provided to non-affiliates who have a question related to CSU or materials found in CSU Libraries. The page (which has a form to fill out) specifies that complex research needs should be asked of subject librarians (link to names and phone/e-mail), renewals and circulation concerns should be asked of Access Services (phone number provided), and questions about borrowing from other libraries should be asked of Interlibrary Loan (e-mail address provided). The service responds Monday-Thursday within 24 hours except during University holidays. Questions sent Friday-Sunday are answered by the following Tuesday. These time frames are taken seriously by the librarians, and if working on a weekend day librarians will frequently check the service for questions and respond well before the promised Tuesday. The service provides short answers or citations for sources. All information is supplied by e-mail. Ask a Librarian is not for in-depth research (officially), does not renew, retrieve or hold library materials (in practice–these are referred; as a matter of fact, librarians do not have access to these mechanisms anyway), nor does it send information via fax or postal mail (in practice).

CSU's Ask a Librarian form asks for a first name, a last name, CSU status via a drop box (not currently affiliated with CSU, undergraduate student, graduate student, faculty, staff), e-mail address, telephone number with area code, your question, and has a "Send E-mail" submission button. Note that in this article, the detailed information about the types of questions and who sent them covers August 1998-May 2000, or 22 months. Additional raw statistics cover through November 2000.

According to the answers on the forms, the following categories of people asked questions between August 1998 and May 2000:

- 126 undergraduates
- 141 graduates
- 59 faculty
- 113 staff
- 179 non-CSU
- 11 unknown
- 629 total

(Note: These self-defined categories are used for the breakdown of types of questions.)

Upon examination of the questions–people will occasionally talk about themselves or have revealing e-mail addresses–the actual breakdown is slightly different. Fourteen "staff" are not staff at CSU, but elsewhere (should be Non-CSU). Three "graduates" are alumni (Non-CSU), and three others are really Non-CSU. Therefore, Non-CSU should be an additional 20 people and the breakdown should look like this:

- 126 undergraduates
- 138 graduates
- 59 faculty
- 99 staff
- 196 (+ 3 from others) non-CSU
- 11 unknown

The people asking questions did not limit themselves to distant locations. Sixty-two of the questioners asked from within the library building itself; 219 asked from somewhere else on campus. Asking from the library were:

- 38 undergraduates
- 11 graduates
- 5 staff
- 3 faculty
- 3 non-CSU
- 2 unknown
- 62 total or 10%

The statistics end up being misleading (as they frequently are) because at least two of the staff and faculty questions were from library staff and faculty, and related to the service itself being set up and tested.

Asking from on campus were:

- 60 undergraduates
- 78 graduates
- 29 staff
- 44 faculty
- 7 non-CSU
- 1 unknown
- 219 total or 34%

The non-CSU questions appear to indicate that in spite of being limited to CSU affiliates only some of the workstations are being used by others. It could simply be a friend of an affiliate using a staff or faculty workstation, or be a question asked when non-affiliates are being shown what the university has to offer them should they become members of the community. The library computers have open access, so questions sent from those locations are easily explained.

The off campus questions can be separated: from the United States (341 or 53% of the total) and from other countries (17 or 3%). CSU's Ask a Librarian has been contacted by people from over fifteen different countries in both hemispheres. Along with e-mail addresses the phrasing of the messages indicate foreign origins. Occasionally local e-mail addresses are sent from afar, according to their senders–for example, CSU students studying abroad.

Another category of question origins is reference questions not sent directly to the Ask a Librarian service. These are forwarded to the service by the recipients. The address for the Libraries' Web technicians got 5 questions, the Web Librarian 3, the CSU Webmaster (not even sent to someone in the library) 4, and others 2. Not part of the other totals, in the same time frame the author got four questions sent directly to her e-mail that were not related to her subject specialities. It is probable that colleagues get similar reference requests.

When are the questions sent? A large number, 510 (81%) were sent when the library was open and there was a librarian at the Reference Desk. Thirty questions (5%) were sent when the library was open, but there was no librarian at the desk. The final category, when the library was closed was 89 (14%). Thus it appears that the majority of questions were sent when the option of asking a Reference Librarian in person or via the telephone was available. The CSU Reference Desk does default to answering the people at the desk first, then answering the phone, but at a guess much more than half of the time the telephone is answered. A good part of the time, the librarian or staff member ends up forwarding the telephone call to another service desk, usually Access Services. The telephone, when not answered, does offer a menu that includes some of these services, so callers don't necessarily need to call back or e-mail

to get answers to their questions. At any rate, the high number of e-mail questions while there is someone at the Reference Desk is intriguing. Do we have shy users? Long lines at the Reference Desk? (It does not seem like there are long lines all that often.) The questions have not seemed to be at all personal or potentially embarrassing.

TYPES OF QUESTIONS

To see what types and how many questions were asked, questions were categorized; in addition, who asked them was noted. A question could be placed in more than one category, but no more than three. The largest category, Reference, was interpreted generously. Directly following are the totals in the categories; a breakdown of who asked what for the larger categories is found after this list.

Type of Question/Number

Reference	431
Morgan Library (CSU's main library) related	28
Library department	13
University related	8
Bibliographic citation	9
Loan/reserve	60
In depth	43
SAGE–library catalog	29
Dissertation found here	29
Own dissertation	4
PIN #	8
Interlibrary Loan	
Refer out of library	6
Access to databases	26
Database specific	20
World Wide Web	3
Re: service itself (other librarians)	2
Selling own book	1
Donation	10
Empty (no question)	3

In addition there was some self-provided information:

For a faculty member	7
Distant Education Student	6

The categories of questions were then broken down by who asked that type of question. The categories were determined as:

Undergraduate student
Graduate student
Faculty
Staff
Non-CSU questioner, with the question related to CSU (part of service)
Non-CSU questioner and the question was something his/her own library could have helped (not part of service). There *are* libraries in other states.

BREAKDOWN OF QUESTIONS/PERCENTAGES

Basic Reference

The most frequent category of question was the basic reference question. As mentioned earlier, this category was generously interpreted. It also most frequently overlapped with another category.

98	22%	Undergraduate
90	21%	Graduate
42	10%	Faculty
69	16%	Staff
56	13%	Non-CSU-Related
76	18%	Non-CSU–Own Library could have helped

Loan and Reserve (Access Services)

In general, although not officially part of the Ask a Librarian service, these questions were answered when possible. Reference staff cannot access individual records, place holds, etc. The responses always referred to Access Services as the appropriate source for the information. The telephone number, mentioned on the question form, was supplied.

11	18%	Undergraduate
18	30%	Graduate
10	17%	Faculty
6	10%	Staff
14	23%	Non-CSU-Related
1	2%	Non-CSU–Own Library could have helped

Morgan Library Related

These questions had to do with types of collections and services available. It makes some sense that most of the questions come from non-affiliates interested in what the library might have to offer them.

4	14%	Undergraduate
1	4%	Graduate
1	4%	Faculty
1	4%	Staff
21	74%	Non-CSU-Related

Colorado State University Related

2	24.3%	Undergraduate
1	12.5%	Faculty
2	24.3%	Staff
2	24.3%	Non-CSU-Related
1	12.5%	Non-CSU–Own Library could have helped

Interlibrary Loan

This category was one that if Ask a Librarian only received service-related questions would not exist. Because the author did try to answer questions–even non-covered questions–she visited the Interlibrary Loan staff for more than just a few of these questions. The author referred to these visits as "answer a librarian." One complication for the time of the survey was that Interlibrary Loan was not loaning *anything* to anyone outside of CSU because of the devastating impact of the disaster of July 28, 1997 when the basement of the library was inundated with 8 1/2 feet of water. It has only been recently (beginning November 2000) that CSU began loaning its own dissertations to other libraries.

6	21%	Undergraduate
9	32%	Graduate
1	4%	Faculty
5	18%	Staff
5	18%	Non-CSU-Related
2	7%	Non-CSU–Own Library could have helped

Database Specific

This category was surprisingly little used. Few people wanted help in using a given database (most of these at CSU are indexes or abstracts). The author thought that database questions would be one of the main uses for the service–that is, affiliates would frequently wonder which index or electronic source would be recommended for a particular research project. It is possible that the subject categories on CSU's "Databases" page suffice for many of our users.

5	25%	Undergraduate
9	45%	Graduate
4	20%	Faculty
2	10%	Non-CSU-Related

SAGE–Library Catalog

This is another category with surprisingly few questions.

7	24%	Undergraduate
9	32%	Graduate
7	24%	Faculty
3	10%	Staff
3	10%	Non-CSU-Related

Own Dissertation (CSU Alum) and Dissertation Found Here

These categories were combined to assure statistical confidentiality of the four asking about their own dissertations.

1	3%	Graduate
2	6%	Faculty
6	18%	Staff
20	61%	Non-CSU-Related
4	11%	Non-CSU–Own Library could have helped

In-Depth Reference

This is a category that should not have existed. It is possible that people either (1) don't know what in-depth reference is or (2) think it is worth a try anyway. There were 43 questions that fit here. A disturbing number were non-affiliates

asking questions that were not CSU-related. (And when the author would answer anyway, mentioning that these were outside the scope of the service, she *rarely* got thanks for the special favor.) Officially these non-affiliate questions can be ignored.

6	14%	Undergraduate
9	21%	Graduate
2	5%	Faculty
6	14%	Staff
5	12%	Non-CSU-Related
15	34%	Non-CSU–Own Library could have helped

Access to Databases

These questions related to being able to remotely search the indexes and informational databases available to CSU affiliates. CSU currently has remote searching capabilities for over 300 different indexes and other types of databases. If the user is off campus, his/her computer needs to be configured properly if s/he does not have a CSU e-mail account (which has a fee attached to it). Non-CSU affiliates were told that they cannot remotely access most of these databases (there are a few that allow anyone to search them).

4	15%	Undergraduate
11	42%	Graduate
3	12%	Faculty
3	12%	Staff
5	19%	Non-CSU-Related

Donation to Library

These questions had to be referred outside of the service to the appropriate subject specialist or gifts and exchange staff. There were many months during the time of the survey when no gifts were being accepted, period (the library had to catch up with the numerous gifts generously given after the disaster). During that period the potential donor was informed of this policy.

1	10%	Graduate
1	10%	Faculty
4	40%	Staff
4	40%	Non-CSU-Related

Refer Out of Library

2	34%	Undergraduate
2	33%	Staff
2	33%	Non-CSU-Related

Bibliographic Citation

This is also the category frequently mentioned specifically as part of Colorado e-mail reference services.

4	45%	Undergraduate
2	22%	Graduate
2	22%	Staff
1	11%	Non-CSU-Related

Library Department Related

These fell into the "who does what within the library" category.

1	8%	Undergraduate
2	15%	Graduate
4	31%	Staff
6	45%	Non-CSU-Related

Electronic Journal

Most of these questions concerned an electronic journal that had been available but had since disappeared or had some barrier and why can't I access it?! In most cases, the journal was one CSU subscribed to so that a link could be established (after negotiation, which took varying time periods to conduct). In other instances access was denied because CSU did not subscribe to the journal. Non-affiliates don't have remote access to password-protected journals.

5	39%	Graduate
2	15%	Faculty
4	31%	Staff
2	15%	Non-CSU-Related

Seeing the questions and answering them is a learning experience. The number of non-service questions is very high:

- 207 (32.9%) of the questions were types *specifically excluded* from the service
- 76 were reference questions from non-affiliates
- 43 were in-depth (15 of these from non-affiliates)
- 60 were loan/reserve related
- 28 were Interlibrary Loan questions

Very unexpected were:

- So few bibliographic citations questions–only 1.4% of the total
- So few database questions–3% of the total
- So very few WWW questions–3 or 0.47% (not worth breaking down)
- So many non-affiliates asking questions; 196 (31%)–the largest category of Ask a Librarian user

The bibliographic citations and WWW are what librarians perceive as good questions to ask a librarian in this type of service. For the most part these are genuinely short answer questions, relatively fast to find, although there can be tricky ones.

YEAR TO YEAR COMPARISONS

CSU's Ask a Librarian service experienced a great drop in numbers from the first year to the second. The probable reason was the removal of a direct link from the library's home page to the service. In the first year of Ask a Librarian (August 1998-July 1999), there were 463 questions asked; in the second year (August 1999-July 2000), there were 181 questions asked. (The change took place on August 16th, so at the beginning of the month Ask a Librarian was prominent on the home page.) In addition to having a direct link from the home page, the first year of the service included a promotional write up in the faculty newsletter and in the library newsletter sent to members of the campus community. Also noticed is that in the second year, non-CSU questioners dominated those asking questions. It is possible that there are links with lists of "Ask a Librarian" services, and Web surfers are coming across these lists and asking their questions (without reading about who is "officially" eligible to use the service). Month to month, the numbers looked like this:

Month/Year	First	Second	Third
August	13	22	19
September	36	18	17
October	52	20	39

November	58	11	14
December	36	13	
January	44	10	
February	57	17	
March	45	26	
April	37	15	
May	33	14	
June	23	6	
July	29	9	
Totals	463	181	

The anomaly month of October 2000 was very likely because "Ask a Librarian" was featured on the library home page that month as part of a rotating "Current Highlights" feature. This evidence points strongly to the necessity of having a direct link from the library's home page if the library wants its e-mail reference service to get used. The author is going to petition for a permanent place on the library home page–and for placement on other pages throughout the site, such as on the "Databases" page. Whether these efforts will be successful is yet to be seen.

The totals by user category looked like this:

First Year Second Year

Undergraduate	103	23
Graduate	97	44
Faculty	44	15
Staff	100	13
Non-CSU	108	71
Unknown	11	0

Graduate students appear to be the most likely campus group to track down this service. Their numbers dropped the least of any of the affiliate categories.

INTERPRETING QUESTIONS

Part of the challenge of answering the e-mail reference questions is interpreting them. The "reference interview" is cut short here; it is an option to ask for further information or clues, but the author's preference is to reply with some kind of answer, instead of with questions. Technical considerations can create one kind of confusion when the lines in the e-mail message are scattered about and are difficult to read. Or, when the questioner's first language is not

English (or it is, but it is not clear English), an amount of interpretation needs to take place. Sometimes the only option is to reply with possible answers, as in, "if you are asking A, the answer is B; if you are asking C, the answer is D; if it is neither of these, please try to ask your question another way." Other questioners ask a series of questions and the reply needs to be broken up in the hopes that the answer to each question is clear. Sometimes the questioner will even number the questions, which makes it easier when replying.

IMPLICATIONS BEYOND CSU

The number of questions from non-affiliates, whose questions could surely be answered by a local library, raises some concerns. Who are libraries with e-mail reference services serving? (At CSU the number of non-affiliate questions are the most prominent category.) Are one's own affiliates at a public institution anyone in the state? What about the numerous questions from out of state? Are the taxpayers going to approve of this use of resources? Should libraries simply ignore non-affiliate questions? Ignoring the questions completely is an option (and fits the parameters of the service), but just because someone isn't an affiliate now doesn't mean that this person might not, if treated courteously, become an affiliate. These might be parents paying tuition for current or potential students. As a public relations tool, as long as the service is manageable, it seems that answering the questions is the choice at CSU.

To complicate the situation, there is growing competition from question answering services found all over the World Wide Web. These tell searchers that they can "Ask an Expert." The "experts" could be librarians working for the companies or a staff member who may or may not have research skills or experience. In addition, it is unknown whether or not these experts use only their Web's sites to find information. No one search engine covers everything, and some questions are best answered using traditional printed sources. Students may be turning to these services because they are apparent (through ongoing advertisements), and might even be answered 24 hours a day. Do libraries care? Should libraries care? It depends. Maybe students are happy with the answers they get (but then they were happy when they got ten thousand citations in electronic indexes too–never mind that the majority of the results had nothing to do with their topics). The quality of research itself is in question. Some of the free material on the Web is worth what is paid for it; other free material is highly reputable and valuable–but the free materials do not cover everything, and "free" sometimes changes, as some of the researchers who have sent questions to CSU's Ask a Librarian discovered. Libraries also purchase and make accessible to their communities electronic sources; and, not to be forgotten, there are the thousands of books and other materials that libraries purchase

that are not available on the Web. Affiliates of our libraries have access to our databases; we hope that they will make use of these sources.

What does the public sector e-mail reference service offer that commercial services probably don't? We offer the world as we find it. We don't limit ourselves to one search engine or one vendor's products or databases, but to the broadest range we can access, which includes our printed collections. We even search for answers outside of our collections, searching local or distant libraries' online catalogs. Our only limit is our budget and time. Another advantage is that confidentiality is part of our service. Some search engines have a "what are they asking now" feature so questions can be seen by others. This might not matter for the most part, but when privacy matters, it matters a great deal. At present we don't have advertisements as part of our replies (the author hopes this is permanent, but there are murmurings that this could change in order to continue the service); there is no implicit or explicit pressure to purchase a service or product. In addition, we will go beyond the scope of the service and consult with a teacher or professor who has assigned an impossible research project. We can give advice on approaches to topics (again, not limiting ourselves to one search engine or database). As PR for affiliates, it means that they can type their questions whenever they have them and know that the person responding is familiar with the library they are using.

THE FUTURE

The future of e-mail reference is still open. See-you-see-me technology, as well as technology that allows remote users to see the librarian's screen and vice versa, exists. However, it is expensive, and in some cases requires special software to be loaded on the user's terminal. While e-mail reference requires technology not available to everyone, it is available to the user with a basic computer and e-mail access. A major concern for some librarians is turnaround time; 24/7 reference would mean a reply within a very short time frame. This may or may not be an essential service. At academic institutions most of the questions are not literally life and death (and would not even be "urgent" if the questioner had started the research project in a more timely fashion) and the expense involved to support these technologies may not be an effective use of resources in a time of tight budgets.

How many people will be served by these advanced options? Are the equipment and staffing costs worth it? Suppose at CSU that the number of questions to this service is ten times the number of questions sent in the first year of basic e-mail reference–that is 4,630 questions–it still amounts to under thirteen questions a day. In the first 22 months, 81% of the questions were asked when a librarian was at the reference desk, so it seems like there is a large potential

for many idle (or doing non-reference activities) in late night/early morning hours for 24/7 librarians. There are the beginnings of libraries across the country and the world banding together to provide 24/7 reference services, and this may help make the services cost effective. However, sometimes we send proprietary database information sources to users–if they are affiliates–and copyright issues may loom large in these scenarios. Nevertheless, libraries with joint use of proprietary databases can band together and avoid these copyright concerns. Some questions deal specifically with a local collection and a remote 24/7 librarian may not have access to this kind of information (that is only gained by asking someone–during regular library hours). It will be interesting to see how these services develop. They may become part of the fabric of our everyday lives or be a small part of some lives and not of others. Or they may disappear entirely. Stay tuned.

REFERENCES

1. Joseph Janes et al. "Digital Reference Services in Academic Libraries," *Reference & User Services Quarterly* 39.2 (1999): 146.

2. Kristine K. Stacy-Bates. "Ready Reference Resources and E-Mail Reference on Academic ARL Web Sites," *Reference & User Services Quarterly* 40.1 (2000): 71.

3. Joseph Janes. "Associating Continually with Curious Minds: The Evolution of Reference," Presentation. *Reference 24/7: High Touch or High Tech, RUSA President's Program 2000.* Chicago, Illinois. 10 July, 2000.

4. Janes et al. 148.

5. Janes.

6. Source for population: Colorado Municipal Population 1990-1999, draft July 1999. http://www.dlg.oem2.state.co.us/demog/muni.htm.

7. http://www.boulder.lib.co.us/ask/index.html.

Internet Engineering Reference–
An Academic Strategy

Susan B. Ardis

SUMMARY. The McKinney Engineering Library has always been an activist library–we play to win and winning means providing users with high quality help whenever and wherever they need it. This paper describes a multi level strategy for reaching out to engineering users wherever they are. This strategy includes the creation of several kinds of web based tools including: a full online tutorial aimed at new graduate students, specialized exploratory tutorials aimed at users who need only a quick introduction in how to use a specific tool, and topic guides on cross disciplinary design topics. An integrated part of our strategy is an aggressive marketing plan geared toward reminding our users that the Engineering Library and its website are THE places to find information and help. We have changed our thinking–the web makes the library remote from its users, not the other way around. *[Article copies available for a fee from The Haworth Document Delivery Service: 1-800-342-9678. E-mail address: <getinfo@haworthpressinc.com> Website: <http://www.HaworthPress.com> © 2001 by The Haworth Press, Inc. All rights reserved.]*

KEYWORDS. Internet, Web-based instruction, online tutorial, reference service, marketing, Engineering Library

---

Susan B. Ardis is Head, Science Libraries Division and Engineering Library–The General Libraries, The University of Texas at Austin, ECJ 1.3, University of Texas, Austin, TX 78712 (E-mail: s.ardis@mail.utexas.edu).

[Haworth co-indexing entry note]: "Internet Engineering Reference–An Academic Strategy." Ardis, Susan B. Co-published simultaneously in *The Reference Librarian* (The Haworth Information Press, an imprint of The Haworth Press, Inc.) No. 74, 2001, pp. 75-89; and: *Evolution in Reference and Information Services: The Impact of the Internet* (ed: Di Su) The Haworth Information Press, an imprint of The Haworth Press, Inc., 2001, pp. 75-89. Single or multiple copies of this article are available for a fee from The Haworth Document Delivery Service [1-800-342-9678, 9:00 a.m. - 5:00 p.m. (EST). E-mail address: getinfo@haworthpressinc.com].

BACKGROUND

The McKinney Engineering Library (www.lib.utexas.edu/Libs/ENG/engin.html), part of the General Libraries, is a stand-alone collection located about 1/2 mile north of the main library. The library serves a user population of approximately 360 faculty, 1900 graduate students, and 4600 undergraduate students in the College of Engineering. Historically, graduate students have constituted 48% of our user activity, such as circulation reference, and library visits. The remainder of usage breaks down as follows:

Faculty   13%
Undergraduates   29%
Community users   10%

Real estate salesmen have had a saying, "location, location, location," and location is just as important to academic science libraries. Historically, at UT Austin, 80% of our faculty had offices and labs within one block of the Engineering Library. This central location has been a real advantage in providing service to faculty and could be quantitatively measured by the number of "drop-ins" by faculty per day. This is beginning to change, as more and more faculty and their graduate students move to our research campus eleven miles north of campus. The importance of our location is also diminished by the increasing urbanization of Austin and the lack of on-campus housing. The vast majority of our students reside in private off-campus housing, most of it in "student ghettos" three to four miles south of the campus.

With so many of our users miles away from the campus and the library, Internet access to our catalog, indexes and electronic journals has been a real boon because it allows access to information from home, remote labs and computer facilities. This improved access is having a dramatic impact on traditional library services, which is good for users but problematic for reference staff. This article is about how reference staff must reach out to users; we cannot wait for them to find us.

WHAT HAS CHANGED

Like many libraries we are experiencing a decline in traditional library traffic statistics such as: reference, circulation, and photocopies made. The decline in library visits means that it will be more difficult for staff to directly experience:

- Student information gathering behaviors
- Specific language used by researchers
- "Oddities and strengths" of specific indexes and other tools

But the most important changes have been the creation and heavy use of web search engines such as Yahoo! and AltaVista, and the "ask an expert" services provided by numerous proprietary products. These changes have caused many of our users to confuse a search engine's results with results from an index or abstracting service. They have also confused library reference help with Aska services.

WHAT HAS NOT CHANGED

Even though the number of questions has decreased, the nature of the questions we continue to get has not really changed (except in one instance and this will be discussed). The vast majority of our questions can still be characterized as:

- I have an idea for a patent
- I need information on
- Do we have? And its friend, how can I get?
- What does this abbreviation mean?
- Where can I find the property, structure, cost, procedure, etc., of a known material, technique, etc.?
- Which index should I use?

The good news is that we still get lots of questions and our tools are being used. Interestingly, we get just about as many "Do we have, I need information on, and what does this mean" questions as we used to get. What has dramatically declined is "What index should I use?" This is sad because experience shows users, especially in interdisciplinary areas, often don't select the best index for their needs.

The one instance of real change is the increasing number of questions dealing with log-ins and other computer access problems. These highly technical and individualized remote access problems are beyond the scope of this paper because they involve interactions between library, university and departmental web servers and computer access providers.

WHAT DOES ALL THIS MEAN?

In other words, our users seem to have the same kind of questions whether they are in the library or at home. They need answers to specific questions or

problems, strategy suggestions, as well as instructions about how to use a particular tool.

By now it is pretty clear that we've made it quicker and more convenient to access our catalog, abstracts and electronic journals, and users are taking advantage of this in droves. It is just as clear that many continue to be as confused as they were in the past. Both of these coupled with the noticeable decline in library visits means we still have a job to do. The rest of this article is about our response–what we are doing to provide remote reference assistance.

HISTORICAL SOLUTIONS TO REMOTE REFERENCE

Historically, the General Libraries have been very active in undergraduate Bibliographic Instruction. We have integrated library instruction into hundreds of classes and offered thousands of library tours. We have held thousands of "Classes of the Day" (http://www.lib.utexas.edu/Libs/UGL/cod/) and created TILT, Texas Information Literacy Tutorial (http://tilt.lib.utsystem.edu/), a general introductory library tutorial that aims to "prepare students to explore and research the online world."

All of these assume that users know that libraries are a place to get information either in person or remotely because they are all advertised in the library or on our websites. Users must visit the library or our websites regularly to see the advertisements. Another problem is that these are fairly generalized approaches–to reach large audiences they must cover the basics–they cannot and do not cover highly specialized tools. For example, TILT does not cover the complexity of scientific tools, free websites, etc.

Our first attempt at offering tool or subject specific help has been through the addition of ASKA buttons on our websites. These are a good first step but they make several assumptions. First they assume that information seekers know how to ask for help from the library, and secondly, they assume users are familiar with the library's website and tools. They do not address users' confusion between library tools and search engines.

Among UT students there is a widely held belief that search engines such as *www.Google.com* also search our library's catalog, full text journals, and abstracts and indexes (A&I). This is absolutely not true at UT. Confusion is further enhanced by the sheer number of ASKA buttons embedded in tools and services accessible through the web. It is now possible for users to ask for help directly from the information product provider or from one of the growing "ask a question" services on the web such as Ask Jeeves.

Product based ASKA buttons provide product specific help, but they cannot be expected to offer assistance with or even suggest the use of competing products. Nor can they be expected to:

- Explain the complexities, oddities, and values of good information searching
- Announce the availability of new resources and explain the multiplicity of tools, search locations, and access points
- "Aggregate" engineering information

But from our point of view another limitation is that none of these really deal directly with the specialized information needs of engineering students. To solve these problems we decided to develop and then aggressively market three kinds of web-based instructional aids: Exploratories, Guides, and Tutorials. Each would deal with a definite problem and each would be aimed at a specific segment of our audience.

TUTORIALS; SUBJECT AND FAQ GUIDES; AND EXPLORATORIES

Tutorials

The first and most ambitious part of our strategy was the development of a subject specific tutorial aimed at engineering graduate students. We chose graduate students because they are heaviest users of the library's collection and web resources. This is because they are involved with both faculty and independent research. They are, in fact, often the research employees of faculty. This places a tremendous responsibility on graduate students to find good, relevant information quickly.

Even though today's engineering graduate students are part of a generation that has been using computer technology for a lifetime to communicate, for entertainment and a source of information, we know from experience that they have a limited idea of what specialized engineering tools exist, where to find them, or even how to use them. Their Internet experience has convinced them that finding information is easy–it's all just a couple of "clicks" away on the web.

All this led us to create an integrated tutorial. We wanted to take advantage of the Internet and use the electronic medium to explain how to use tools accessible through the library's Internet site. Another advantage of the Internet is that it essentially places responsibility for finding information on the user. We decided to work with this and provide active learning to graduate students using the web. We also felt that our tutorial should allow students to learn at their own pace.

This decision was not taken lightly–a tutorial that is boring, irrelevant, and badly marketed and therefore poorly used is a waste of everybody's time and

money. Therefore, once the decision was made to develop a tutorial, we began immediately in tandem to work on attention getting devices and a marketing strategy.

Goals

The tutorial has two sets of goals. The first is what the users should be able to do after using our tutorial, and the second is what the tutorial should do for the library. You do not go to all this work without expecting some benefit for the library. We quickly delineated one area that was important to both groups–improving information access skills. Students want to find what they need quickly and without a lot of trauma. Staff wanted to improve users' information access skills. Both needs led to the decision to teach:

First set:

- The strengths and limitations of web search engines
- The strengths and limitations of the online catalog
- The availability of highly specialized tools
- Where and how to go for additional help
- The nature of proprietary information

Second set:

- Promote services
- Demonstrate the usefulness of "paid tools"
- Improve actual usage of these tools

Once we were clear on our goals we decided what areas to cover and what areas to rely on other tutorials such as TILT that are already in existence. Therefore, we decided not to cover:

- Nature of call numbers
- Concept of a bibliographic record
- Nature of LC subject headings
- Organization of the university's library system

Instead we would cover specifically:

I. Searching the Internet–What's Free on the Web

- Search Engines–Overview and Advice
- Search Tips

- Evaluating Websites
- What the Search Engines Do Not Find

II. UT Library Online–UT Austin Library Website

- Using UT Library Online Resources to Find Free Resources on the Web
- Finding Books and Conference Proceedings
- Finding Scientific and Technical Articles
- Taking the Guesswork Out of Abbreviations
- Journals–Full-Text vs. Paper
- What does a reference librarian do?

III. Tips and Advice–Resources to Keep in Mind

- Patents–A Great Source of Information
- Finding Data and Specific Properties or Facts
- Company Information/Proprietary Information
- Product Information/Specifications
- Industry Standards
- Finding Images on the Web

The tutorial was called "Information Excavation." From our experience we know that most of our students are fascinated by heavy equipment and we thought this image would get their attention. Working through "Information Excavation" from start to finish provides a user with a thorough introduction to finding information. While new students and foreign students find it helpful to work through the session step by step, graduate students with some experience using the library may prefer to work through only selected sections. Students who just need a refresher can choose the Frequently Asked Questions option of navigating through the tutorial to get the highlights.

How It Was Developed

Over a three-month period of time, the tutorial was developed using Microsoft FrontPage. The focus at this phase of development was content, so limited attention was given to creating graphics, animation and complex page designs. When a draft was completed, librarians and other staff at the Engineering Library edited the pages and suggested additional topics that needed to be addressed.

Once we received input on the tutorial from the library perspective, we were anxious to find out what representatives from our target audience thought of the tutorial. Graduate student volunteers reviewed the draft tutorial and pro-

vided excellent feedback. Overall, the response was positive and made us feel that we were on the right track with the tutorial.

In the early planning stages for a Web-based tutorial, the theme of digging or mining for information was proposed and from this came the "Information Excavation" concept. Not only is this suitable for our engineering audience, it also provides countless options for graphics and logos to be used in the promotion of the finished product. We also hoped that this might provide us with financial sponsorship possibilities from the construction industry.

Future Plans

Plans are afoot to provide links within the tutorial to our other reference products: Topic Guides and Exploratories. With the content of the tutorial determined, the intention now is to focus on developing a look and feel for the tutorial. These graphics will also be used on our websites, Aska button, premiums, handouts, banners and posters, and on in-library signage. The idea is to form an integrated graphical look for our reference products and services. This is an iterative process and therefore a work-in-progress. It can be seen at: *http://www.lib.utexas.edu/Libs/ENG/grad/gradtips.html.*

Subject and FAQ Guides

The second portion of our strategy is the creation of a series of Subject and FAQ guides. Both are really a twist on the old pathfinder idea. There are two major differences between Subject guides and FAQs. First is format. The FAQ series is in the Internet question and answer format while the subject guides are not. The second difference concerns coverage. The Subject guides cover fields of study and the FAQ series covers categories of material or problems. To get "more bang for our buck," the first topics selected in both categories were those most relevant to our technical writing and engineering design classes. In both cases every undergraduate must take both a design and a technical writing course. Students in these classes are heavily stressed by the need to either produce a major report or solutions to real engineering problems. As a result, in the past these students have been heavy library users because they need all kinds of technical, scientific, and business information, much of which is often very removed from their primary field of study. As a result our first set of Subject guides covered topics such as: ergonomics, transportation, and materials science where we knew there was a tremendous interest. On the other hand, the FAQ series covered such topics as "How to select an index" and "Finding Technical Reports."

Audience

We see these guides as class based and highly related to our hands-on Bibliographic Instruction program. However, another audience is engineering reference staff. These guides have been extremely useful in sharing experience and knowledge among staff because they have served as a place to store useful URLs, titles of handbooks, as well as information about what is in specific tools and books. Another important use has been in training new staff. Interestingly, recent experience has shown that staff value Subject guides and FAQs more than was at first expected.

Goals

- Provide information on topics of interest to our design and technical writing classes
- Share information among Engineering reference and other reference desks
- Provide users with an intersection between web and paper tools
- Remind users that "we are here to help"

Future Plans

We have other Subject guides in the works including space exploration, weather and biomedical engineering. We have proxy server, password, and hook-up FAQs in the works as well. With both our Subject and FAQ Guide series we are really sharing our knowledge with each other and with our users. An example can be seen at: *http://www.lib.utexas.edu/Libs/ENG/techrept.html*.

Exploratories

The third part of our strategy may be the most creative and that is the development of our Exploratory series. The Exploratory series is designed to give users a web demonstration of how to use a specific tool, along with advice on any special aspects or oddities found in the tool. They are not intended to cover all uses of a specific tool or to offer individual or personalized help. Rather, the Exploratory series is designed to offer quick, guided interactive instruction on the use of specific engineering tools.

The instructions guide users through specific searches. Once they have results, they are asked to examine these results. Additional guidance, opinions, usage tricks, etc., may be offered. Once users have completed an Exploratory they should be able to use the tool quite efficiently. We chose the title Exploratory as a way of letting users know these are intended to give quick help on the topic being covered.

There are additional uses as a:

- Training tool for new library staff.
- Part of telephone reference. Users who can talk on the phone and use the computer can be walked through a relevant Exploratory. We know what they are seeing, the results retrieved, and then we can help them analyze their problem.
- Part of email reference. Users who email us with questions get the URL of the relevant Exploratory as part of their answer.

Frankly, our Exploratory Series is nothing more than a web version of our answer to the traditional reference question–"Can you show me how to use xyz?" In the past, users who asked this question wanted a quick hands-on demonstration rather than to be shown the *User Guide*. The point of this series is to provide a remote version of a traditional demonstration.

Our first two in this series cover U.S. and international patent searching. These topics were selected because we are a Patent and Trademark Depository Library and as such had wide experience providing patent and trademark reference service. In fact we had gained some web visibility through the development of an in-depth U.S. patent tutorial that dealt with searching patents using a CD-ROM product. This web-based tutorial was still being used but it was not helpful for patent searching using the USPTO website. Besides, our CD-ROM tutorial was initiating a lot of user calls asking for a quick guided tour of the various Internet patent sources. We used this experience to develop our first Exploratories.

Both of our new patent Exploratories have been very popular both with UT users and with the general public. This popularity is measured by the number of log-ins. We were not surprised by the use because patent searching websites can be very complex. The USPTO site, for example, is very dense, and users often become quite confused and cannot find where to look for what they need. The Exploratories were designed to alleviate some of the confusion by:

- Highlighting the different types of intellectual property and what is covered or not covered by each type
- Demonstrating the various navigation elements on each website
- Demonstrating the different kinds of searches that can be done
- Pointing out the potential need for a trained patent professional

Reference librarians have always considered patent searching to be the ultimate "reference trip." This is because a patent is the intersection of the law, technology, and business; therefore, all of these aspects are important in patent searching. Go to *http://www.lib.utexas.edu/Libs/ENG/uspatents/index.html* to see our first Exploratory.

Development

The Exploratory series was developed using Microsoft FrontPage and frames. We chose Microsoft FrontPage because it is easy to use. Ease of use meant that the person developing the intellectual content could do some of the rough design work while also working on the content. This speeds up development.

We also decided to use Frames even though at first UT was very much against this. However, once we demonstrated that our proposed Exploratory series was the perfect use of Frames and that there really was no other way to accomplish the same results, we were given permission to go ahead. The real strength of Microsoft Frames is that it allows us to demonstrate or highlight the actual site while commenting on what is being seen. We chose to use two horizontal frames on one screen so that we can put instructions in one frame and an introduction in another. Once the user enters the instruction frame and begins following the directions, they will see the tool being discussed displayed in the former introduction frame. The introduction frame merely serves to get users started.

Once users enter the instruction frame, they are led through an actual demonstration of pre-selected search topics. Frames allow us to make suggestions concerning who and when to call or email for additional personal help. One of the best things about using a Frames template is that it is easy to produce Exploratories on hot topics quickly.

Future Plans

Our first two Exploratories dealt with publicly available websites. In the near future we plan to produce Exploratories that cover other publicly available tools (such as DTIC and search engines), as well as tools that are available only to our own students. Topics being considered include: how to use specific indexes (citation searching) and product searching that compares search engines, the Thomas Register with CatalogXpress.

EVALUATION OF THE TUTORIAL, SUBJECT AND FAQ GUIDES AND EXPLORATORIES

Every web page at Engineering is edited and tested. During the editing process students on our staff evaluated each product for:

- Utility
- Clearness

- Appropriateness
- Functionality
- Search engine access
- Attractiveness

Once our student employees have had their input, then each web product is tested in our hands-on Bibliographic Instruction classes prior to being made available to the public. Once our websites are publicly available, another group of student employees is put on the job. The job this time is to determine if our products will be retrieved using UT licensed search engines. This testing is an important precursor to our marketing program because there is no point marketing something that users cannot find easily.

HOW ALL OF THESE NEW TOOLS ARE MARKETED

Even the best web-based tutorial, topic guide or exploratory will be value-less if no one uses them. Most of our users have busy schedules. We also know from experience that they won't use tutorials, topic guides, pathfinders or any other "help" aids if they are time-consuming or boring. Our tools must catch their attention and demonstrate value immediately. The latter is important because we know from experience users do not really believe that there is much to learn–they believe they can just "parse" or "gut" it out and find what they need. Our users have great faith in their own ability to figure things out–after all, "finding information is easy, you just need a couple of keywords." In short, fun and interesting are important.

Our aids are being heavily marketed through the College of Engineering, the Engineering Library, and the General Libraries. This marketing has several thrusts:

- Mass mailing (email and paper) to all engineering students
- Announcements in every library user education presentation made by staff
- Display of construction toys (e.g., front loaders, excavators) in the library–this points to our website
- A premium given when the user presents the "successful completion" tutorial coupon in the library. Actually we'll give the premium to anybody who asks for one.

However, if our aids are to be successful, we must have faculty and college administrator "buy-in," as well as student use. We assumed that faculty recommendations plus student "word-of-mouth" about the availability of a premium would encourage student use. To get College and faculty buy-in we are:

- Visiting every graduate advisor and demonstrating the tutorial, guides, etc. We know that if a graduate advisor makes a recommendation, students, especially new students, take it seriously.
- Making presentations to the Council of College of Engineering (COE) Chairmen
- Giving a letter, a copy of the flyer, and a premium to all:
  - College of Engineering deans
  - Directors and associated directors of the General Libraries
  - Relevant UT Austin vice-presidents
- Sending a copy of the flyer and letter offering to demonstrate the tutorial to all COE student organizations

Premium

We decided early on that a premium might get through the miasma of research and overconfidence by playing on a desire to get something free, and we know most everyone likes freebies. Our premium had to play a several roles–it should be desirable, it should re-enforce our message, and it needed to be free to us. We gave a lot of thought to which freebie would be the most compelling–pens, mouse pads, bags or insulated cups–and how to go about getting the premium.

Actually, it did not take much thought or research to come up with cups. At the time of our discussion Austin had just gone through one of the hottest summers on record–over 40 days above 100°. Carrying a cool drink had become a necessity. We decided to play on this and give out insulated cups. To carry our message these cups had to have on one side:

- Our name and logo
- Physical address
- Email address
- Reference phone number
- Quotation "your place for engineering information"

On the other side the provider could have a "brought to you by" or "in support of" statement along with the:

- Name and logo of provider
- Address
- Web address

We contacted several vendors and local companies we thought would be interested in advertising their services to engineering students. One was not in-

terested, and, in fact, specifically said that they did not see engineering students as a potential market. This surprised us, since they hired over 100 UT engineering students last year–well, "Tant pis," or there is no accounting for how some companies think. Another company did not respond even though we asked for help from the College's Corporate Relations officer; note he was very surprised by the lack of response–oh, well. Lastly, we contacted a library vendor and they responded almost immediately. They produced 500 red insulated cups with their logo on one side and our information on the other side in less than five weeks.

Even though this premium was originally aimed at graduate students who completed our tutorial, we decided not to discriminate. If an undergraduate completes the tutorial–great, they can get a cup, too. If any student comes in and asks for a cup, they get one too, and we began giving them out at the end of our hands-on classes. These cups have been reasonably popular and none has shown up in our "lost and found" yet.

CONCLUSION

Times are changing in the information world and libraries and librarians must change with them. Users expect and now demand convenience and ease of use as they search for information. The good news is that the Internet makes it easier. It is easier to reach more people at more times. It also makes it possible to show them how to use electronic tools, electronically.

However, we must assume that the library is NOT the first place our users look for information. Therefore, we must market our services in the actual place, the Internet, where they will look for information. We cannot be passive, relying only on word-of-mouth, and our physical location to get our message to our users. The Engineering Library has done this through an active marketing campaign of reference services, whether they are Exploratories, Subject or FAQ guides, our tutorial, or our traditional reference services.

The McKinney Engineering Library has always been an activist library–we play to win and winning means providing our users with high quality help whenever and wherever they need it. We won't just wait for users to visit the library–and hope that they also have questions. We will reach out. We will think of ourselves as being remote from our users rather than thinking of our users as being remote. No longer are our users remote from information; instead, it is reference librarians who are now remote.

Visitation and access may have changed, but what has not changed is our responsibility to provide our users with high-quality help. We may not have the staff for 24-hour reference, but we do have the staff and the expertise to share our experience and knowledge with our users by creating different levels of

topical help. Exploratories, Subject and FAQ guides and tutorials should be included as part of the mix of help offered to users—along with email, telephone, and in-person reference. We must aggressively demonstrate the value libraries and librarians bring to our organization and our students by manufacturing aids and then marketing the aids and the services everywhere.

Link: *http://www.lib.utexas.edu/Libs/ENG/engin.html* Engineering Library Homepage

Meeting Reference Responsibilities Through Library Web Sites

Michael Adams

SUMMARY. Among the many ways the World Wide Web has changed libraries are the additional tools gained by librarians and library users for answering reference questions. In addition to the growing number of licensed resources providing the full text of articles from newspapers, magazines, academic journals, and reference works are the millions of free Web sites offering an incredible variety of information about everything. Locating the most useful of these sites and organizing them into categories on library Web sites can be enormously beneficial both to patrons and libraries. After deciding to make their sites reference portals, librarians must make a number of important decisions. *[Article copies available for a fee from The Haworth Document Delivery Service: 1-800-342-9678. E-mail address: <getinfo@haworthpressinc.com> Website: <http://www.HaworthPress.com> © 2001 by The Haworth Press, Inc. All rights reserved.]*

KEYWORDS. Evaluating Web sites, library newsletters, library patrons, library publicity, marketing libraries, reference questions, reference sources, search engines, Web design, Web directories, Web portals, Web searching, Web sites

---

Michael Adams is Reference Librarian, Mina Rees Library, City University of New York Graduate Center, 365 Fifth Avenue, New York, NY 10016-4309 (E-mail: madams@gc.cuny.edu).

[Haworth co-indexing entry note]: "Meeting Reference Responsibilities Through Library Web Sites." Adams, Michael. Co-published simultaneously in *The Reference Librarian* (The Haworth Information Press, an imprint of The Haworth Press, Inc.) No. 74, 2001, pp. 91-101; and: *Evolution in Reference and Information Services: The Impact of the Internet* (ed: Di Su) The Haworth Information Press, an imprint of The Haworth Press, Inc., 2001, pp. 91-101. Single or multiple copies of this article are available for a fee from The Haworth Document Delivery Service [1-800-342-9678, 9:00 a.m. - 5:00 p.m. (EST). E-mail address: getinfo@haworthpressinc.com].

91

INTRODUCTION

Most academic, public, and school libraries have World Wide Web sites, but do these sites just provide information about collections and services or do they do more? As a means of helping patrons, whether inside or outside the library, find answers to their questions, helping librarians also locate these answers quickly, and promoting awareness of the library, why not make your site a portal or gateway to the vast world of information available on the Web? The following explains some of the benefits when libraries make their sites reference portals and how this can be achieved.

The arrival of the World Wide Web transformed library services and practices in innumerable ways, and one of the most profound has been the ways reference librarians respond to patrons' needs. In the pre-Web days, library users looking for biographical information about a historical figure, a bibliography about international environmental policies, or a map of Pakistan would either be referred to the appropriate reference book or shown how to find it in the card catalog or OPAC. The only available resources would be those in the library and, possibly, those in nearby libraries, if the reference librarian had access to their catalogs. This procedure, taken for granted by generations of librarians, has, of course, changed drastically. Now, reference librarians, faced with questions such as those above, must decide whether to limit themselves to resources within the physical library or to find (or, better, show the patron how to find) the information on the Web.

PRINT OR WEB?

Deciding which way is best depends upon the nature of the question, the completeness of the library's collection, and the ease of finding the information electronically. The library certainly has a map of Pakistan, and if it has been published in the last twenty years, it should be fairly accurate. But what if the patron needs a map of a central European country whose boundaries and even name may have changed in the past decade? In such cases, a map ten or even five years old may not be sufficient. If a recent map is available, how easy is it to photocopy, if that is what the patron needs? Will the library's photocopiers produce a clean, readable image? Will the map have to be reduced, making the text portion less legible? Is the map on two pages, making the center of the photocopy difficult or impossible to decipher? Is color photocopying possible? The same sorts of concerns apply when the best available map can be found on the Web. Is the map current, if that is what is needed? Does the library allow printing from Web sites? What is the quality of the printout? Size and color may also be factors.

A patron looking for biographical information about an American president can probably find sufficient material about Washington, Lincoln, Wilson, and Eisenhower in most libraries, but what about more recent presidents? Few reference books available in 2001 will have any detailed information about George W. Bush. In the pre-Web days, librarians would have to help patrons track down newspaper and magazine articles. This task is much easier with online databases, the more with full text the better, but printing policies may come into play here as well. Then there are the numerous Web sites providing such biographical information. Books and articles by scholars and journalists are one thing; sites created by amateur enthusiasts another. While evaluating the reliability of Web sites has become an important issue in the profession, it is much easier to deal with in an instructional setting than with a patron who demands an immediate answer. And are the amateurs always inferior to the professionals? Individuals with passions for their subjects may actually do more complete jobs in some instances. Meanwhile, your patron is growing impatient about finding something about Bush's economic policies while governor of Texas. What are reference librarians to do?

This situation is not really a dilemma. The Web–and the electronic resources that preceded it–have not made our jobs more complicated; they have just altered our options. Deciding whether a print or an electronic resource is best depends upon the size of the library's collection on the subject in question, the librarian's knowledge of this subject collection, the librarian's ability to find the information electronically, and the availability as well of an appropriate electronic solution. What if the best source is on the Web, but the patron must wait for a half hour for an available PC? The librarian may be able to show the patron how to reach the appropriate site at the reference desk, but the reference PC cannot be tied up for the patron's use. Sometimes, a less complete, less up-to-date print resource just has to do, especially when the library's computer network goes down.

Many readers of essays like this one may occasionally become annoyed because the supposed experts explaining how things should be or could be done imply that their way is the only way or that all patrons or librarians are the same. Such expert advice often overlooks practical considerations. Faced with ten patrons with similar questions during a two-hour stint at the reference desk, a librarian may not deal with each equally. Experienced librarians develop the ability to read quickly their patrons' personalities: recognizing which will be more comfortable with print resources and which with electronic ones, which ones will have the patience to explore several options and which will settle for nothing less than an immediate solution, which will be receptive to having a quick information-seeking tutorial while the question is explored and which are too impatient. Academic librarians are also well familiar with the faculty members offended by the most benign suggestions that they may not be

knowledgeable about something. Then there is the fatigue factor. After two or three or four or more hours on the desk, as often happens in small libraries and even in larger ones on nights and weekends, librarians may seek not the answer best for the patron but the one easier for them. Then there are the librarians resembling the clerks in Herman Melville's "Bartleby, the Scrivener," who are at their best before or after lunch but not all day. These practical, often invisible (especially to administrators) considerations affect how reference librarians perform their jobs.

Then there are the growing number of patrons who never make it to the reference desk, those who assume that computers are smarter than librarians and that anyone can bang on a few keys and easily find whatever information is needed. Increasingly, these patrons searching the library's catalog and licensed resources, whether inside or outside the library, never pose their questions in person. More and more libraries try to meet the needs of these patrons through remote contacts: allowing their users to ask reference questions by e-mail through creating electronic reference-question forms, with some libraries attempting real-time electronic conversations between patrons and librarians.

TO SEARCH OR NOT TO SEARCH

Many of these remote patrons, perhaps most, take matters into their own hands by attempting to use search engines to find whatever they need. Too frequently, typical Web users select one search engine, usually by happenstance, and stick with it. If that search engine cannot find what they are looking for–or if they do not know how to interpret the results they get–they assume the information is not available on the Web. At the other extreme, those who assume everything is on the Web become frustrated or angry when they cannot find the name of Shakespeare's cousin's brother-in-law's cow and turn against the Web as an important source of information. Even college students seeking information about subjects such as developmental psychology can become bewildered when search engines lead them not to useful information but to publishers' advertisements for books about this subject or course syllabi at other colleges or announcements about academic conferences. Such are the unavoidable pitfalls of using search engines to find information about academic topics.

Librarians can counter the limitations of search engines through making their patrons aware of the alternative: directory sites arranging links into categories. While many popular search engines, such as Yahoo!, are directories as well–and while many directory sites have copied or been influenced by Yahoo!'s directory structure–often the best resources for library users with refer-

ence questions are sites which have attempted to organize Web sites into logical categories. These include Academic Info (www.academicinfo.net), the Big Eye (www.bigeye.com), Digital Librarian (www.digital-librarian.com), Education Index (www.educationindex.com), Infomine (infomine.ucr.edu), the Internet Public Library Reference Center (www.ipl.org/ref), Librarians' Index to the Internet (lii.org), Martindale's The Reference Desk (www-sci.lib. uci.edu/~martindale/Ref.html), refdesk.com (www.refdesk.com), Resource Discovery Network (www.rdn.ac.uk), Voice of the Shuttle (vos.ucsb.edu), and the World Wide Web Virtual Library's General Reference site (home.istar.ca/~obyrne).

Such sites vary greatly in the types of sites they index, some emphasizing academic sites, others those of interest to the general public, and in their thoroughness. Then there are the hundreds of sites attempting to be portals for a particular topic or academic subject. All of these are extremely useful in varying degrees, but because of the ever-expanding nature of the Web, none can list every good site about every subject.

BECOMING A PORTAL

Libraries attempt to address this matter by having links to such portals on their Web sites. Libraries have quickly evolved from being repositories for information to being doorways which users can enter electronically to find virtually anything. There are many approaches to alerting patrons to the availability of reference resources on the Web. Most library Web sites, whether academic, public, or school, have links to general reference sites like those listed above. Other library sites will go the next step and include links to subject-specific sites, generally portals. A more adventurous approach is to make the library site one of these portals itself.

Many libraries refrain from making their sites reference portals by proclaiming, "Why reinvent the wheel?" Why must we find and organize sites into categories when Digital Librarian, Infomine, and Voice of the Shuttle have already done so? The wheel analogy works only in those instances in which what is being compared has reached a level of perfection like the wheel. Are these reference portals perfect? As soon as a brilliant site about European immigration to North America before 1920 appears, does it automatically jump into all the reference portals? Even with its level of perfection, the wheel must still be a certain size and color. The same is true of reference portals: Decisions have to be made about the content and its organization. Are the results of these decisions necessarily reflected in the way patrons of a particular library–or even librarians themselves–seek information?

Let's say the person looking for the name of Shakespeare's cousin's brother-in-law's cow actually comes to the reference desk. The librarian knows that such information is unlikely to be found easily, if at all, but does remember seeing a Web site with information about Shakespeare's family that may be of interest to the patron. But where was it? Was it in the Internet Public Library? Or LookSmart? Or a literary portal? If this library's Web site had a collection of Shakespeare links, the librarian's job would be easier because there would be fewer steps in the process. If the librarian was involved in deciding which sites to link to, the task could be even simpler, not to mention rewarding. All librarians experience a degree of pleasure when a question can be answered with a book purchased for the library on their recommendation. The same applies to the Web when the librarian chose to add the site providing the patron with needed information.

When a library's Web site includes sufficient useful and reliable links, it can become a portal where its users automatically begin their searching. The entire library benefits as a result because visitors to the site learn more about the library's collection, services, programs, and staff than they would otherwise.

WHAT TO INCLUDE?

The next question is obviously what sites should be included in the library portal. Links to the major reference sites and search engines are obvious. Library users should be trained to try directories first and use search engines only when the directories fail. This matter involves more than traditional library instruction sessions, though all library users on all levels can benefit enormously from such formal training. In helping the patrons who come to the reference desk, the librarian trains them by showing that if they first go to the library's site which leads to a large site which leads to a smaller one which leads to the specific one the patrons need, the logic of the way information is organized on the Web comes across. Visitors to the site from outside the library who find what they are looking for in this way will be impressed by the site–and those who created it–and return again. Becoming a reference portal for your school or community is a way of marketing awareness of the library.

After the reference portals and search engines come the subject-specific directories. Why are these specific sites necessary if they are included in the reference sites to which the library has already linked? Because some may be listed in reference portal A, some in B, others in C, but not all in one place. Your goal is to try to round up all the best sites your patrons need and keep them in one place–your library's site. This is particularly important when the community of a public library has certain specific interests: the oil industry,

say, or forestry or high-school basketball statewide. The reference portals may not have links to such topics or may have them deeply imbedded within other subjects.

There are many useful academic portals, but each tries to cover all academic subjects or all subjects within an area such as the humanities, sciences, or social sciences. If you are an academic reference librarian, you want your library's Web site to reflect the particular needs of your users. A small liberal arts colleges may not need links to engineering sites. Library Web sites must be customized to the needs of their constituents. For example, if a renowned scholar of medieval French architecture is on the faculty and teaches courses in this area, the library's Web site may include more links to sites related to his field than most comparable library sites would. Again, the public-relations/marketing aspect of the library site comes into play.

As the previous example implies, a good academic library portal should not just include general architecture, French, and history sites but specific ones, sometimes very specific ones, in fact. The procedure for developing a good library portal is similar to the collection-development methods for purchasing books. Professor K teaches courses in L, M, and N, so we need books to support the research his students are performing. Comparable Web sites are also needed. The main difference in the two collection-development practices is that while the acquisition of books, periodicals, audio-visual materials, and electronic databases is defined by budgetary restrictions, the Web, except for those expensive databases, is free. There may be some snobbery inherent in some dark recesses of librarianship suggesting that if something is free it cannot be that valuable, but even a glance at the sites developed by faculty, students, and even those amateur enthusiasts mentioned earlier undermines this attitude.

In addition to sites arranged by subject, you can create an interdisciplinary category, perhaps labeled excellent or recommended or useful sites, to showcase ones to which you wish to call special attention. These sites may include those created by your institution or community, other sites of local interest, and sites with unique features likely to appeal to your patrons. Having a site-of-the-day feature is another way of luring visitors to your site.

FINDING SITES

Well, where do these sites we are collecting come from? Many come from the reference and subject-specific portals themselves. Academic Info may include hundreds of mathematics sites, but not all of them may be helpful to your patrons. Choose the ones you want. Another way to develop appropriate links is to visit sites that recommend new sites or list their new additions. Academic

Info and Digital Librarian perform the latter service. Yahoo! has a daily list of additions by category: dir.yahoo.com/new. Sites such as the Chronicle of Higher Education (chronicle.com/infotech), Political Site of the Day (www.aboutpolitics.com), Scott's Botanical Links (www.ou.edu/cas/botany-micro/bot-linx/), Translators' Site du Jour (home,ncia.com/~slarsson/sitejour.htm), and USA Today (www.usatoday.com/life/cyber/ch.htm) recommend sites daily with annotations. Our professional colleagues also call attention to useful sites. The Machine-Assisted Reference Section (MARS) of the Reference and User Services Association (RUSA) annually creates a list of the best free reference sites. (The list for 2000 can be found at www.ala.org/rusa/mars/best2000.html.) Each issue of *College & Research Libraries News* offers an annotated list of useful sites in a particular subject. These lists are also available on this publication's Web site: www.ala.org/acrl/c%26rlnew2.html.

CRITERIA FOR INCLUSION

What are the criteria for inclusion? Beyond the obvious usefulness for your patrons, you might consider the following criteria for an academic library site:[1]

1. Is it scholarly? For some academic subjects, there are many more sites aimed at the K-12 level than at college and university students and faculty. This does not mean, however, that the K-12 sites should automatically be rejected. Such a site explaining the basics of particle accelerators may, after all, be helpful to a beginning physics student. For the most part, however, the language and design should clearly indicate the seriousness of the site. Those created by faculty and graduate students generally have an advantage over those from amateurs.

2. What about the language? Is it too technical? If it is too technical for undergraduates, is it still likely to be of interest to faculty and graduate students? Are there typographical errors? The most important language requirement may simply be literacy. If the first page of the site has *it's* when it should be *its*, the scholarly content of the site is seriously in doubt.

3. Too many Web designers try too hard to be flashy. Sites should be easy to read and navigate. If it is too difficult to find your way back after penetrating several layers into the site, it is badly designed. Every page should have a way to get back home. The graphics should not take an inordinate amount of time to load. There should be no unnecessary distractions such as exploding rainbows that allow the designer to show off but achieve little else. Red text on a black background is difficult to read. Advertisements are unfortunate, but sometimes that is the only way the site can keep in operation. Weigh the value of the con-

tent against the negatives of the ads. The types of ads, dating services, for example, may also be negative factor.[2]

4. Sites should be up-to-date. A site created by students for a class four years earlier is unlikely to be the best available on the particular subject. A site whose links have not been checked in two years may be not very useful. There are problems, however, with the dating of sites. Webmasters are trying to be helpful when they indicate when the site was last changed, but what do the changes involve? Just adding or removing one or two links does not mean much unless all the links are checked regularly. Some unscrupulous Webmasters may even not be entirely honest about the dates on their sites. The best determiner in many cases is simply looking at the site's content and comparing it to similar ones.

5. Too many library sites play the linking game too conservatively. If they have one Virginia Woolf link, that is enough. But is that Woolf site that seemed to be the best available when added two years ago still the best? It offers information not available on other Woolf sites, but what about this one that not only has a bibliography but annotates it as well. One site is heavy on text but has no graphics. Another has links to ten Woolf photographs, the title pages of her books, etc. Rarely will one site about any subject be the last word. Again the specific needs of your likely visitors must be taken into consideration. And sites, even authoritative ones, have a habit of disappearing. Students graduate, and their sites are removed from the university's server. A site's creator may decide a site is too time-consuming and take it down. If your users have a serious interest in biotechnology, links to five general biotechnology sites and twenty specific ones might not be enough. If a site has useful content and is navigable, add it.

6. If a site takes a controversial stance on a sensitive issue, do not automatically reject it if it has other virtues and is not clearly offensive to a large percentage of your patrons. Librarians are information providers, not censors.

CATEGORY CONCERNS

After sites have been selected, they must be organized. Most headings are obvious, but you must be cognizant of users' searching patterns. If you have only a category called medicine, where does the visitor looking for health information go? The solution is one category with alternative names in the index of your categories. You may decide to include anthropology and archaeology within the same category, but you list both in your index. You have a category labeled reference that includes quotations, but will your visitor automatically look under reference to find quotations? Such subcategories can be listed separately in your index. Subcategories are necessary for some subjects. An alpha-

betical list of over one hundred or even fifty or twenty-five history links may be unwieldy. Dividing the larger category into such subcategories as American history, European history, organizations, teaching history, etc., may be necessary.

What about a site such as Rutgers University's Alcohol Studies Database (scc01.rutgers.edu/alcohol_studies)? Does it go under medicine or sociology or psychology? What is wrong with all three? Try to look at the subject from the point of view of a user approaching alcoholism from different angles. Consulting the Library of Congress Subject Headings for a book with similar content may be helpful.

Why not simply use LCSH? Again, look at matters as the visitor to your Web site might. As long as LC uses *Afro-Americans* instead of *African-Americans*; *United States–History* instead of *American history; Art–History* instead of *Art history; Motion pictures* instead of *Movies, Films,* or *Cinema,* and other headings that do not reflect the way most library users search for information, the answer is obvious. The LCSH model can be followed, however, in terms of cross-references. Refer visitors to the economics links to those for business, government resources, and statistics, visitors to film studies to performing arts and theater, visitors to history to political science, and so on.

The best approach to determining how to organize and label your links is simply to look at how other sites do it and borrow from their approaches, combining what you learn with your awareness of how your patrons seek information and with your creative impulses. The same borrowing strategy applies to the overall look of your site, especially the necessary signposts telling visitors where they are and how to get back to where they were. Even librarians without formal HTML training can follow this approach by looking at the codes used by pages they admire and adapting the design to their needs.

Once the sites have been found and organized, they must be kept up to date. There are several software products for checking links. Some libraries may run into difficulty, however, with network administrators who resist adding such programs. Such software can track dead links, but what about those sites that simply change names or URLs? The reference librarians should share the responsibility for keeping the reference portal vital.

The reference portal can, of course, include more than links to outside sources. Original resources such as guides to the library's most significant reference works can be included. Such guides, especially when annotated, can help your patrons remember that Web and print resources can be equally essential to their research. A particularly good example of such a research-guide site is Auburn University's: www.lib.auburn.edu/hum/humweb/researchguides.html.

FINDING THE TIME

How do I find time to do all this, you ask? I have funds that must be spent by a certain date, workshops to conduct, meetings to attend. Creating and, especially, maintaining the reference portion of a library Web site obviously takes time and should not be undertaken by any individual or group of librarians who cannot commit themselves to the project. If you see a need for making your library's site a reference portal for your users and want to do it, you may have to decide to take time away from other duties. Dividing the responsibility with like-minded librarians works only if all are equally committed. Academic librarians may use student assistants for some tasks such as checking links.

Try to be realistic about what you can accomplish, what you need to do. The best possible reference portal will have annotations of all sites, but if you absolutely do not have the time, do what you can. If a site's name does not clearly describe its content, provide a simple phrase that does so: indicate that Domestic Goddesses, for example, refers to nineteenth-century writers of "domestic fiction." When a site is officially sanctioned by an institution, organization, or business, including the name of such bodies can help your users see the difference between such generally reliable sites and those created by enthusiasts.

EVERYBODY'S HAPPY

Making library Web sites into information portals helps everyone. They benefit patrons by showing how the seemingly chaotic world of the Web can be organized into logical divisions to help them find what they need. Libraries benefit as more visitors come to their sites. Reference librarians can better help their patrons and experience a sense of achievement. Such librarians are not mere information gatekeepers but information architects.

NOTES

1. A different set of criteria are offered by Kristine K. Stacy-Bates, "Ready-Reference Resources and E-mail Reference on Academic ARL Web Sites," *Reference & User Services Quarterly* 40 (fall 2000): 61-73. The MARS criteria for the sites it recommends can be found at www.ala.org/rusa/mars/criteria.html.

2. There are dozens of good articles about designing library Web sites. See Kim Guenter, "Designing and Maintaining Your Digital Library," *Computers in Libraries* 20 (January 2000): 34-39. Most of this issue deals with library Web site design.

EVALUATION AND ANALYSIS

Evaluating Electronic Reference Services:
Issues, Approaches and Criteria

Eric Novotny

SUMMARY. As electronic reference services become routine in many libraries, it is time to systematically examine how they are being implemented and used. Unfortunately, few libraries have rigorously examined their electronic reference services. We still know very little about who uses electronic reference services or why. We also do not know how satisfied our users are with the new services we are providing. This article provides an overview of the chief methodologies available for conducting assessments of electronic services (e.g., surveys, usability studies, observation, etc.). Existing criteria for evaluating reference services are discussed with suggestions for how they can be applied or adapted to the online service environment. *[Article copies available for a fee from The Haworth Document Delivery Service: 1-800-342-9678. E-mail address: <getinfo@haworthpressinc.com> Website: <http://www.HaworthPress.com> © 2001 by The Haworth Press, Inc. All rights reserved.]*

Eric Novotny is Humanities Librarian, Arts and Humanities Library, University Libraries, The Pennsylvania State University, University Park, PA 16802-1803 (E-mail: ecn1@psu.edu).

[Haworth co-indexing entry note]: "Evaluating Electronic Reference Services: Issues, Approaches and Criteria." Novotny, Eric. Co-published simultaneously in *The Reference Librarian* (The Haworth Information Press, an imprint of The Haworth Press, Inc.) No. 74, 2001, pp. 103-120; and: *Evolution in Reference and Information Services: The Impact of the Internet* (ed: Di Su) The Haworth Information Press, an imprint of The Haworth Press, Inc., 2001, pp. 103-120. Single or multiple copies of this article are available for a fee from The Haworth Document Delivery Service [1-800-342-9678, 9:00 a.m. - 5:00 p.m. (EST). E-mail address: getinfo@haworthpressinc.com].

KEYWORDS. Assessment, evaluation, reference, e-reference, electronic reference, chat reference, research methods, methodology/methodologies

INTRODUCTION

While still a relatively recent development, the provision of reference service via electronic means is by now well established in the majority of American libraries. Ninety-six percent of the libraries responding to an Association of Research Libraries survey reported that they offered reference assistance electronically.[1] For the purpose of the survey, electronic reference was defined as "reference service designed for remote users and identified by a specific link from a library's website." Thirty percent of these services were more than five years old, while another fifty percent had been established more than three years ago. Only a small minority of libraries had established their online reference services in the last year.[2]

As electronic reference matures it is time to take a more pragmatic look at the way it is used. Unfortunately, very few libraries have consistently and rigorously examined their electronic reference services. Only 13% of the libraries responding to the ARL survey indicated that they conducted any assessment of their electronic reference services. Judging by the sparse professional literature on the topic, very few of the assessments that have been done have made it into print.[3] This has left librarians and administrators with more questions than answers. We still know very little about who uses electronic reference services or why they choose to do so. We also do not know how satisfied our users are with the new services we are providing.

The goals of this paper are: (1) to convince librarians that they need to conduct ongoing assessment of reference services, including those delivered online, (2) to provide an overview of the chief methodologies available for conducting such assessments, and (3) to review existing criteria for evaluating reference services and suggest how they can be used to judge the efficiency and effectiveness of electronic reference services. It is hoped that readers will not only be better informed, but also inspired to closely examine their services and ways to improve upon them.

Before proceeding it is prudent to clarify terms. What is a reference service generally, and more specifically, what is an electronic reference service? There are many definitions for both terms in the library literature. Some emphasize the act of answering questions, while others are broader. The more expansive definitions include pathfinders, bibliographies, FAQ databases or tutorials as reference services. For this article I will rely on a definition formulated by Chris Ferguson and Charles Bunge. They identify the defining characteristic

of "traditional" reference service as "answering questions posed by users."[4] This model emphasizes human attention and interaction. It excludes non-human, purely technological approaches to public service. Resources such as databases and instruction modules also fall outside the scope of this article. I believe this definition of reference service captures the essence of the reference encounter, whether in-person or online. The interaction between users and information professionals remains the most important relationship, and the one most deserving of attention. Of course in order to be an electronic reference service the information must be conveyed electronically in some way, either via e-mail, chat room discussion, web form, or some other from of digital communication.

Evaluation also requires a precise definition. Much like "electronic reference services" the term can be used to describe many things. Evaluation can include everything from a telephone survey, to gathering usage statistics, to making a mental note of a user's comments at the reference desk. Charles McClure defines evaluation as "the process of identifying and collecting data about specific services or activities, establishing criteria by which their success can be assessed, and determining both the quality of the service or activity and the degree to which the service or activity accomplishes stated goals and objectives."[5]

WHY EVALUATE?

The evaluation process described by McClure is a time-consuming one. It is not enough to simply conduct one study and analyze the results. Evaluation must be integrated into the library's operations, and built into the implementation of any new service. It is also not enough to merely gather quantitative measures such as the tabulation of reference desk statistics. To truly evaluate a service it is necessary to gauge the quality of what is being offered as well as the quantity. Quantitative measures tell us little about the value of the service to the users. An increase in recorded desk activity may not be a positive thing. It may reflect greater user frustration with a poorly designed library.

Quality can be a difficult concept to measure, requiring greater efforts on the part of investigators. Why do we need to expend this effort to evaluate electronic reference services? After all, isn't it obvious that high-tech service provision is the wave of the future? This may well be, but it does not release us from our professional obligation to provide the highest level of service to our users. New services do not magically appear without cost. Every new offering represents a loss of resources in some other area. An hour spent staffing an online chat service is an hour that cannot be used to accomplish other important library goals.

Any introduction of new services should be done with a clear accounting of the costs and benefits involved. To paraphrase a famous saying, there is no such thing as a free service. Even if there is no money expended, the involvement of staff represents an opportunity cost to the institution. The opportunity cost is the value of the services that could have been provided with the time and resources devoted to the new service.

Some librarians may counter that they are not cutting other services, that electronic reference services are simply being added to their existing workloads. If true, this is not without its own costs. The phenomenon of librarian burnout is hardly a new one, but technology seems to have exacerbated the problem. The trend towards increasing workloads and expectations was identified as early as 1984 by Bill Miller. In his article entitled "What's Wrong with Reference: Coping with Success and Failure at the Reference Desk," Miller noted that librarians are expected to maintain existing services while adding new ones. In an effort to keep pace with rapid technological changes, librarians found themselves working longer hours. This was not a sustainable solution. The end result was an increase in stress and a decline in job satisfaction.[6]

Ironically the problem of burnout is caused by our successes, not our failings. Librarians have emerged as leaders and experts in the information realm. We have eagerly taken on new responsibilities, while at the same time maintaining our existing services. This is only natural. It is often easiest to delay hard decisions by offering a new service without eliminating or reducing existing responsibilities. While this may work for a while, it is not a recipe for long-term job satisfaction. It is not possible to work longer and harder indefinitely.

Inevitably choices need to be made. We can offer many services that are of value to our users. We cannot, however, provide every potentially useful service our users might want. In an environment of fixed resources, libraries cannot be all things to all people. There is a need to prioritize amongst the many service options available. A consistent, coherent program of evaluation can make choosing amongst the available options easier by providing sound data on which to base decisions.

EVALUATION METHODS

While many librarians acknowledge the benefits of evaluating their services, they face obstacles that prevent them from implementing such a program at their institutions. Designing and carrying out an evaluation project can be a daunting task. Fortunately a number of guides exist which offer advice on how to get started. The *Reference Assessment Manual*,[7] compiled by the ALA Evaluation of Reference and Adult Services Committee, examines at the state

of assessment in all areas of reference services. This includes training, the reference environment, what reference services should be offered, costs and outcomes, and reference effectiveness. A more recent text that updates the *Reference Assessment Manual* is *Evaluating Reference Services: A Practical Guide* by Jo Bell Whitlatch.[8] As the title suggests, this book is aimed at busy librarians in the field. It offers advice on how to plan an evaluation, select an appropriate research tool, and deliver quality reference service.

It is not possible for this article to describe in detail the many research methodologies available for evaluating reference services. It is desirable, however, to briefly present the advantages and disadvantages of each approach. The most widely used research methodologies are: case studies, focus groups, individual interviews, and surveys. Other methods that have been used to assess electronic reference services are cost-benefit analysis, usability studies, web log analysis, and statistics. The most appropriate method for your situation depends on the type of information you are seeking. Do you want a large number of responses, or would you prefer more in-depth analysis from a few sources? Do you want emotions and opinions, or would you prefer to collect numbers that are easily tabulated and analyzed? These are the sorts of questions you need to consider as you ponder which methodology to use.

- *Case Studies*–A case study is an intensive examination of a particular situation or environment. The intent is to gain a deep understanding of the individual circumstances in a unique setting. A well-done case study employs a variety of methods, e.g., surveys, interviews, observations to thoroughly explore the issue being examined. The main drawback is that the narrow focus may mean that the results are only relevant to the particular case being researched.[9]
- *Cost-Benefit Analysis*–This type of analysis seeks to measure the value of services, or the cost of reducing an existing service. Various methods have been devised to estimate user benefits. One approach is to ask patrons to place a dollar value on a service such as personal assistance at the reference desk. Other measures may be substituted for dollars, such as asking users how a change in service might affect their happiness, efficiency, or productivity. A related methodology is contingent valuation method in which users are asked about their willingness to pay for library services. Conjoint analysis involves asking users to rank competing service levels or options. The advantage of these methods is it shows what users value most. It also assists librarians who must make choices about expanding or reducing programs, all of which have some merit. The disadvantage is that users may be overwhelmed by the complexity of the task. Considering and comparing more than a few programs at the same time can be mentally taxing for the average library user.[10]

- *Focus Groups*–A focus group is a group interview. Focus groups have the advantage of allowing users to interact, remind, reinforce, and reflect upon the views of others in the group. You can usually obtain richer, more detailed information than from a written survey. The disadvantages are that some individuals may be reticent to express their true opinions in front of others. Especially vocal members may hijack the session, dominating discussion. Avoiding these problems requires a carefully trained interviewer. Finally, it may be difficult to convince administrators and colleagues to act based solely on information obtained from such a small number of people. For these reasons focus groups are often used early in the process, and then supplemented with another research method such as a general survey.[11]
- *Individual Interviews*–Interviews have similar advantages to focus groups. Interviews allow participants to express their opinions and concerns in their own words. They allow you to explore a particular issue, i.e., why people do not use e-mail reference service, in considerable detail. Individual interviews do have their disadvantages. They can be time-consuming to set up and conduct. They also require careful staff training. A poorly prepared interviewer can seriously bias the results obtained. In particular, if you use staff members, they must be wary of defending existing policies or services from criticism. They must appear receptive to negative as well as positive comments.
- *Observation*–As the name suggests, this brand of research involves observing users in real-life situations. This may be done obtrusively, where the person being studied knows they are being observed, or it may be done unobtrusively without the knowledge of the other participants. The advantage of unobtrusive observation is that you are able to measure actual behavior, unlike surveys and interviews which involve people trying to predict their behavior or attitudes. The predictions may not always be accurate indicators of what someone will actually do in a given situation. A concern with the observational method is the potential for bias. Observer bias can taint the results, especially if staff enter into the study with preconceived notions of how users will behave. In an obtrusive observation, subjects who are aware they are being monitored may alter their behavior as a result of being under scrutiny. Finally, observational studies tell us what a person has done. They do not often reveal why they acted as they did, how they felt about it, or how they might act if presented with alternatives.[12]
- *Surveys*–Surveys are probably the most common data collection method used in libraries. Examples of surveys include a questionnaire distributed after an in-library instruction session, a user satisfaction form given to every person entering the library, a telephone survey of a random sample of the city's residents, and an e-mail feedback form on the library's web

page. The fixed format of most surveys provides consistency in responses. Everyone receives the same questions and the same set of instructions. The choices of answers can be standardized, making it possible to analyze a large number of responses efficiently. The anonymity of most survey methods can encourage honest responses. Surveys will not typically reveal the depth of information you can obtain from interviews or focus groups. Standardized responses may leave little room for respondents to accurately express their thoughts. Finally, question design is important. Respondents will usually not be able to ask for clarification if a question is poorly worded or ambiguous.[13]

- *Usability Studies*–Usability studies combine the features of observation and individual interviews. Usability studies have been conducted by libraries seeking to evaluate the design and utility of their web pages. Typically they involve giving a user a set of tasks, such as locating a book in the online catalog, or identifying where to go for assistance. Users are monitored while they attempt to complete the tasks. The session may be followed by individual or group interviews where participants are asked to explain their actions in more detail. The prominence and ease of use of an online reference service can be assessed using a usability study. The disadvantages to this approach are similar to those of focus groups. It can be difficult to set up a useful number of user sessions. Recording and analyzing the sessions can also be time-consuming.[14]

- *Web Log Analysis/Statistics*–Web log analysis is a variant of an observational study. Usage of a library's web page can be tracked. Basic data recording the number of times a page has been accessed, from where, and for how long can be relatively easy to obtain. It may be useful to determine which pages on your library's site receive the most traffic, and include links to your electronic reference services from these high-use pages. The downside of web logs and usage statistics is that they tell us little about the motivations of users. Web statistics can be inaccurate due to browser caching features that store frequently accessed pages on the user's own computer. Future visits to the same web page will not be counted if the page is obtained from the user's cache. If logs or statistics are used, they are best supplemented with surveys, or interviews.

Selecting a research tool is an important step, but before you can make a final decision, you will need to consider what exactly you are trying to measure. Are you trying to gauge usage, user satisfaction, librarian workload, or the efficiency of your service? This will inform your choice of methodology. You will also need to decide whether to conduct a quantitative study, or whether your focus will be more on the quality of the service.

QUANTITATIVE MEASURES AND BENCHMARKS

Quantitative measures are probably the most widely used approach to assessing electronic reference services. They measure how much, by whom, when, and where a service is used. Anyone who has made hash marks counting the number of questions at a reference desk is familiar with this form of assessment. Also well known are the drawbacks of this method. Knowing how many people asked a reference question, whether at a reference desk, or online, does not tell us much about the quality of the service. In fact, as has been noted earlier, more activity may be an indication that there is a problem in the library.

Statistics are also limited without a context to place them in. Are four e-mail questions a day indicative of a good, poor, or average service? How many questions does it take to make an electronic reference service a success? The answer to that question depends upon the goals and objectives of your service. If you are planning to conduct quantitative assessment, there are some recently published measures that can be used as benchmarks to compare your service.

Beth A. Garney and Ronald R. Powell conducted a survey of public libraries in the United States. Twenty-two libraries provided information about their e-mail services. The average number of e-mail reference questions received was 5.6. The modal, or most frequent response was 3 questions per week.[15] Academic libraries do not appear to be generating much more in the way of e-reference activity. A survey of Association of Research Library members revealed that the average number of questions submitted via formal electronic reference services was sixty-seven per month, or barely more than two per day.[16]

While libraries anticipate increasing demand for electronic reference services, the current numbers reported are almost uniformly low. An active electronic reference service would appear to be one that receives any more than a handful of questions per day. There are a few notable exceptions, however, that illustrate the potential audience for online reference services. The Library of Congress receives over 2,500 questions per month, surpassed in the library world only by the 3,200 questions per month sent to the National Library of Medicine.[17] Even this impressive volume of activity is exceeded by certain non-library based services such as AskERIC, which receives about 4,000 questions per month.[18]

The reasons some services are well-trafficked, while others receive minimal usage, deserves additional scrutiny from librarians. Many of the users of national services such as AskERIC have access to excellent local public or academic libraries. Judging by the relative levels of activity, libraries are not the first choice for many of their online patrons. Any evaluation of digital reference service should include some sampling of non-users to determine why it is that they are opting to bypass their local libraries and using other services in

such large numbers. Is the library service not advertised enough, is the link to reference assistance too hard to locate, are libraries seen as "uncool" by our Internet savvy users? Until we actually ask someone these questions, the answers will remain merely speculative. Libraries need more research to uncover the reasons why some services thrive while others are ignored.

QUALITY MEASURES

Of course statistics are not the only, or even the best, way to measure the utility of a library's services. To adequately assess most library endeavors it is necessary to go beyond the numbers. An effort must be made to determine the quality of the service as well as the quantity. Quality can be difficult to define and measure, but this has not stopped many librarians from offering their own suggestions. A somewhat utopian vision of electronic reference services was envisioned by Chris Ferguson and Charles Bunge. They urge libraries to move towards "delivering high quality reference through the network to all users at all times and from all locations."[19] Others have proposed more modest goals. Acknowledging the widespread phenomenon of limited usage of electronic reference, proponents insist that such services are a success because they extend the reach of the library. The Santa Monica Public expresses this sentiment when it asserts that ". . . anytime we can extend the reach of our services to our clients . . . we think it is a success."[20]

Most librarians are probably between these two extremes. Few would regard a service that does not reach "all users at all times and from all locations" as a failure. The low usage of our electronic services does concern many, however. With limited staff and personnel resources it is not prudent to consider a service a success merely because it reaches a few users. We need a better gauge of the costs and benefits of electronic reference services in order to efficiently allocate resources to maximize benefits to our users. For this we need to go beyond merely gathering statistics on the usage of electronic reference services.

Fortunately there are a number of criteria that can be used to assess new and longstanding services (see Table 1). Many of the methods developed for traditional reference services will still apply to evaluating newer offerings. A starting point for discussing what constitutes quality electronic reference services may be to use the values proposed by Ferguson and Bunge. They identify the features of traditional reference service quality as access, equity, and professional personalized service.[21]

How might these traditional service values be measured in the digital environment? For electronic reference services access can mean many things. The option of e-mail or chat reference service extends access to users who may not have approached a librarian previously. A recent study of e-mail reference

TABLE 1. Criteria for Evaluating Reference Services

FERGUSON AND BUNGE	RUSA ELECTRONIC INFORMATION GUIDELINES	RUSA BEHAVIORAL GUIDELINES	MCCLURE AND LAPOTA	SERVQUAL
Access	Response time	Approachability	Extensiveness	Reliability
Equity	Accessibility/Convenience	Interest	Efficiency	Assurance
Personalized Service	Value	Listening/Inquiring	Effectiveness	Empathy
	Effectiveness in meeting needs	Involves patron in search process	Service Quality	Responsiveness
	Effectiveness in anticipating needs	Follows-up	Impact	Tangibles
			Usefulness	

found that international students were heavy users of electronic reference services. These students may have felt more comfortable writing than speaking English.[22] It is speculated that the Internet can be used to reach other library users who may be reluctant to ask for help at a traditional reference desk. These groups might include the elderly, handicapped, or particularly shy individuals.[23] These examples illustrate the potential for reaching a larger group of users. Further research is needed to see if this potential is being reached, and if not, how it can be. One approach might be to target specific populations using surveys to ascertain users' attitudes toward the service.

Equity is the ethic of ensuring that all users are able to locate the information they need. This does not mean that everyone receives the same *amount* of service. The needs of a faculty member will often differ from those of an undergraduate. What is important is that each receives the level of service appropriate to their needs. The existing evidence suggests that electronic reference services may not fare well in evaluations based on considerations of equity. This inequity is due to socioeconomic factors that are largely beyond the control of libraries. While computer ownership and Internet access are increasing at a rapid rate, troublesome gaps persist. This is reflected in the user demographics of a recent survey of public libraries. The users of the e-mail reference service were primarily highly educated computer scientists and information professionals. It is unlikely that these groups have more of an information need than other segments of the population. More likely they have better access to computer technology. These results suggest that online reference services may not be reaching users who are in need of information services.

Measuring the equity of your service probably requires a combination of approaches. An analysis of your current users can be conducted if you collect demographic data from those submitting requests. This can be done easily if users are asked to complete a form as part of the service. From this you can determine if your questions are coming from a particular group of users. A focus group of selected non-users can help to determine if there are obstacles to use in the community. Libraries can engage in outreach efforts to members of the community whose information needs are not being met through the library's online information services.

Equity can also refer to the level of service that is offered. Can users expect consistent, high-quality assistance from your digital reference service? The equity of your digital reference service can be evaluated by comparing it to your reference desk service. Do you treat users of your online service in the same manner as you do your in-person users? Many institutions appear to have intentionally created distinctions between the service they offer at the desk, and the services they offer online. Forty-one percent of the ARL libraries surveyed indicated that they only accept basic, factual questions online. It is common for academic institutions to only accept questions from the general public if they pertain to local resources.[24]

It may be necessary to limit service for pragmatic reasons, but at a cost in quality. The ideal service environment is one in which a user of your electronic reference service receives the same consideration as someone who asks a question at the reference desk. When establishing policies the potential impact on the equity and quality of your service should be considered.

Other measures of reference quality focus on inputs and outcomes. McClure and Lopata suggest concentrating on the following areas:[25]

> *Extensiveness:* How much of the service is provided? Measures of this would be the number of users and the type and status of users.

> *Efficiency:* How well are the resources devoted to the service being used? How much does it cost to provide the service? One measure of efficiency would be to determine how much each online reference transaction costs. This could be compared to the costs of other alternative service options.

> *Service Quality:* How good is the service provided? User satisfaction is one measure of service quality. Peer comparison is another method of determining if a service is of high quality.

> *Impact:* Does the service make a difference to the user? For example, does the user produce a better paper as a result of the citations suggested

by the librarian? Users can provide an estimate of the impact of a service, or it can be observed through other means (improved grades, citation analysis of papers, etc.).

Usefulness: How well does the service meet the needs of the user? This information can be readily obtained using interviews or surveys to discover how well existing services are of value to library patrons. Conjoint or trade-off analysis can also be used to measure the relative usefulness of competing service delivery methods.

BEHAVIORAL ASPECTS OF QUALITY: THE LIBRARIAN-PATRON INTERACTION

A high quality electronic reference service requires a human touch. Automated systems and online help screens have their uses, but they can only go so far in assisting our users. This is not an opinion that is universally shared. Some have argued that in the digital age personalized assistance will be judged too costly and inefficient. Individualized attention from a librarian has been compared to handcrafted furniture, which was largely displaced when mechanized production of furniture became possible. The author of this analogy suggests that librarians face a similar predicament. We may find ourselves replaced by automation, not because computers are better searchers, but because they are faster, and cheaper.[26]

While automation may be inevitable, it appears that for the present most people still prefer human interaction and guidance. A recent marketing survey determined that 90% of online shoppers want human assistance available while they make their purchases.[27] If you want to measure the human element of your online service, there are criteria you can use. Some have been created specifically for the digital environment, while others need adaptation. Among the latter category are the RUSA Behavioral Guidelines (see Table 1). These were developed to describe the best practices for face-to-face interaction at a reference desk. In many ways, however, they are applicable to an asynchronous reference environment.

The main evaluation criteria for the RUSA Behavioral Guidelines are Approachability, Interest, Listening/Inquiring, Involving the patron in the search process, and Engaging in follow-up. Approachability in an online environment translates to how easily your service is located, and how user-friendly it is. A long, complicated form can discourage patrons from submitting their questions. The appearance of the page can suggest approachability, or it can act as a deterrent. Many pages devote their first paragraphs to telling users what questions cannot be asked, and who cannot use the service. This is the electronic equivalent to sitting at the reference desk with arms folded and a

stern look on your face. The location of the page can also mimic approachability. Is your online service as easily located as your reference desk? Most users can probably identify your reference desk, but are the online service links as obvious?

Interest can be harder to determine. In an online environment the closest characteristic may be response time. Users do not necessarily expect an instant response, but a rapid response is a way to assure the patron that the question is important to the library. This does not mean that the question must be *completed* quickly, simply that initial contact be made in a timely fashion.

Listening and inquiring relate to the reference interview. It is well established that the reference interview can be difficult to conduct online. What takes place instantly in person can require several exchanges online conducted over a period of days. Even instant messaging or chat services can be awkward. The lack of visual cues such as body language, facial expressions, or tone of voice can lead to false starts and miscommunication.

Eileen Abels has proposed a model for communicating effectively online. She examined numerous reference encounters conducted online and identified distinct patterns of communication. Based on these patterns, she suggests that an efficient e-mail reference interview should consist of no more than three stages: an initial problem statement by the patron, a quick response containing a summarization by the librarian, followed by a confirmation by the patron. This need not be the end of the communication, as the answer may not yet be obtained, but if done correctly the interview should be completed at this point. If the interview proves to be more complicated, Abels recommends using another medium (telephone, or in-person) to complete the interaction.[28]

The last two RUSA Behavioral Guidelines stress the importance of involving the patron in the process, and engaging in follow-up. These should be a part of any reference interview. Reference service is more than simply a correct answer. Just as important are what market researchers refer to as "dirty bathroom" factors. Users are unlikely to return to a restaurant with dirty restrooms, even if the food was acceptable. Similarly, research by Joan Durrance has found that 90% of users would not return to an unfriendly librarian, even if they were satisfied with the information obtained.[29] One way to measure the behavioral aspects of your electronic reference service may be to record the number of repeat users. If your patrons are not returning, this could indicate that the service is perceived to be unfriendly.

An assessment focusing on behavioral issues can be conducted a number of ways. An unobtrusive method might involve asking people to pose as users of the service. The responses sent to these users can be examined by library staff to see if proper reference interview and follow-up techniques were used. This technique can be problematic, however, as reference staff may become resentful if they feel they are being spied upon. These issues can be minimized if it is

made clear that the assessments are being done to improve services and not to punish or penalize individual librarians. Finally, the users are the ultimate judges of performance. A survey or interview can be conducted to ask users whether they felt the librarian involved them in the process, or asked follow-up questions.

ONGOING AND FUTURE DEVELOPMENTS
IN ASSESSING ELECTRONIC REFERENCE SERVICES

It is clear from the preceding discussion that the library profession does not lack criteria with which to assess electronic reference services. What is scarce, however, are standards or benchmarks with which to compare one's institution. For example, if your library's policy is to respond to e-mail questions in 24 hours, is this good, bad, or about average? The profession needs more researchers working on developing specific measures that can apply to a variety of library environments.

An excellent model to emulate is provided by the Virtual Reference Desk AskA consortium. The quality standards for the consortium are outlined in the Summer 2000 issue of *Reference and User Services Quarterly*. Members in the consortium agree to provide a service that has the following features: Accessible, Prompt Turnaround, Clear Response Policy, Interactive, Instructive, Authoritative, Private, Reviewed, Referrals, Publicity.[30]

What makes the VRD document outstanding are two features. One, it provides detailed measurement criteria for each element of quality service. For example, "Prompt Turnaround" is defined using specific percentages of questions that should be answered in a defined period of time. Another excellent feature of the standards is that they are flexible. For each element there is a base target required of all members, a current practice that reflects the current level of services offered, and a future goal, which corresponds to the optimal level that members should strive to achieve over time. This built-in flexibility is key. As technology changes and improves, it is important that our service expectations do not remain static.

The future of electronic evaluation offers many exciting possibilities. One interesting endeavor is the Association of Research Libraries New Measures Project. The ARL is investigating the feasibility of establishing ServQual criteria as a de facto national library standard. Briefly, the ServQual criteria are:

- *Reliability*; i.e., ability to perform the promised service dependably and accurately.
- *Assurance*; i.e., knowledge and courtesy of employees and their ability to convey trust and confidence.

- *Empathy*; i.e., the caring, individualized attention the firm provides to its customers.
- *Responsiveness*; i.e., willingness to help customers and provide prompt service.
- *Tangibles*; i.e., appearance of physical facilities, equipment, personnel, and communications materials.[31]

The elements of the ServQual assessment are being modified and tested within ARL Libraries. The proposed new instrument has been named LibQual+. If LibQual+ is widely adopted by ARL libraries, it may lead to the collection of standardized quality measures. These will allow libraries to compare their performance with peer institutions.[32]

Another initiative of interest is the Digital Library Federation's Discussion Group on Usage, Usability, and User Support. The members of this group are surveying libraries to determine what evaluation needs exist. They are seeking to determine the gaps in the research with a goal of devising new research methods to address these information gaps.[33]

Technology offers additional cause to be optimistic about the future. Most interactive software packages include built-in mechanisms for capturing and recording vital transaction data. The software can automatically record information such as the number of interactions, the length of each transaction, and average wait time for a session. The quality of the interaction can be observed as session transcripts are automatically generated. Privacy concerns can be addressed by stripping out names from the record before it is analyzed. Below is an example of statistics and a session transcript from the University of Chicago's online reference service:

Ask a Librarian Live
Statistics for September 2000.[34]

Number of Chat Sessions	143*
Total Time in Chat	12:39:42
Average Time in Chat	00:05:18
Average Time in Queue	00:01:00

*This number also includes the practice session that were done to get familiar with the service

Ask a Librarian Live
Sample Session Transcript.[35]

Operator Librarian is connected to The Business and Economics Resource Center I-Operator.
Patron is connected to The Business and Economics Resource Center I-Operator.

Librarian: Hello. You have reached the Business & Economics Resource Center at The University of Chicago. How may I help you?

Patron: I was wondering if it is possible to obtain an economics paper titled "Economics of Superstar" written by Sherwin Rosen (UofC Professor) in 1981?
Librarian: Do you know what journal it was published in?
Librarian: Nevermind, it is in American Economic Review.
Patron: You are great, thank you . . . how would I be able to get a copy?
Librarian: You will have to order it via Interlibrary Loan through your company or public library. Licensing restrictions don't allow me to send it to you. The full citation, however, is: Rosen, Sherwin. "The Economics of Superstars" American Economic Review; v71 n5 Dec. 1981, pp. 845-58.
Librarian: Are you a University of Chicago faculty, student or staff member?
Librarian: If you are, I can tell you how to get access to the databases.
Patron: It is actually for my boss, who did get his undergraduate degree from UofC–his name is XXXXXXX.
Librarian: Alumni with current borrowing privileges are eligible but must pay $5 per transaction.
Librarian: The number for Interlibrary Loan is: 773-702-7031
Librarian: Call them. I'm not sure if their service includes possible faxing this article to you; definitely ask.
Librarian: Is there anything else I can help you with?
Patron: I really appreciate all your help, I will give them a call. Thanks again and have a good day.
Librarian: Please click "quit" and fill out the end-user survey (it would help us out!)
Librarian: Thanks!

The transcript and statistics above demonstrate the potential for quantitative and qualitative evaluation of online reference services. What are needed in the future are benchmarks based on the results of research conducted in a wide variety of library settings. More libraries need to evaluate their electronic reference services, and the results must be widely disseminated. Only by sharing our successes (and failures) will the profession move forward. It is hoped that this article has motivated at least a few researchers to begin seriously assessing services at their own institutions.

ENDNOTES

1. Association of Research Libraries (1999), *SPEC Kit #251: Electronic Reference Service*, Washington, DC, p. 7.

2. *Ibid.*

3. Among the formal evaluations conducted are: Lara Bushallow-Wilbur, Gemma DeViney, and Fritz Whitcomb, "Electronic Mail Reference Service: A Study," *RQ* 35 (Spring 1996): 359-371; Ann Bristow, "Academic Reference Service over Electronic Mail: An Update," *College and Research Libraries News* 7 (1995): 460; Julie M. Still and Frank Campbell, "Librarian in a Box: The Use of Electronic Mail for Reference," *Reference Services Review* 21, no.1 (1993): 15-18; Beth A. Garnsey and Ronald R. Powell, "Electronic Mail Reference Services in the Public Library," *Reference & User Services Quarterly* 39, no. 3 (Spring 2000): 245-252.

4. Ferguson, Chris D. and Charles A. Bunge, "The Shape of Services to Come: Values-Based Reference Service for the Largely Digital Library." *College & Research Libraries* 58, no.3 (1997): 257.

5. McClure, Charles R., "User-based Data Collection Techniques and Strategies for Evaluating Networked Information Services," *Library Trends* 42: 592.

6. Miller, Bill, "What's Wrong with Reference: Coping with Success and Failure at the Reference Desk," *American Libraries* 1984: 303-306, 321-322.

7. Evaluation of Reference and Adult Services Committee. American Library Association (1995), *Reference Assessment Manual,* Ann Arbor, Michigan.

8. Whitlatch, Jo Bell (2000), *Evaluating Reference Services: A Practical Guide,* American Library Association: Chicago.

9. For examples of case studies see Whitlatch, Jo Bell, *Evaluating Reference Services: A Practical Guide,* p. 91-97.

10. For a discussion of the various cost-benefit methods, see Chapters 3 and 14 in *The Reference Assessment Manual.*

11. For additional information on focus groups see David L. Morgan & Richard A. Krueger (1998), *The Focus Group Kit,* Sage: Thousand Oaks, Calif.

12. Examples of studies using observational techniques are: Childers, Thomas, "The Test of Reference," *Library Journal* 105: 924-928, and Patricia Dewdney and Catherine Sheldrick Ross, "Flying a Light Aircraft: Reference Service Evaluation from a User's Perspective." *RQ* 34: 217-230.

13. For additional information on conducting surveys see Suskie, Linda (1992), *Questionnaire Survey Research: What Works,* 2nd ed., American Association for Institutional Research: Tallahassee, Fla.

14. Chisman, Janet, Karen Diller, and Sharon Walbridge, "Usability Testing: A Case Study," *College and Research Libraries* 60, no. 6 (1999): 552-569.

15. Garnsey, Beth A., & Ronald R. Powell, "Electronic Mail Reference Services in the Public Library," *Reference & User Services Quarterly* 39, no. 3 (Spring 2000): 245-252.

16. *Reference Assessment Manual,* (1995): p. 7.

17. *Ibid.*

18. Mon, Lorri, "Digital Reference Service," *Government Information Quarterly* 17, no. 3, (2000): 310.

19. Ferguson & Bunge (1997).

20. Richardson, Joanna, *"Ask a Librarian" Electronic Reference Services: The Importance of Corporate Culture, Communication and Service Attitude.* Online, *<http://www.bond.edu.au/library/jpr/ausweb2k/>* Accessed: 12-15-2000.

21. Ferguson and Bunge (1997).

22. Johnston, Pat & Ann Grusin, "Personal Service in an Impersonal World: Throwing Life Preservers to Those Drowning in an Ocean of Information," *The Georgia Librarian* 32 (1995): 45-49.

23. Straw, Joseph E., "A Virtual Understanding: The Reference Interview and Question Negotiation in the Digital Age," *Reference & User Services Quarterly,* 39, no. 4 (Summer 2000): 376-379. Also, Myoung C. Wilson, "Evolution or Entrop: Changing Reference/User Culture and the Future of Reference Librarians," *Reference & User Services Quarterly* 39, no. 4 (Summer 2000): 387-390.

24. Association of Research Libraries (1999), *SPEC Kit #251.*

25. McClure, Charles R. and Cynthia L. Lopata (1996), *Assessing the Academic Networked Environment: Strategies and Options.* Washington, DC, Coalition of Networked Information: 5.

26. Arms, William Y., "Automated Digital Libraries: How Effectively can Computers Be Used for the Skilled Tasks of Professional Librarianship?" *D-Lib Magazine,* 6, no. 7/8 (July/August 2000). Online, *<http://www.dlib.org/dlib/july00/arms/07arms.html>* Accessed: 12-08-2000.

27. Statistic cited in, Gray, Suzanne M., "Virtual Reference Services: Directions and Agendas," *Reference & User Services Quarterly* 39, no. 4 (Summer 2000): 372.

28. Abels, Eileen G., "The E-mail Reference Interview," *RQ* 35, no. 3 (Spring 1996): 345-358.

29. Durrance, Joan C., "Reference Success: Does the 55 Percent Rule Tell the Whole Story?" *Library Journal* 114 (April 15, 1989): 35.

30. Kasowitz, Abby, Blythe Bennett, & R. David Lankes, "Quality Standards for Digital Reference Consortia," *Reference & User Services Quarterly* 39, no. 4 (Summer 2000): 355-363.

31. Cook, Colleen, Fred Heath, Bruce Thompson & Russell Thompson, "The Search for New Measures: The ARL LibQual+ Project–A Preliminary Report," *portal: Libraries and the Academy* 1, no. 1 (2001), 65-74. Online, <*http://muse.jhu.edu/journals/portal_libraries_and_the_academy/v001/1.1cook.html*>. Accessed: 12-20-2000.

32. For additional information on LibQUAL+ see: *http://www.arl.org/libqual/*.

33. Digital Library Federation, "Usage, Usability, and User Support: Report of a Discussion Group at the DLF Forum on 2 April 2000," Online: <*http://www.clir.org/diglib/use/useframe.htm*>. Accessed: 12-20-2000.

34. "About Ask-A-Librarian Live," University of Chicago, Business and Economics Resource Center <*http://www.lib.uchicago.edu/e/busecon/aboutask.html*>. Accessed 1-20-2001.

35. "About Ask-A-Librarian Live," University of Chicago, Business and Economics Resource Center <*http://www.lib.uchicago.edu/e/busecon/aboutask.html*>. Accessed 1-20-2001.

Historical Fabrications on the Internet: Recognition, Evaluation, and Use in Bibliographic Instruction

John A. Drobnicki

Richard Asaro

SUMMARY. Although the Internet provides access to a wealth of information, there is little, if any, control over the quality of that information. Side-by-side with reliable information, one finds disinformation, misinformation, and hoaxes. The authors of this paper discuss numerous examples of fabricated historical information on the Internet (ranging from denials of the Holocaust to personal vendettas), offer suggestions on how to evaluate websites, and argue that these fabrications can be incorporated into bibliographic instruction classes. *[Article copies available for a fee from The Haworth Document Delivery Service: 1-800-342-9678. E-mail address: <getinfo@haworthpressinc.com> Website: <http://www.HaworthPress.com> © 2001 by The Haworth Press, Inc. All rights reserved.]*

John A. Drobnicki is Associate Professor/Head of Reference Services, York College Library/CUNY, Jamaica, NY 11451 (E-mail: drobnicki@york.cuny.edu). Richard Asaro is Reference Librarian, Queens Borough Public Library, Central Library, Social Sciences Division, Jamaica, NY 11432 (E-mail: rasaro@mindspring.com).

The authors would like to thank the many members of H-HISTBIBL (the H-Net Discussion List for the Study and Practice of History Librarianship) who suggested possible sites for inclusion in this article, especially David Durant, Debra Kimok, Michael Levine-Clark, Aaron Marrs, Kurt Metzmeier, Amy Mussell, Patrick Seigler, Diane Trap, and Alan Unsworth, as well as Mary-Jo Kline, whose earlier posting on that listserv initially piqued the authors' interest in this topic.

[Haworth co-indexing entry note]: "Historical Fabrications on the Internet: Recognition, Evaluation, and Use in Bibliographic Instruction." Drobnicki, John A., and Richard Asaro. Co-published simultaneously in *The Reference Librarian* (The Haworth Information Press, an imprint of The Haworth Press, Inc.) No. 74, 2001, pp. 121-164; and: *Evolution in Reference and Information Services: The Impact of the Internet* (ed: Di Su) The Haworth Information Press, an imprint of The Haworth Press, Inc., 2001, pp. 121-164. Single or multiple copies of this article are available for a fee from The Haworth Document Delivery Service [1-800-342-9678, 9:00 a.m. - 5:00 p.m. (EST). E-mail address: getinfo@haworthpressinc.com].

KEYWORDS. Censorship, fabrications, misinformation, disinformation, hoaxes, Afrocentrism, Holocaust, denial, conspiracies, Internet, World Wide Web, evaluation, genocide, Revisionism, intellectual freedom, famine, Nanking, cybersquatting, domain names, bibliographic instruction

Although librarians pride themselves on building their collections and choosing materials wisely, misleading and inaccurate information has always found its way into those very collections. This is even more true in the age of the World Wide Web, when librarians have very little (if any) control over the quality of what our patrons access electronically, and the growth of the Web continues, nearly tripling over the last two years to contain about 7 million distinct sites; and when one counts the so-called "Deep Web" (i.e., content retrievable by direct query from searchable databases), it is 400 to 550 times larger.[1] As has been pointed out elsewhere, the Internet "is a work in progress, and anyone is free to publish information or an opinion on it."[2] Or, to put it more bluntly, the "Internet may be loaded and fast (sounds like a used car ad, doesn't it?), but it's also filled with gargantuan amounts of trash."[3] The accuracy of medical information in libraries and on the Web is of critical importance, since it could result in illness and/or death. This paper, however, will deal with a subject that it is not quite a matter of life and death–it will seek to identify some glaring examples of historical fabrications on the Web, and how librarians (and students) can recognize and determine their unreliability. The present authors believe, however, that these websites *can* (and *should*) be used in bibliographic instruction classes to demonstrate the necessity of critically evaluating *all* information accessed via the Internet.

FABRICATIONS IN LIBRARY COLLECTIONS

There have been many famous *literary* hoaxes over the years–Clifford Irving's *Autobiography of Howard Hughes* immediately jumps to mind[4]–but this paper will deal with *historical* fabrications rather than literary ones.[5] By "historical fabrications," the present authors are referring to materials that *deliberately mislead* the reader by presenting false information as if it were true. It is acknowledged that many historical topics are open to debate, such as the origins of the First World War, the causes of the American Civil War, and the merits/shortcomings of various politicians and famous persons. With this in mind, then, an example of a fabrication would be Parson Mason Weems' *A History, of the Life and Death, Virtues and Exploits, of General George Washington,*[6] which went through numerous editions even though many of the "facts" were entirely anecdotal or invented, such as the famous cherry tree incident.[7]

Weems' book is by no means the only historical fabrication that is present in many libraries–others are simply not as well known. For example, *Appleton's Cyclopædia of American Biography*[8] is a staple in many reference collections around the country, owned by over 300 libraries according to OCLC. Nevertheless, *Appleton's* contains at least 21 spurious articles, and the authenticity of 62 more has been seriously challenged.[9] A recent study of articles in just Volume 3 of *Appleton's* found 37 authenticated articles, but 6 spurious articles, 13 suspicious ones, and 9 unconfirmed ones.[10] As Allan Nevins explained, the "unknown author of these sketches was paid by space, and to obtain a larger remuneration coolly created heroes out of thin air."[11] Another historical set known to contain forged materials is *The Horn Papers: Early Westward Movement on the Monongahela and Upper Ohio, 1765-1795*, by W. F. Horn,[12] which actually resulted in the establishment of a committee of historians to investigate its authenticity a half-century ago.[13] David Rorvik's 1978 book, *In His Image: The Cloning of a Man,* claimed that a human being had actually been *successfully* cloned. The publisher, J. B. Lippincott, was sued for defamation in federal court by a British scientist that Rorvik mentioned in the book as having developed the scientific basis for human cloning. Although a judge ruled that the book was "a fraud and a hoax" in 1978, [14] over 1400 libraries own it, according to OCLC.

An early example of fraudulent hate literature is *Awful Disclosures of Maria Monk as Exhibited in a Narrative of Her Sufferings During a Residence of Five Years as a Novice, and Two Years as a Black Nun, in the Hotel Dieu Nunnery at Montreal*.[15] The author claimed to have been a novice and then a nun's in Montreal, and described lurid details of routine sexual encounters with priests; any babies born of these illicit encounters would be baptized and then immediately killed. The book was actually a hoax, an example of anti-Catholic bigotry that was widespread in the United States at the time.[16]

Holocaust-denial is perhaps the most widely publicized example of spurious historical literature that librarians come into contact with. These deniers (known in France as negationists), who prefer to call themselves "revisionists" in an attempt to gain scholarly legitimacy, claim that the Holocaust is either a hoax or, at the very least, a great exaggeration that "Zionists" (i.e., Jews) use to extort money and to legitimize the existence of the State of Israel. Holocaust-denial is based on deliberate falsifications of the historical record, twisting and/or ignoring the testimony of perpetrators, victims, witnesses, and bystanders.[17] Probably the most famous work of denial is *The Hoax of the Twentieth Century: The Case Against the Presumed Extermination of European Jewry,* by Arthur R. Butz, an Associate Professor of Engineering and Computer Science at Northwestern University.[18] A few other notorious revisionists are Austin J. App,[19] Paul Rassinier,[20] Wilhelm Staglich,[21] Michael A. Hoffman II,[22] and Robert Faurisson.[23] Challenges faced by librarians include

whether or not to purchase (or accept donations of) Holocaust-denial, where to classify it, and where to shelve it (e.g., open shelves or restricted access).[24]

Ironically, two of the most recent controversies regarding allegations of fabricated work also relate to the Holocaust. Binjamin Wilkomirski's book *Fragments: Memories of a Wartime Childhood* [25] was hailed as among the most moving Holocaust memoirs, and received the 1997 Jewish Quarterly-Wingate Literary Prize for non-fiction. Investigators, however, have accused Wilkomirski of being a fraud, saying that his name is really Bruno Grosjean, the son of a Protestant Swiss woman, and that he actually was in Zurich during World War II.[26] Questions were also raised regarding the authorship of *Man of Ashes.*[27] Supposedly written by Salomon Isacovici, a Romanian Jew who later emigrated to Ecuador, publication of an English-language edition was delayed because Juan Manuel Rodriguez, an ex-Jesuit priest, claimed to have written the book and said that it is fictionalized, while Isacovici's family insisted that Rodriguez had only been hired to polish-up the original Spanish text. The English edition, however, lists *both* men as authors.[28]

A more controversial, and politically charged, example of material already present in many libraries whose scholarship has been questioned is the emerging field known as Afrocentrism. Afrocentrism is "an insistence by a growing number of black Americans to see the world from an 'African-centered' perspective in response to the dominant 'European-centered' perspective to which they feel they have been subjected throughout their lives."[29] When this philosophy is applied to the writing of history, it tends to stress the Black African origins of civilization, as exemplified by the title of George G. M. James' book, *Stolen Legacy: The Greeks Were Not the Authors of Greek Philosophy, But the People of North Africa, Commonly Called the Egyptians,* which is owned by over 700 libraries, according to OCLC.[30]

Although different Afrocentric authors make different claims, the following quote from John G. Jackson is fairly representative: "For the first two or three thousand years of civilization, there was not a civilized white man on the earth. Civilization was founded and developed by the swarthy races of Mesopotamia, Syria, and Egypt. It was southern colored peoples everywhere, in China, in Central America, in India, Mesopotamia, Syria, Egypt and Crete who gave the northern white peoples civilization."[31] Thus, Egypt was a Black civilization, and the Egyptians spoke an African, rather than an Afro-Asiatic, language. Some other prominent Afrocentric authors are Martin Bernal,[32] Molefi Kete Asante,[33] Cheikh Anta Diop,[34] Chancellor Williams,[35] and Yosef ben-Jochannan.[36] Many scholars and teachers have criticized both Afrocentrist writings and attempts to include it in public school curricula.[37]

Aside from outright fabrications like Holocaust-denial, librarians have also had to deal with government-sponsored "official" publications, ranging from annual yearbooks that gloss over the excesses of authoritarian regimes to oth-

ers that twist history, to McCarthy-era propaganda.[38] Because of the presence of controversial and unreliable information in libraries, some have called for placing warning labels on these materials.[39] The American Library Association, however, strenuously opposes labeling, which it considers to be both prejudicial and a violation of the "Library Bill of Rights." Warning labels are also misleading, since they imply that all materials *without* a label are therefore accurate and reliable, which would be an impossibility to assure.[40]

WORLD WIDE WEB IN LIBRARIES

As has already been pointed out, the quality of information available on the Web runs the gamut from very high to very low, since, in the words of one author, "this unbiased medium will voice the opinions of Ivy League professors, as well as your next-door neighbors."[41] In many ways, this is a gold mine for Bibliographic Instruction librarians, since it provides much fodder for use in classes dealing with evaluating websites (and sources, in general).

Since the introduction of Internet access in libraries, much of the debate and controversy has centered around questions of *access,* rather than on the issue of quality per se. Because of the tremendous range of materials out there, there have been disagreements among libraries and librarians as to whether or not library patrons should have unlimited access to Internet sites; access to chat rooms and/or e-mail; and printing privileges. And, of course, should children have the same privileges (or, rather, no restrictions) that adults have with regard to computer use?

Filters are software programs that block access to certain websites, based on either a predetermined set of criteria or on information that the purchaser of the program inputs. Many parents, of course, have the right to use filters on their *home* computers to prevent their children from gaining access to materials that they find objectionable (which often means pornography). Some groups, however, have called for the installation of filtering devices in libraries, which has been opposed by the American Library Association.[42] Several U.S. court decisions have struck down attempts by legislators to impose mandatory filtering in libraries, including the U.S. Supreme Court in Reno v. ACLU, where the court sided with the ACLU and found that communications on the Internet warrant the same constitutional protections as the written and spoken word, ruling that the provisions of the Communications Decency Act (CDA) relating to "indecent" or "offensive" speech were unconstitutional. A pedigree of CDA, The Child Online Protection Act (COPA), was declared unconstitutional by the Third Circuit Court of Appeals in June 2000.[43] Since the courts have left it up to parents to monitor their children's viewing habits, software companies can expect to profit from these rulings. As the Center for Me-

dia Education (a non-profit public interest group) reported in 1999, the sales of Windows and Macintosh filtering software was projected to reach $75.9 million by the year 2000.[44]

Critics have pointed out that many software filters block more than just porn and violence, and often also single out websites that espouse left-leaning political views–for example, some sites blocked by four popular filtering programs include *Mother Jones* magazine, Hasbro Toys, the official Pokémon website, and the Smith College Astronomy Department.[45] In one case, which won a "Foil the Filters" contest run by the Digital Freedom Network, a high school student could not access his own school's website from the school's library, because the filtering program recognized the word "high" as an offensive drug word.[46]

Although pornography and sexual predators might be the main concern of those who call for filters in libraries, those people might *also* be surprised to see some of the "facts" freely available on the Web.

MISINFORMATION, DISINFORMATION, AND HOAXES

Today, when someone shops in a giant supermarket, one is presented with an unbelievable array of choices that were not available to our parents or grandparents–and the quality of the products varies in principle to the price. If the product is defective, the shopper can return it to the store and receive a replacement/refund. The World Wide Web is a mega-supermarket of information at incredible bargain prices: free. However, it is home to unreliable and sometimes dishonest information providers. Unless one is a subscriber to an information broker service, one cannot get a "refund" for acquiring bad information. Exercising skepticism in reading information over the Internet is incumbent on the user, even more so than on the supermarket shopper. It should be part of basic computer literacy.

The Internet is an effective transmitter of all types of propaganda, and members of organized groups (both legitimate and questionable) know that they can reach a potentially vast audience. The Web makes it possible for anyone with access to simultaneously become writer, editor, and publisher, with few consequences to themselves since there is no profit margin to worry about. An accidental click on the keyboard while surfing the Internet can retrieve a well-designed and/or alluring website; however, the content might be saturated with misinformation.

The tremendous increase in the use of e-mail has greatly exacerbated the spreading of misinformation, rumors, and urban legends.[47] Not only false virus rumors are passed along by well-meaning people to all their friends and co-workers, but also chain letters, false medical information (e.g., antiperspi-

rants cause breast cancer), and urban legends (such as the notorious "kidney snatchers"). There are numerous websites devoted to debunking them.[48]

Several authors have addressed the problem of misinformation on the Internet, which can be either accidental or deliberate. In an early article on the topic, Luciano Floridi hypothesized that the Internet, by its very nature being unregulated, had the potential to be a "disinformation superhighway," although he pointed out, "at the moment [1996] there seem to be no reasons to be worried."[49] Mary Ann Fitzgerald pointed out that censorship is "a non-solution" and proposed nine skills for electronic information evaluation, most of which centered on users adopting critical skills when using the Internet.[50] Philip J. Calvert has pointed out that "misinformation can be information that is incomplete, out of date, confused, or low consensus 'knowledge,'" most of which pertains to human error. Calvert also presented the results of focus group discussions on the topic conducted with Information Science (IS) faculty and research students at Singapore's Nanyang Technological University, and IS faculty at Temasek Polytechnic. The consensus seemed to be that teaching information literacy and critical thinking to students would be the most effective way to combat misinformation.[51]

Ann Scholz-Crane conducted a survey of 49 lower-level undergraduates (divided into two groups) and had them evaluate two websites, which she then compared with evaluations of those sites done by four librarians. Her findings indicated that students needed more concrete instruction in evaluating websites than was provided in a simple checklist of evaluation criteria.[52] To test the accuracy of information retrieved from the Web using a popular search engine, Tschera Harkness Connell and Jennifer E. Tipple chose 60 ready-reference questions to use as their sample. They found that, considering *all pages retrieved* in a search, 64% of the pages contained *no* answer to their query at all (either right *or* wrong), wrong/mostly wrong answers were found 8.8% of the time, and correct/mostly correct answers were found 27.2% of the time. When excluding the pages that contained no answers, the percentages changed to 24.5% wrong/mostly wrong, and 75.5% correct/mostly correct.[53]

CRITERIA FOR EVALUATING INTERNET RESOURCES AND RECOGNIZING FABRICATIONS

In many ways, the same criteria that one uses to evaluate websites in general are also used to detect historical fabrications on the Internet. What follows are some general guidelines for evaluating websites, based on the abundance of articles, books, and Web pages on the subject.

"Don't check your common sense at the keyboard!" is probably the best (and simplest) advice given in the literature.[54] Just as consumers in the marketplace should keep in mind the motto "buyer beware," so should Web surfers

memorize "reader beware," especially since there is no authority to seek redress over misinformation unless there is sufficient evidence to show criminal intent. If you ask yourself, "who, what, where, when, and (most importantly) context" each time you read something on a Web page, it is a first step in developing a critical sensibility to evaluate the meaning and tendentiousness of what's being said.

When people are in a hurry—and, let's face it, that covers virtually all college students—they are prone to simply use the first item they locate, be it a book, article, or Web page. One of the problems for students with viewing materials online is that "it takes real effort to distinguish among magazines, trade journals, and peer reviewed journals, especially when all you can see is the full-text transcript and not the lurid cover or staid publisher responsibility statement."[55] If and when one has (or makes) the time, there are several criteria that one should use when determining the value of an Internet site.[56]

The first step is "to recognize that information does not gain or lose credibility simply by virtue of its format (print or electronic),"[57] so in many respects, one should ask the same critical questions of Internet materials as one would ask of print materials, beginning with the author. With online resources, "author" can mean the person who wrote the specific item being accessed as well as the person who runs the website. Most reputable sites will list a name, preferably with an e-mail link, as a contact person. The background and credential of the author can be checked in standard biographical sources. If no name is given, another strategy is to check the domain name's owner through WHOIS <http://www.whois.org>, a directory of over 25 million domain and user names. One can possibly find a real address, contacts with phone numbers, domain date origin and updates, and the numerical IP address.

Analysis of the website's URL (Uniform Resource Locator), or "address," is another factor in determining the reliability of the information source. The suffix at the end of the URL provides a clue whether the document's origin is from a government site (.gov), an educational institution (.edu), a commercial site (.com), or from a non-profit group (.org). Combined with information on the author/owner, the domain name will help one to determine the authoritativeness of the information.

The currency/timeliness of the site is important, as well. Many website administrators will place a line somewhere on the page telling the reader the date the site was last updated. Admittedly, this is not *always* important for a site dealing with historical information, but can be crucial for sites dealing with business and medical data.

Links are also very important, meaning both "to" and "from" the site. The other pages that are linked to and from the site you are evaluating tell you something about its quality; but even more important are the other sites that link to this one. Many search engines, such as Google <http://www.google.com/>,

enable you to retrieve Web pages that link to a URL you enter. The quality (or lack thereof) of *those* sites, in turn, can tell you about the original one. Also, the other sites might provide a qualitative or evaluative annotation in addition to simply a link.

Perhaps the most important factor to consider is accuracy, which consists of not only the truthfulness/reliability of the data presented, but also the bias or objectivity of the author/owner of the site. One must determine if the material consists of objective research or personal opinion. Does the author cite sources/references for his/her conclusions? Check them for accuracy. Is it an advocacy site, championing the viewpoint of a particular organization, or the result of a researcher that has carefully sifted through the sources and arrived at various conclusions? With regard to the historical sites and topics discussed further in this paper, the present authors needed to consult print sources, electronic sources, and even use personal contacts to determine the accuracy/inaccuracy of the material.

Often it is necessary to look for site reviews, which can range from using (online or print) periodical and newspaper indexes, to website directories that evaluate other websites, such as *The Argus Clearinghouse* <http://www.clearinghouse. net/> or *Magellan* <http://magellan.excite.com/>. *The Internet Scout Project* <http://scout.cs.wisc.edu/index.html> consists of "the best resources on the Internet," selected by librarians and educators; its weekly *Scout Report* <http:// scout.cs.wisc.edu/report/sr/current/index.html>, which can either be subscribed to via e-mail or read directly on the Web, helps one be assured of getting quality control over the information passing over the net without fear of being duped by hoaxes or misinformation.

Clues to a site's accuracy and validity can also be gleaned from the way that it is categorized by some of the many Web directories, such as *Yahoo!* <http://www.yahoo.com/> or the *Open Directory Project* <http://dmoz.org/>. For example, *Yahoo!* uses both "Revisionists" and "Revisionism" as part of their directory structures.

Although there is no absolute, guaranteed way for users of the World Wide Web to protect themselves from hoaxes and historical fabrications, using the above criteria will certainly improve one's chances of accepting reliable information from a website. As has been discussed above, even those democratic societies manifesting authoritarian tendencies realize their attempts to control information though Internet filters has yielded mixed results.[58] The question remains unanswered whether the Internet will liberalize society or will it become a tool in the arsenal of Big Brother governance. In some cases, even pure democracies have panicked and threatened boycotts of e-commerce companies or taken portals to court for allowing hate literature, forbidden by law, to be sold and disseminated in their homelands.[59] Whether totalitarian societies can simultaneously enter the information age and tightly control information

for its Internet user population is still in question. And as the porousness of information over the net only accelerates with the increase in growth of a Web audience, can government stand idle and ignore pressure to control and change ultimately the nature of the Internet? The following suggestions recognize these paradoxes and are more in the form of aids developed by information professionals to sharpen awareness in detecting hoaxes and misinformation along your ride on the information highway.

The Web itself is replete with information professionals eager to guide the novice searcher. The knowledge that some of these guides have been prepared by experienced persons affiliated with established institutions in the fields of education and information management is itself a comfort when attempting to sharpen one's awareness in detecting hoaxes and misinformation along the information highway. Some valuable websites which discuss criteria for evaluating materials on the Internet, and provide links to other such sites, are:

- "Evaluating Quality on the Net" <http://www.hopetillman.com/findqual.html>, by Hope N. Tillman, Director of Libraries at Babson College [Accessed 4 Sept. 2000].
- "Evaluation of Information Sources" <http://www.vuw.ac.nz/~agsmith/evaln/evaln.htm>, maintained by Alastair Smith (Senior Lecturer at the School of Communications and Information Management, Victoria University of Wellington, New Zealand), part of the *Information Quality WWW Virtual Library* [Accessed 4 Sept. 2000]. Smith's article, "Testing the Surf: Criteria for Evaluating Internet Information Resources,"[60] is also very helpful.
- "Evaluating the Quality of Information on the Internet" <http://www.virtualchase.com/quality/>, maintained by Genie Tyburski of Ballard Spahr Andrews & Ingersoll, LLP, part of *The Virtual Chase: Legal Research on the Internet* site [Accessed 4 Sept. 2000].
- "Evaluating Web Resources" <http://www2.widener.edu/Wolfgram-Memorial-Library/webevaluation/webeval.htm>, by Jan Alexander and Marsha Ann Tate of Widener University [Accessed 5 Sept. 2000], who have also written a book on the subject.[61]
- "ICONnect-Evaluator" <http://www.ala.org/ICONN/evaluate.html>, developed by the American Association of School Librarians, a division of the American Library Association, to support "school library media specialists as they assume leadership positions in the use of the Internet in the school community" [Accessed 4 Sept. 2000]. Some of the materials, such as "How to Tell if You Are Looking at a Great Web Site" <http://www.ala.org/parentspage/greatsites/criteria.html>, would benefit anyone learning to cope with the massive bits of data overloading the Internet.

B.I. librarians should also familiarize students with the use of virtual libraries in addition to merely using search engines. Although many academic and public libraries have constructed their own virtual libraries (i.e., lists of recommended sites arranged under subject categories), the most famous is *The WWW Virtual Library* <http://vlib.org/>, "the oldest catalog of the web, started by Tim Berners-Lee, the creator of html and the web itself."[62] Volunteers create and maintain pages of links to sites in their areas of expertise, assuring users of a degree of safety and authority that is usually lacking from search engines, which usually only rank sites according to "relevance," i.e., the number of times the keyword entered by the searcher appears on the retrieved page.

HISTORICAL FABRICATIONS ON THE INTERNET

In an excellent article on Internet misinformation, Paul S. Piper of Western Washington University Library divided these problematic sites into several (sometimes overlapping) categories: counterfeit, parodies and spoofs, fictitious, questionable, malicious, and product-related.[63] The present authors will now examine some malicious and/or counterfeit Web sites that deliberately mislead the public by providing false historical information. As the reader will see, many of these sites deny the actuality of recognized and accepted historical events, either for personal or ideological reasons.

Holocaust-Denial

1. Institute for Historical Review <http://www.ihr.org/>
[Accessed 9 June 2000]

According to a literature search, the Institute for Historical Review (IHR) was founded in 1978 by Willis A. Carto (who had earlier founded the Liberty Lobby), whom the Anti-Defamation League of B'nai B'rith once described as "the leading anti-Semitic propagandist in the United States," and Lewis Brandon, who in reality was William David McCalden, a British neo-fascist.[64] The IHR publishes the *Journal of Historical Review (JHR)*, holds conferences, and is affiliated with Noontide Press <http://www.noontidepress.com/> [Accessed 9 June 2000], publisher and/or distributor of many "classic" volumes of anti-Semitica, such as the *Protocols of the Learned Elders of Zion*, and was affiliated with Carto and the ultra-right Liberty Lobby until mid-1993, when they broke over alleged financial improprieties.[65] The bulk of the IHR website is devoted to reproducing articles from the *JHR* and other IHR leaflets. Although the IHR's slogan is "Bringing history into accord with the facts," the IHR focuses almost exclusively on World War II and the Holocaust. Indeed, a

literature search quickly located a content analysis of their journal which showed "that more than half (51.9 percent) of all articles, essays, book reviews, commentaries, and editorials are about revisionism and the Holocaust, with another fifth (20.2 percent) allocated to the Nazis and the equivalency argument that their [i.e., the Nazis'] government was no different from others. We thus argue that the *JHR* could just as accurately be called the *Journal of Holocaust Revisionism*."[66] The IHR website is linked to from at least 436 other sites, according to the Google search engine.

A background search on the Web easily located relevant information regarding the IHR, which casts serious doubts on the accuracy and reliability of any information that they provide on their website:

- "Willis Carto and the IHR" is available on the Nizkor Project site <http://www.nizkor.org/faqs/ihr/index.html>, and provides information on the backgrounds of Carto and many members of the IHR's editorial board and their ties to fringe groups, raising issues relating to bias and objectivity [Accessed 12 June 2000]. While some contributors to the *JHR* have advanced degrees (e.g., Arthur R. Butz), those degrees are not in history.
- "Holocaust Denial: Anti-Semitism Masquerading as History" is available on the ADL's website <http://www.adl.org/frames/front_holocaust_ denial.html>, and contains information on both Carto, whom it describes as "perhaps the most influential professional anti-Semite in the United States,"[67] and the IHR, which it refers to as "the world's single most important outlet for Holocaust-denial propaganda"[68] [Accessed 12 June 2000].
- "Encountering Holocaust Denial," by Lin Collette <http:// www.publiceye. org/magazine/v08n3/holodeni.html>, originally published in the September 1994 issue of *Public Eye,* details the connections between Carto, the Liberty Lobby, and the IHR, and notes that the "IHR presents a public face that avoids overt anti-Jewish bigotry. However, its fund-raising letters, mailed to 'supporters of truth in history,' reveal its directors' prejudices quite clearly" [Accessed 6 Nov. 2000].

A quick search on *Lexis-Nexis Academic Universe* found numerous relevant court cases, including one where the Liberty Lobby sued Dow Jones & Company (publisher of the *Wall Street Journal*) over an article which called the organization anti-Semitic. In dismissing the case, Justice Robert Bork of the U.S. Court of Appeals, District of Columbia Circuit, wrote that, "We tend to agree with the district court that if the term 'anti-Semitic' has a core, factual meaning, then the truth of the description was proved here."[69]

The present authors feel that it is not necessary to go into great detail refuting the Holocaust-denial arguments promulgated on the IHR website. To save space, we will point out that there are numerous refutations available online:

- One of the IHR's most frequently reproduced pamphlet, which is available on the websites of many other sympathetic organizations, is "66 Questions and Answers on the Holocaust" <http://ihr.org/leaflets/66qna. html> [Accessed 10 June 2000]. The Nizkor Project has answered the IHR with a document entitled "66 Questions & Answers About the Holocaust: Nizkor's Response" <http://www.nizkor.org/features/qar/>, which provides detailed, documented answers to the IHR's questions [Accessed 14 June 2000].
- Another handy site is the Simon Wiesenthal Center's "Responses to Revisionist Arguments" <http://www.wiesenthal.org/resource/revision.htm> [Accessed 1 Dec. 2000].
- Many arguments expounded by deniers regarding gas chambers and chemistry are refuted by Richard J. Green (PhD, Chemistry) on his Web page <http://www.holocaust-history.org/~rjg/>, part of The Holocaust-History Project's website [Accessed 12 Dec. 2000].
- "Gravediggers of Memory" <http://www.usfca.edu/fac-staff/neamane/history210/> is a wonderful website consisting of student essays refuting Holocaust-denial arguments from a Historical Methods class at the University of San Francisco [Accessed 14 Nov. 2000]. Several of the essays deal with materials published by the IHR.

2. Zündelsite <http://www.zundelsite.org/>
[Accessed 19 June 2000]

Though dedicated to the work of Canadian Ernst Zündel, a German national living in Canada, a WHOIS search shows that this site is actually run from California by Ingrid Rimland, no doubt to take advantage of the United States' liberal freedom of speech provisions rather than the more restrictive Canadian environment. According to HateWatch, "Rimland has been one of the most visible figures in [the] Holocaust denial movement since 1995, when she appeared on the Internet and other media as the 'press secretary' for Ernst Zundel. . . . Today Rimland is openly anti-Semitic and pro-Hitler, but these are views she hid or suppressed for some time before stating them openly at the 'Zundelsite.'"[70] Zündel "gained recognition originally on his bizarre 'flying saucer' claims, that the Nazis had manufactured 'flying saucers' in order to escape Germany as the Allied forces were conquering it during World War II. He speculated that it was possible that Hitler escaped in such a craft and was hiding out in, perhaps, Antarctica."[71] Zündel is the co-author (using the pseudonym Christof Friedrich) with Eric Thomson of *The Hitler We Loved & Why* (Reedy, WV: White Power Publications, 1980), and he created his own pub-

lishing house, Samisdat Publications, to publish and distribute materials both inside and outside Canada. For publishing the book *Did Six Million Really Die?*, Zündel was found guilty in 1985 of publishing "false news"; it was over-turned on appeal, and a second conviction was also overturned when Canada's Supreme Court ruled that the false news statute was unconstitutional.[72] The Zündelsite contains both original materials as well as reprints of information from other websites (such as the IHR), and Rimland sends out daily Z-grams via email (which are also posted on USENET). The Zündelsite (including its various mirror sites) is linked to from over 1,000 other websites, according to the Google search engine.

A search on the Web for background information to see if either Zündel or Rimland can be trusted to provide accurate historical information located much relevant information, including an interesting interview with Zündel by Frank Miele of *Skeptic* magazine. Miele writes, "Zündel's 'game plan,' as he calls it, is to 'first, bring down Jewish suffering in terms of numbers and events, both real and imagined, to what it really was, not what they say it was, what they exploit for their own political, financial, and geopolitical purposes.' When asked to be more precise, he estimated total Jewish deaths from all causes under the Nazi regime as only about 300,000. His second goal is to make the world look at German suffering and the Allied brutality toward Germany and realize that both peoples were victims."[73]

Some other informative documents on Zündel and/or the Zündelsite are:

* "Notes on a Discourse Analysis of Selected Zündelsite Materials," by Gary D. Prideaux, Professor of Linguistics at the University of Alberta, available from Nizkor <http://www.nizkor.org/hweb/people/p/prideaux-gary/> [Accessed 22 June 2000]. Prideaux analyzes several documents and concludes, "These analyses lead to the conclusion that the writers of the passages have in numerous instances singled out Jews as a special, identifiable group. Moreover this group is asserted to possess highly negative and criminal attributes as a group, thereby targeting the group for, e.g., hatred, revulsion, contempt, and loathing. In some passages, overt threats of violence are uttered toward Jews as a group."[74]
* "Ernst Zundel, Douglas Christie, and the Conspiracy of Holocaust Denial in Canada," by Gregory Paul Michael Hartnell <http://www.usfca.edu/fac-staff/neamane/history210/greghartnell_canada.html>, and "A Look at Holocaust Denial Through the Works of a Propagandist, Ernst Zundel," by Shanti Pappas <http://www.usfca.edu/fac-staff/neamane/history210/shanti_zundel.html>, both of which are from the aforementioned "Gravediggers of Memory" site and contain valuable information on Zündel [Accessed 14 Nov. 2000].

Denial of the Armenian Genocide

1. *Armenian Allegations: The Facts Concerning the Alleged Armenian Genocide*, by Hasan Ozbekhan, President of the Turkish American Friendship Society of the United States, and Professor Emeritus and Chairman of the Graduate Group in Social Systems Sciences at the University of Pennsylvania <http://www.turkey.org/politics/p_armn00.htm> [Accessed 25 Aug. 2000]. Ozbekhan rejects the charge of "genocide," calling it rather an "inter-communal war," and states that, "Armenians lost between 525,000 to 600,000 people, and the Turks and other Muslims in Eastern Anatolia lost, say between 2 and 2.5 million."

According to a WHOIS search, the domain turkey.org is registered to the Foreign Ministry of the Republic of Turkey (i.e., Turkey's embassy in Washington, DC). As an official site of the Turkish government, it should be assumed that it only provides information approved by, and supporting the positions of, that government. Its objectivity must be questioned.

2. *A "Statement" Wrongly Attributed to Mustafa Kemal Atatürk*, by Türkkaya Ataöv of Ankara University <http://inter.mfa.gov.tr/grupa/ad/adf/mfa276.htm> [Accessed 13 Nov. 2000]. Ataöv disputes the legitimacy of a document in which Atatürk, the founder of the Turkish Republic, acknowledged Ottoman responsibility for the Armenian genocide. He argues that the famous quotation is actually from one of Atatürk's enemies, Nemrud Mustafa Pasha, and he presents quotations from Atatürk regarding the Armenian "exaggerations," with the purpose of casting doubt on the genocide. This document is on the website of the Ministry of Foreign Affairs of the Republic of Turkey, and, as with any such document, one should examine it closely for bias before accepting its assertions completely. Thus, a literature search was performed.

The attempted genocide of Armenians during 1915-1917 by the Young Turks continues to be a controversial subject, even though in the opinion of many historians it is well documented. As one author has pointed out, "Unlike the Holocaust, which has been denied by individuals, the Armenian genocide has been continuously denied by Turkish *governments* for eighty years."[75] The position of the Turkish government has been summed up as, "it never happened, Turkey is not responsible, the term 'genocide' does not apply," even though a June 1915 telegram from one of the Turkish leaders carrying out the genocide asked, "Are the Armenians, who are being dispatched from there, being liquidated? Are those harmful persons whom you inform us you are exiling and banishing, being exterminated, or are they being merely dispatched and exiled? Answer explicitly. . . . "[76]

While those who deny the Jewish Holocaust often are members of fringe groups and have no academic credentials, several of those who deny the Armenian genocide are scholars who hold academic positions–however, their

motives for denying the genocide have been questioned. According to an article in the *Encyclopedia of Genocide,* "By the 1970s a handful of scholars emerged in U.S. universities who were working in some capacity or other with the Turkish government in order to help Turkey absolve itself of responsibility for the extermination of the Armenians. Bernard Lewis (Princeton University), Justin McCarthy (University of Louisville), Stanford Shaw (UCLA) and most recently Heath Lowry (Princeton University), are among the most vocal genocide deniers."[77] In the 1980s, the Turkish government gave financial assistance to support the establishment of various institutes to further research on Turkish history. Heath Lowry became the first executive director of the Washington, DC-based Institute of Turkish Studies, before becoming the first incumbent of the Atatürk Chair in Turkish Studies at Princeton, also financed through a grant from the Republic of Turkey. It has been documented in memoranda published in the journal *Holocaust and Genocide Studies* that "Lowry has been engaged in an ongoing relationship with the Turkish government, and that he has regularly offered advice on denial both to the Turkish ambassador to the United States and to other persons in Turkey," and "that Lowry apparently seeks to discredit the work of any author who treats the Armenian genocide as historical reality."[78] Bernard Lewis was actually found guilty in June 1995 by a court in Paris on civil charges that had been brought against him of denying the Armenian genocide, and was ordered to pay court costs and a symbolic punitive damage of one franc.[79]

There are numerous scholarly books that document the Armenian Genocide, such as those by Richard G. Hovannisian,[80] Donald E. Miller and Lorna Touryan Miller,[81] and Vahakn N. Dadrian,[82] as well as collections of documents.[83] Robert F. Melson has stated flatly, "The Armenian genocide and the Holocaust are the principal instances of total domestic genocide in the twentieth century. In both cases, a deliberate attempt was made by the government of the day to destroy in whole an ethno-religious community of ancient provenance."[84]

Among the numerous websites with further information on the Armenian Genocide are:

- Armenian National Institute <http://www.armenian-genocide.org/>, a non-profit organization based in Washington, DC, "dedicated to the study, research, and affirmation of the Armenian Genocide. Its overarching goal is affirmation of the worldwide recognition of the Armenian Genocide" [Accessed 13 Nov. 2000].
- Armenian Genocide <http://www.genocide.am/>, which includes the text of several valuable articles, including "Remembering and Understanding the Armenian Genocide," by Rouben Paul Adalian, and "The Turkish Military Tribunal's Prosecution of the Authors of the Armenian

Genocide: Four Major Court-Martial Series," by Vahakn N. Dadrian [Accessed 13 Nov. 2000].

- Armenian Genocide Home Page <http://www.armeniangenocide.com/>, operated by Reynold E. Khachatourian. Extremely valuable, especially for its disturbing photographs [Accessed 15 Nov. 2000].
- Armenian Research Center <http://www.umd.umich.edu/dept/armenian/>, located at the University of Michigan-Dearborn [Accessed 13 Nov. 2000]. Contains a valuable page "Useful Answers to Frequent Questions on the Armenian Genocide."

While some of *these* sites are also affiliated with organizations and therefore should themselves be critically evaluated by any users, the historical information they present is corroborated by the aforementioned books and articles, leading the user to believe that the preponderance of evidence for the Armenian genocide is great.

Denial of the Ukrainian Famine/Genocide

1. *Lies Concerning the History of the Soviet Union*, by Mario Sousa, Member of the Communist Party Marxist-Leninists Revolutionaries Sweden, from the December 1999 issue of Northstar Compass <http://www.northstarcompass.org/nsc9912/lies.htm> [Accessed 18 Aug. 2000]. The author writes that, "There is a direct historical link running from: Hitler to Hearst, to Conquest, to Solzhenitsyn," and blames Nazi propaganda minister Joseph Goebbels for spreading the story about a genocidal famine, in order "to prepare world public opinion for the 'liberation' of the Ukraine by German troops." A clue that this site might have a particular bias is evident on its main page, where it states that it is operated by the "Organizing Committee for International Council of Friendship and Solidarity with Soviet People," which is "Dedicated to the Re-Establishment of the Soviet Union as a Socialist State," as well as its own description that "Northstar Compass is a monthly magazine containing the latest news and views of the struggles of the Soviet peoples against Yeltsin's capitalist regime and its imperialist backers."[85]

2. *The Hoax of the 1932-33 Ukraine Famine* <http://www.plp.org/cd_sup/ukfam1.html>, which originally appeared in the 25 Feb. 1987 issue of *Challenge-Desafio,* newspaper of the Progressive Labor Party [Accessed 13 Nov. 2000]. Concentrating on trying to debunk both the acclaimed film *Harvest of Despair,* and Robert Conquest's book *Harvest of Sorrow,* the author of this Web page asserts that, "This film is a fraud. This essay will show that it uses lies, misleading film, and Nazi collaborators, to attack Stalin, the Soviet Union, and the whole idea of communism, while promoting nationalism and fascism." Wanting to absolve Stalin and the Soviet Union of any blame, the au-

thor openly admits that "any attack on the then-socialist Soviet Union is an attack upon all workers today." This website is operated by the Progressive Labor Party (PLP), which also publishes a political journal called *The Communist,* as well as *PL Magazine: A Journal of Communist Theory and Practice.* The purpose of the PLP can easily be summed up from one of its Web pages: "The historical experience of revolutionary communist movements shows that the dictatorship of the proletariat turned into its opposite because of key weaknesses within the old communist parties and their strategic political line. These weaknesses eventually led to the re-establishment of full-blown capitalism in once-socialist countries. The obscene anti-communist, anti-worker lies and actions of a Gorbachev or a Deng have their roots in these weaknesses."[86]

It should be fairly obvious that any information from these two sites questioning the Ukrainian famine should be considered biased and unreliable, since it is clear that both would like to rehabilitate the image of Soviet-style communism. A search of the literature reveals that the question of the Ukrainian famine was thoroughly investigated and documented in a report to the U.S. Congress in 1988.[87] There seems to be little scholarly debate over the *actuality* of the Ukrainian famine–a 1987 book by Canadian Douglas Tottle was the only book located supporting the view echoed on the aforementioned websites[88]–although scholars differ in their opinions regarding how much–grain Stalin was sitting on (i.e., how much he was holding back from Ukraine), and whether or not the famine constitutes *genocide.* Robert Conquest is a strong and convincing proponent of the relationship between official Soviet policies and the famine.[89] Conquest also located a document in (then-) newly opened Russian archives from Stalin and Molotov to local party officials, in which those local officials were ordered to *prevent* a mass exodus of peasants from Ukraine and Kuban' in search of bread.[90] Mark B. Tauger has argued that the 1932 grain harvest was much too small, which caused the famine on its own, rather than being a result of a deliberate decision by Stalin.[91] A later article co-written by Tauger demonstrates that "Stalin was not hoarding immense grain reserves in these years," although the authors admit, "These findings do not, of course, free Stalin from responsibility for the famine."[92] Barbara B. Green has argued that the famine was not an intentional act of genocide, but rather a result of Stalin's forced collectivization.[93] See also the aforementioned award-winning documentary film, *Harvest of Despair: The 1932-33 Man-Made Famine in Ukraine,* produced by the Ukrainian Famine Research Committee of St. Vladimir's Institute, Toronto.[94]

On the Web, the following sites offer information on the famine:

- Several relevant articles, including a bibliography on the famine, are available from InfoUkes, a Canadian-based information resource about Ukraine and Ukrainians, at <http://www.infoukes.com/history/famine/

index.html> [Accessed 7 Sept. 2000]. (Aside from the two sites discussed above, InfoUkes also provides links to some other sites that deny the Ukrainian famine at http://www.infoukes.com/history/famine/ revisionists/ index.html.)

* The website of *The Ukrainian Weekly* <http://www.ukrweekly.com/ Archive/Great_Famine/index.shtml>, published by the Ukrainian National Association, contains a wealth of information, including a chronology, numerous articles, and eyewitness accounts [Accessed 15 Nov. 2000].

Although *these* sites must also be critically evaluated by any users, especially since some are affiliated with organizations, the historical information they present is corroborated by the aforementioned books and articles, leading the user to believe that the preponderance of evidence for the actuality of the Ukrainian famine/genocide is great.

Denial of the Nanking Massacre/the Rape of Nanking

The Japanese government has steadfastly refused to apologize for the so-called Nanking (or Nanjing) Massacre, where as many as 300,000 Chinese noncombatants were slaughtered in cold blood, and tens of thousands of Chinese women were raped, some of whom were then forced into sexual slavery as "comfort women." The wartime atrocity was thrust into the public sphere with the publication of Iris Chang's book, *The Rape of Nanking: The Forgotten Holocaust of World War II* (New York: BasicBooks, 1997). The book was hailed in the media as a fair and balanced portrayal of that terrible event. However, Chang and the book were attacked in the Japanese press. Japanese revisionists claimed that Chang inflated the number of those killed, used unreliable sources, and placed false captions on the photographs in the book.[95] Japan's ambassador to the United States told reporters, "The book contains many extremely inaccurate descriptions and one-sided views on the case. It's not a good thing that such a book has been published and has attracted great attention."[96] Writer Akira Suzuki's 1973 book, *The Nanking Massacre Illusion*, was revised and republished to answer Chang.[97] There are also several websites that echo these charges against Iris Chang:

1. *Iris Chang's Errors* <http://www.jiyuu-shikan.org/nanjing/> [Accessed 7 Sept. 2000] states that, "Iris Chang's 'Rape of Nanking' is a book that fails to heal but rather sears all efforts for good international relations because it prioritizes passion at the cost of basic historical facts." The bulk of the site consists of quotations from Chang's book, followed by refutations from primarily Japanese sources. This site is operated by the "Association for the Advancement of Liberalist View of History," whose purpose is "getting different view-

points together, free, active, rational debate, and overcoming taboos and restraints of ideology to pursue historical truths."[98]

2. *The Other Side, Nanking Massacre* <http://members.tripod.com/~funkytomoya/massacre/sample01.htm> [Accessed 7 Sept. 2000]. The unnamed author of this site blames the Chinese for the massacre, saying that the Chinese used guerrilla warfare where the soldiers pretended to be farmers, so the Japanese had no alternative but to treat the farmers as if they were soldiers. The author states that General Matsui "never encouraged his soldiers to execute the civilians, to rape ladies and children, and to rob civilian's properties . . . [but rather] ordered [them] to treat the civilians as kindly as the troops could," and concludes that less than 2,000 innocent civilians were killed.[99]

Deniers of the Nanking Massacre use the same methods as deniers of the Holocaust: look for any error or inconsistency and then try to cast doubt on the entire event (*Falsus in Uno, Falsus in Omnibus*). While the merits of Iris Chang's volume can be debated, there are many *other* books that document what happened in Nanking,[100] including the diaries of eyewitness John Rabe, a Schindler-like Nazi industrialist who helped to set up an "International Safety Zone" to shelter and protect the victims.[101] Chang's book received many favorable reviews–Peter Li, Professor of East Asian Studies at Rutgers University, commented that "Chang has produced, as much as possible, a balanced and multi-sided view of the tragedy at Nanking"[102]–although errors have also been pointed out. As Jeff Kingston of Temple University Japan observed, "In writing such a flawed and sloppy work, Chang inadvertently provided ammunition to the denial camp, allowing them to sidetrack the debate into arguments over details, numbers, dates and locations that attempt to distract attention away from the overwhelming evidence of widespread atrocities."[103] A planned Japanese-language version of the book was canceled.[104]

Among the many websites that document the tragedy are:

- Nanking 1937 <http://www.princeton.edu/~nanking/html/main.html>, which is a companion website to a conference and exhibition held at Princeton University to commemorate the massacre's sixtieth anniversary [Accessed 15 Nov. 2000]. There is only brief textual material, but fourteen photographs and links to other sites with information on the massacre.
- WWW Memorial Hall of the Victims in the Nanjing Massacre (1937-1938) <http://www.arts.cuhk.edu.hk/NanjingMassacre/NM.html> [Accessed 15 Nov. 2000] contains many photographs, articles, and links to other sites, as well as three brief video clips (in .mov format) taken from a 16mm film that missionary John Magee made during the massacre[105] to document the Japanese crimes.

It seems clear to the present authors that the preponderance of evidence for the Nanking Massacre is great, despite any alleged flaws in Iris Chang's book, and that several people have attacked her book as a convenient smokescreen, attempting by doing so to cast doubt on the Massacre itself.

Afrocentrism

The World Wide Web is an important forum for competing claims among disenfranchised groups. Certain African-Americans espousing an idealization of Africa and its history, and the legacy of slavery here, feel other groups (even those who have also been historically mistreated) are given undue attention at their expense. Afrocentrists of different varieties feel particular frustration with the Jewish-American community. Some of these websites promote their agenda in addition to books written (or endorsed) by professors whose scholarly patina adds intellectual and monetary value to the websites' agendas. Some unwary readers might assume the irrefutability of arguments advanced on a site simply because it includes footnotes or endnotes. A few interesting manifestations of this type of website are discussed below.

1. *The Blacks and Jews Newspage* <http://www.blacksandjews.com/> is unguarded in its Afrocentric sentiments [Accessed 9 Sept. 2000]. The origins of slavery in the New World is a particular focus of this Web page, and among its aims is the "dissemination of accurate information about the historical relationship between Blacks and Jews."[106]

Although a disclaimer states the site does not belong to the Nation of Islam (NOI), one can nonetheless easily link from this site to the NOI homepage. The reader can order a copy of the NOI's controversial (and anonymously written) *The Secret Relationship Between Blacks and Jews,*[107] with 1,275 footnotes among its 334 pages. A WHOIS search reveals that this site is registered to "Latimer Associates," the publisher of *The Secret Relationship*. According to the unnamed author of this Web page, the book's footnotes show that "the irrefutable record of Jewish historical compliance with Black oppression is no longer a 'secret.'"[108] Scores of Jewish scholars are selectively quoted on this Web page lending credence to the Afrocentrists' claims. Moreover, this website claims that both *The Washington Post* and a Professor Ralph A. Austen (whose Jewish religion is apparently of importance to the online author) somehow confirm the scholarly accuracy of the NOI's book. Here is a classic example of using an *argumentum ad verecundiam*: the respected authority of an institution and an academic to bolster a problematic position among scholars. So why should an unsuspecting reader question the accuracy of the claims made on this website and in *The Secret Relationship* (which it wholeheartedly promotes)? Should one believe the quotations are accurate and not taken out of their original context? How many Web readers have the time

to verify the accuracy and context of the quotes, rather than just accepting them on face value?

From the many instances cited of Jewish participation in the slave trade to the Americas, what time period is being referred to? Sixteenth, seventeenth, or eighteenth century? Many of the quotes from the Jewish scholars are in the seventeenth century, yet it was in the *eighteenth* century when the largest number of African slaves reached the Americas, mainly from *British* ships and sponsors who were predominantly *Christian*.[109] Who were these slave traders even if some were of the Jewish faith? When they acted as slave traders why is their Jewishness singled out and not their national origin? Is the author suggesting the slave traders' Jewishness contains a genetic or religious component compelling them to become slave traders in the first place? Was a genetic or religious component evident in the behavior of Christian and Muslim slave traders, White and Black, who were numerically more important to the slave trade than the Jews?

During the period leading to the American Civil War, opinion on the morality of slavery was divided across the entire spectrum of ethnic, geographic, racial, and religious groups. Jewish Americans were not monolithic in their opinions on this issue, and geography, not religion, was the key factor in explaining their behavior: The Northern Jews were naturally more sympathetic toward abolitionism than their Southern brethren. Yet the Blacks and Jews Newspage uses *one quote* by Bertram W. Korn to assert the "Jews participation in every aspect and process of the exploitation of the defenseless blacks,"[110] inferring *all* Jews were exploiters of Blacks even though Korn was referring only to *some* Jews.

The Web page author also uses this particular chapter in history as evidence of a continuing history of hostility from Jews toward Blacks. One quote from their online page–"Jews were the only group in this country who arrogantly threatened to protest the visit of revered African National Congress Chairman and now President Nelson Mandela to the United States in 1990"[111]–is a blanket indictment of the *entire* Jewish-American community, and, of course, there is no source identified for this statement. It strains credulity to believe every major Jewish-American organization was opposed to Nelson Mandela's visit. On the same page the social scientist Richard Hernstein, co-author of *The Bell Curve,* is identified as "among the most prominent Jewish scientists and scholars who maintain that Black people are intellectually deficient."[112] No mention is made of the book's other author, Charles Murray, presumably because he is not Jewish.

The author behind the Blacks and Jews Newspage employs similar methodology to deniers of the Holocaust in building his/her argument: Assertions are not always footnoted, such as quotes from various Jewish scholars (e.g., Louis Epstein, Jacob Rader Marcus, and Isaac Mayer Wise); some referenced quota-

tions are sandwiched together although they appear on different pages (e.g., the conflation of quotations by Seymour B. Liebman from *New World Jewry 1493-1825: Requiem for the Forgotten*); and blanket assertions such as the aforementioned one regarding *The Washington Post*. In fact, a search of the *Post*'s archive found quite the opposite: Rather than locating an article that endorsed the ideas behind *The Secret Relationship*, an article by columnist Richard Cohen was retrieved regarding the misuse of academic freedom at Wellesley College, where Professor Tony Martin was using *The Secret Relationship Between Blacks and Jews* as a text for his class. Cohen wrote, "Wellesley and the rest of American higher education cannot allow themselves to be used by bigots who abuse academic freedom."[113] In fact, the outlandish claims made by the author of *The Secret Relationship* and by Professor Martin aroused such anger that the American Historical Association in February 1995 declared "false any assertions that Jews played a disproportionate role in the exploitation of black slave labor."[114] Respected historians of slavery David Brion Davis[115] and Seymour Drescher[116] have written balanced treatments of this subject and rejected as anti-Semitic the claims made in the NOI's book. Both the Simon Wiesenthal Center[117] and Anti-Defamation League[118] have issued exposes of the inaccuracies in *The Secret Relationship*, and it has also been thoroughly debunked in books by Harold Brackman[119] and Saul S. Friedman.[120]

   2. *The Afrocentric Experience* <http://www.swagga.com/> operated by Obi Okara (a.k.a. Everton Swagga Powell),[121] this website's welcome message states that it "is dedicated to the empowerment and the enlightenment processes of all people throughout the world especially those of African descent in Africa and the African diaspora" [Accessed 10 Oct. 2000]. This site, which is linked to from about 237 other sites according to Google, offers an African perspective on the news, commentaries on psychological inferiority, and an array of links with reference information on African kings and queens, slave revolts, timelines, and Black inventors. According to information on this website, all of the following Egyptian rulers are "African": Akhenaton, Hannibal, Imhotep, Khufu (Cheops), Menelek II, Tutankamun, Ramses II, Cleopatra, Hatshepsut, Makeda (the Queen of Sheba), and Nefertiti.[122] It further states that Africans also invented: civilization, democracy, chess, the alphabet, writing, math, engineering, paper, boats, pyramids, calendars, domestication of animals, art, literature, philosophy, spiritual systems, monotheism, mining, medicine, stone architecture, universities, agriculture, labor, and economics.[123] A partial review of some inventors find the site's claims at odds with *Famous First Facts*,[124] a standard reference book on verifying such information. Moreover, this type of exercise of listing firsts in science for personal self-congratulation distorts the contributions of those Black inventors who in

the history of science were involved in other phases of the inventive process, even if they were not part of the invention's genesis.

There are numerous examples on this site relating to Black inventors of stretching the historical truth either by providing incomplete or misleading information, or by making patently false claims. Was the gas mask created in 1914 by the Black inventor Garret A. Morgan? Well, *Famous First Facts* states that the "gas mask resembling the modern type was patented by Lewis Phectic Haslett of Louisville, KY. who received a patent on June 12, 1849."[125] In the book *Black Inventors From Africa to America*,[126] Mr. Morgan is credited with a patent for a safety helmet he called a "Breathing Device" which acted as a gas mask, although he did not originate the idea. The Web page's claim that the mask saved many lives during WWI is also contradicted in *Black Inventors*: "There is no evidence that the army purchased Morgan's inhalator."[127] There are also some uncategorical falsehoods presented regarding Black inventors: The wrench was invented by Solymon Merrick, not John A. Johnson;[128] the elevator was Henry Waterman's invention, not Alexander Miles;[129] the refrigerator was from Thomas Moore, not John Standard.[130] Here the "facts" are stretched beyond recognition and so broadly interpreted that one can conclude that what's here is simply propaganda. Not only is the accuracy of the information in question, but one must also question the integrity of the unidentified Web page author in presenting such distortions to the user.

With regard to claims that the ancient Egyptians were Black, Frank M. Snowden, Jr. (Professor of Classics Emeritus, Howard University) makes a convincing argument that many Afrocentrists mistakenly use "Black," "African," and "Egyptian" interchangeably, ignoring the differences between the Egyptians and their Black southern neighbors, the Nubians.[131] Frank J. Yurco, an Egyptologist affiliated with both the Field Museum of Natural History and the University of Chicago, has argued that the ancient Egyptians were multiracial due to intermarriages, and that their skin colors ranged from very light in the North to much darker in the South. He concludes by saying, "How then can we be so presumptuous as to assign our primitive racial labels onto so wonderful a culture."[132]

Although this is a very touchy subject, the preponderance of evidence seems to be with the critics of Afrocentrism, in the opinion of the present authors, and that the operators of the Blacks and Jews Newspage and The Afrocentric Experience provide opinions rather than objective historical information.

Conspiracy Theorists

Political conspiracy theorists who articulate popular, deep-seated suspicions among the American people, especially over government investigations into

the assassinations of prominent political leaders, can easily be found on the World Wide Web. The ease in registering a website has given the conspiracy theorists a forum that they would not otherwise have, since their theories are not prominently reported in the major newspapers. The murders of John F. Kennedy and Martin Luther King, Jr., have their conspiracy adherents represented by two of the more interesting websites on this topic.

It should be noted that it is not the purpose here to rebut every allegation of a conspiracy because the labyrinthine nature of assassination conspiracies makes it necessary to research many books to find explanations for each of the conspiracy theorist's accusations. Those books are available in many public libraries. Part of the problem in deciphering the mountains of information, most of which comes from government documents and court transcripts, is their presentation on the website. Is there an easy way to evaluate the charges and rebuttals? Can you determine an effort of fairness by the online author in the presentation of just the facts?

1. Citizens for Truth About the Kennedy Assassination
<http://www.webcom.com/ctka/index.html>
[Accessed 16 Sept. 2000]

President John F. Kennedy's assassination is believed by some conspiracy theorists to be the first in a chain of planned deaths orchestrated by powerful individuals in the military-industrial complex, including the murders of Robert Kennedy, Martin Luther King, Jr., and even the attempted assassination of George C. Wallace. You can view these sentiments from the website of the Citizens for Truth, which also published *Probe Magazine* <http://www.webcom.com/~ctka/pr-main.html> [Accessed 16 Sept. 2000], a "publication the national security state does not want you to read," offering archives of free articles on the world of political conspiracy. The melodramatics of the presentation should be the first sign to caution any reader of what is being presented. (Ironically, the national security state obviously is not powerful enough to stop anyone from reading this material over the Internet.)

One of the best sites with information to answer and refute those who promote the JFK conspiracy theories is the Kennedy Assassination Home Page <http://mcadams.posc.mu.edu/home.htm> [Accessed 21 Oct. 2000], run by John C. McAdams, Associate Professor of Political Science at Marquette University (PhD, Harvard). McAdams defends the conclusions of the Warren Commission and provides answers to the major questions that are repeatedly asked by the conspiracy sites, such as whether there were shots fired from the grassy knoll area of Dealey Plaza, and if a single bullet hit both President Kennedy and Governor Connally. McAdams also offers a photo gallery, recom-

mended books on the subject, and links to other assassination sites (including conspiratorial ones). While the author's biases are manifest, there is clearly an attempt to be fair, which cannot be said for many of the conspiratorialists.

2. The Assassination of Martin Luther King, Jr.

The assassination of Martin Luther King, Jr., by the lone gunman James Earl Ray, has been corroborated twice by the U.S. Justice Department, once by the U.S. House Select Committee on Assassinations, and also by the district attorney's office of Shelby County, Tennessee. Nonetheless, even as well-meaning a source as the King family itself and their very worthwhile and admirable organization, the Martin Luther King, Jr. Center for Nonviolent Social Change <http://www.thekingcenter.com/> publicly declared in a June 9, 2000 press release: "This conspiracy involved agents of the governments of the City of Memphis, the state of Tennessee and the United States of America. The overwhelming weight of the evidence also indicated that James Earl Ray was not the triggerman and, in fact, was an unknowing patsy."[133] A Memphis civil jury had promulgated this conspiracy theory in December 1999, which only reinvigorated the family's claims and its continuing search for justice regarding the murder of MLK. Transcripts of the Memphis civil jury trial can be viewed through the King Center website <http://www.thekingcenter.com/transcripts.htm> [Accessed 24 Sept. 2000], and the civil trial and verdict were analyzed (and applauded) by the aforementioned *Probe Magazine*.[134]

Parascope Magazine investigates conspiracies at the normal and para-normal level. Its interest in the King assassination led one of its editors, Charles Overbeck, to write a special report, "The Assassination of Dr. Martin Luther King, Jr: An Overview" on its website.[135] Mr. Overbeck makes a number of charges against both the FBI and individual law enforcement officers, stating, for example, that "in April, Hoover approved the plan which led to King's switch to the Motel Lorraine." No source is cited for this serious allegation meant to implicate J. Edgar Hoover in the King assassination. According to the Rev. Billy Kyles and Ralph Abernathy, two close confidants of Dr. King, the Motel Lorraine was a favorite of King's, and Dr. King always stayed in the same room (number 306).[136] Overbeck writes of a mysterious Memphis city official who on the day of the assassination ordered the relocation of two Black firemen and a Black police officer named Edward Redditt. This is false. It was Officer Redditt who ordered the removal of the firemen because he thought they would interfere with his surveillance of Dr. King.[137] The merits of the government's surveillance and paranoia regarding Dr. King are not the issue here; rather, the issue is, what should one think when, after some quick fact checking, one finds that the "facts" presented by the conspiratorialists to be fictitious? If their methodology is faulty and they provide incorrect information, one must then be concerned with the quality of all the other evidence they present.

The latest investigation by the U.S. Justice Department (DOJ) can be viewed at http://www.usdoj.gov/crt/crim/mlk/part1.htm [Accessed 8 Oct. 2000]. Naturally, neither side of the "MLK conspiracy" presents the opponent's point of view; however, the DOJ's table of contents *does* offer the origin of accusations made by those personally involved in the assassination (Loyd Jowers), and a rebuttal to those allegations by the DOJ. The government's case is laid out with the standard outline of headings and subheadings so the viewer can easily connect to any major headings of the report. In contrast, the King Center only provides links to volume numbers of the civil trial transcripts with additional links to the family press conference and a plaintiff summary and analysis by a reporter from *Probe Magazine*. It's impossible to search by subject because only volume numbers are search accessible.

The plaintiff in the case is the King family, while the defendants are Loyd Jowers and others unknown who played a part in Dr. King's assassination. Oddly enough, Mr. Jowers (now deceased) is the primary witness for the plaintiffs. Mr. Jowers' account of the assassination has changed over the years, but in his last testament he accepted blame for a role in the conspiracy to assassinate Dr. King. On the DOJ website, Mr. Jowers' charges are laid out with counter-evidence contradicting him; in contrast, the transcripts of the Memphis civil trial reveal no contradictory evidence was presented, which would give jurors any reason to doubt a conspiracy existed. In fact, this trial is so stacked against the government that both sides in the case–plaintiff and defendant–provide evidence that support each other's story. The DOJ's report concludes that Jowers "has contradicted himself on virtually every key point."[138]

By providing access to the Memphis civil trial transcripts (and labeling them as the "Conspiracy Trial Transcripts") without mentioning (or providing access to or links to) any of the materials that contradict it, such as those on the DOJ website, the present authors believe that the King Center is only performing a disservice by perpetuating a conspiracy theory, rather than allowing users to see *all* the information and make up their own mind.

3. The Reformation Online <http://www.reformation.org/>
[Accessed 15 Nov. 2000]

This site, registered to Bible Believers Press, consists of ugly anti-Catholic bigotry, blaming Catholics (and/or the Pope) for everything from the Irish potato famine to the assassinations of both JFK *and* Lincoln. The fabrications on this site are self-evident.

Deceptively Named Sites

"Cybersquatting" is the process of registering famous brand names (or in some cases, the names of celebrities) as Internet domain names, either to make

immediate money by generating traffic to a website that users mistakenly go to, thinking that it is an official site for the product or person, or with the intention of trying to make money in the future by selling the name to the appropriate owner or celebrity. This is either entrepreneurship or extortion, depending on which side you're on. In 1998, ten newspapers discovered that fake domain names (for example, atlantaconstitution.com) had been registered to one individual and were linked to White supremacist websites rather than to the newspapers' official sites.[139] In some cases, civil rights organizations and other anti-fascist groups have registered racist and/or offensive domain names in order to keep them unused–for example, the ADL registered kike.com, and the NAACP registered nigger.com.[140]

The parties involved in cybersquatting domain name disputes have begun to turn to the Geneva-based World Intellectual Property Organization (WIPO), a specialized agency under the United Nations system of organizations, which had already established an Arbitration and Mediation Center for the resolution of international commercial disputes between private parties in 1994. WIPO's "Domain Name Dispute Resolution Service"[141] has made numerous high-profile decisions, including ruling in favor of the singer Madonna in her dispute with Dan Parisi, who had registered the domain name madonna.com.[142] Among the many other domain names that Parisi has registered is whitehouse.com, a pornography site.

Some "deceptively named" sites are obvious parodies, and are clearly labeled as such. Others, however, appear to the naked eye to be "official," sometimes mimicking the exact layout of the official site. As one author has noted, the problem with many of these sites is when search engines retrieve underlying pages, which "appear as discrete bits of information divorced from the site as a whole," often making it harder for users to see that the information comes from a parody (or fake) site.[143]

1. RTMark [or ®™ark] <http://rtmark.com/>
[Accessed 6 Oct. 2000]

Reminiscent of the Yippies of the 1960s, the RTMark website practices anti-establishment sabotage, only today it occurs on the World Wide Web. Inviting similar minded pranksters from around the world, RTMark acts as a clearinghouse for projects that simulate legitimate Web pages of corporations, politicians, and governmental organizations which do not meet RTMark's criteria of social responsibility. According to its own website, it "supports the sabotage (informative alteration) of corporate products," and its "only ethical compunction" is that it "will never promote a project that is likely to result in physical harm to humans."[144] It is an amorphous organization without members except for the founder, computer consultant Zack Exley, and several other

spokespersons. According to Exley, the rationale for this is, "We behave like a corporation and stay anonymous to limit liability."[145]

At first sight the World Trade Organization/GATT Web page <http://gatt. org/> displays a World Trade Organization banner and below it a bullet list linking you to a site map or information about the WTO [Accessed 7 Oct. 2000]. A frame to the left provides one with various trade topics and resources. All of this is merely bait, however, for the user who might think that he/she was connected to the WTO's official site. Except for the photograph of the Director-General Mike Moore of the WTO, the rest of the site was created by RTMark and *not* the WTO. If one clicks on the link to the Director-General's homepage, one gets instead a diatribe against globalization. When the Director-General issued a press statement expressing concern over the duplicity practiced by RTMark, their spokesperson Ray Thomas said, "Mike Moore must have a very low opinion of people to think they won't figure it out."[146] The more discerning readers would probably realize this site is a parody, but for others unfamiliar with the issues, it remains problematic. In fact, the RTMark site was chosen as an entry in the prestigious Whitney Biennial because of its artistic design and its effectiveness at mimicry. Exit Art, an avant-garde gallery in Manhattan, presented an exhibition in September 2000 on parodies of bio- and gene technology with RTMark as one of the exhibitors. If Ray Thomas really believes in the sophistication of the reading public, why go through this elaborate charade of verisimilitude?

Other targets of RTMark sabotage have been: Texas Governor (and then-presidential candidate) George W. Bush <http://www.gwbush.com/> (also documented at http://rtmark.com/gwbush/), New York City Mayor Rudolph Giuliani (http://yesrudy.com/), and Shell Oil <http://rtmark.com/shell/> [All accessed 7 Oct. 2000]. Parodies of politicians are fair game according to the Federal Communications Commission and Federal Election Committee, despite Bush election campaign efforts to silence RTMark on grounds of copyright infringement in using the Bush domain name and failure to register as a political committee. First amendment protections got RTMark off the hook in this case, however, but the legality of soliciting actual sabotage of a corporation's reputation has not yet been tested in the courts. If "bad faith" could be legally proven against future cultural saboteurs, this matter might be regulated under the provisions of "The Trademark Cyberpiracy Prevention Act," passed by the 106th Congress and awaiting the President's signature.[147] RTMark sets a precedent where misinformation and calculated hoaxes are openly acknowledged and promoted over the Internet, although their legality as instruments of free speech have yet to be fully tested in the courts.

2. Martin Luther King, Jr.–A Historical Examination
<http://www.martinlutherking.org/>
[Accessed 25 Aug. 2000]

As noted above during the discussion of his assassination, American civil rights leader Martin Luther King, Jr., was a target of J. Edgar Hoover and the Federal Bureau of Investigation (FBI) while he was alive. This website, which was publicized in *Salon*,[148] was established by the racist group Stormfront in order to defame the memory of King. Although many of the allegations about King have been around for years, particularly in White supremacist publications, this site is especially tricky because of the domain name–the suffix ".org" often implies, in many peoples' minds, a legitimate nonprofit organization. However, this site repeats (or links to other sites that repeat) many allegations about King that either can't be proven (for example, that he was a Communist), or that have little relevance to his accomplishments in civil rights, such as the fact that he plagiarized material for his doctoral dissertation.[149] As *Salon* pointed out, "The site uses government documents, such as [Sen. Jesse] Helms' [anti-King congressional] testimony, and information from the FBI campaign against civil rights leaders, as its sources. Civil rights groups and historians fear the appearance of official sources adds to the potential for gullible people to be taken in by half-truths and revisionist versions of history."[150] This site is a favorite of many B.I. librarians, who use it to demonstrate how deceptive domain names, and the opening pages of some websites, can be.

USENET Newsgroups

USENET is a worldwide forum consisting of thousands of newsgroups which operate like electronic bulletin boards. Anyone with access to a newsgroup server can post and read messages, and many ISPs (Internet Service Providers) provide access for their users; for example, the ISP Mindspring.com offers its subscribers access to over 23,000 newsgroups alone. Newsgroups can also be accessed through individual websites like Deja.com <http://www.deja.com/usenet/>, which displays and archives newsgroup postings in a searchable, user-friendly format. Without borders to control delivery of information, the USENET network supercedes what sovereignty a nation's postal service may possess.

USENET newsgroups proliferate each day and the number of articles (i.e., messages) posted to these bulletin boards grows exponentially as every subscriber has instant access to someone else's opinion. The desire to connect to someone, perhaps thousands of miles away, in a matter of seconds, who shares the same interest as you, and get quick feedback, is truly phenomenal, yet the potential to spread hoaxes and misinformation, however unintentional, may be unavoidable. E-mail and Internet netiquette codes of conduct are voluntary

and content neutral. Some newsgroups are moderated by administrators who may put restrictions on message content, especially with regard to advertising, but generally content is not censored. You may be warned by the ISP to be careful out there on the Web not only because of a possible offense to frail sensibilities, but also to ensure the legal liability of the ISP is never in question. With misinformation already common on the Internet, the reader should not be surprised to learn that fraud has followed closely behind, as unscrupulous persons attempt to take advantage of false data for their own financial gain, particularly as e-commerce, online investing, and online auctions continue to proliferate. There have been several cases where people have posted fake messages in order to manipulate stock prices for their own gain.[151]

For Holocaust-deniers, the newsgroup of choice is alt.revisionism, where their messages are also usually challenged and refuted by others. A popular forum for JFK conspiracy theorists is alt.conspiracy.jfk. Another site of interest is soc.history.what-if, but it should be clear from the name that everyone knows that the postings are speculative, discussing alternate history (e.g., "What would have happened if Napoleon won the Battle of Waterloo?"). Information retrieved from USENET newsgroups should be treated as suspect until it can be verified.

Personal Vendettas

As we have seen above, RTMark is one example of an organization specializing in parodies of other websites. However, the Web has also been used to conduct campaigns against specific companies, often providing forums for people to air grievances and complaints against the companies. (The present authors are not making value judgments about the worthiness of such causes, which may or may not be well-meaning.) Perhaps the most famous example is McSpotlight <http://www.mcspotlight.org/>, which brags to be the "biggest, loudest, most red, most read Anti-McDonald's extravaganza the world has ever seen."[152] Other groups register domain names containing the name of the targeted company followed by "sucks," such as AOL Watch <http://www.aolsucks.com/> [Accessed 6 Nov. 2000], which (obviously) is not a fan of America Online. In some cases, the company itself has registered the "-sucks.com" name, to protect its product(s) from being disparaged—for example, Target Corp. owns the rights to targetsucks.com, but (of course) has no intention of ever using the domain name for an actual website.[153]

While the airing of grievances against large, multinational corporations might be accepted (or at least expected), using the Internet to conduct vendettas against specific individuals might not be as well known. In some instances, White supremacists have targeted individuals who have vocally opposed their messages of hate. A recent report by HateWatch detailed several examples of

this, such as e-mail harassment and cyberslander (trying to intimidate someone by making threats or spreading lies about them online), computer hacking, and "webjacking," which involves intervening in the IP name resolution process to automatically redirect users from a website whose address they typed to a different website.[154] Another report explained how a woman who actively opposed Holocaust-deniers on the alt.revisionism USENET newsgroup became the subject of a website that claimed that she "sells her children for sex. Another site listed her home address and the names of her children and neighbors, and used an Internet mapmaker to give directions to her home."[155]

Another frequent target is civil rights attorney Morris Dees, who co-founded the Southern Poverty Law Center (SPLC) in Montgomery, Alabama, in 1971. The SPLC established Klanwatch in 1981 to track KKK activities, publishes *Teaching Tolerance* magazine and a quarterly *Intelligence Report,* and currently monitors more than 500 racist groups. As one might imagine, then, Morris Dees has made many enemies and has himself become a target of those who either oppose his work or his methods. DeesWatch <http://www. deeswatch.com/> [Accessed 13 June 2000], run by Marc Slanger, visually resembles the SPLC's Klanwatch site, which might lead one to believe that its purpose is merely parody. On the contrary, Dees himself is the subject, as the site describes itself as "a clearing house for all anti-Dees information and opinion available" and states that it "looks forward to many more years of being a thorn in the side of this evil demagogue."[156] Many articles critical of both Dees and the SPLC are reproduced, clearly with the intent to damage the reputations of both.

Pseudo-Historical/Scientific Claims

Social scientists are not the only ones subject to controversy over interpretation of past and present events. While the name Immanuel Velikovsky might not have much significance for many people in today's world, and while the controversy he stirred is often a mere footnote in scientific discussions, he created a firestorm beginning in 1946 when excerpts from his forthcoming book appeared in the *New York Herald Tribune,* creating a controversy that would last for decades. To a small group of revisionist researchers who support him–some of whom operate a website devoted to Velikovsky at <http://www.knowledge. co.uk/velikovsky/index.htm> [Accessed 11 Oct. 2000]–he is a modern-day Galileo who was unfairly hounded and persecuted by the mainstream scientific community; to his detractors, he was a quack, a pseudoscientist.

The most intense period of this brouhaha that engulfed the physical scientific community began in 1950 after Velikovsky's *Worlds in Collision* was published.[157] In that book and in several others,[158] Velikovsky, a Russian doctor and practicing psychoanalyst who had been living in the United States

since 1939, argued that the catastrophic events depicted in the Old Testament's Book of Exodus–plagues, floods, volcanic eruption, parting of the sea, all of which contributed to a great disruption in civilization in approximately 1500 B.C.–actually happened and were of a *cosmic* origin. He based much of this on the similarities found in his reading of the literature and myths of ancient Occidental and Oriental peoples, which, to him, indicated that they were witnesses to these cosmic events, since (to him) they were all describing the same events.

Velikovsky's theories have been nicely summarized thusly: "Venus was [a comet] born out of Jupiter, passed close to earth with catastrophic effect several times around 1500 B.C., sent Mars into close encounters with earth in the eighth and seventh centuries B.C., and is now a planet whose characteristics reflect that violent history. The time scale of historical and prehistorical events has to be changed from the conventionally accepted one, particularly for the Mediterranean cultures. The catastrophes caused by Venus were only the latest of a number of similar cosmic events."[159]

This controversial view was challenged as pseudoscience by astronomers, archaeologists, linguistic experts, and historians. Isaac Asimov wrote of Velikovsky, "If anyone reads *Worlds in Collision* and thinks for one moment that there is something to it, he reveals himself to be a scientific illiterate. . . . This is not to say that some of Velikovsky's 'predictions' haven't proved to be so. . . . However, any set of nonsense syllables placed in random order will make words now and then, and if anyone wants to take credit for Velikovsky's lucky hits, they had better try to explain the hundreds of places where he shows himself not only wrong but nonsensical."[160] Many of the responses to Velikovsky's theories were published in the book *Scientists Confront Velikovsky*,[161] including a harsh chapter by Carl Sagan that made him the chief nemesis in the eyes of Velikovsky's supporters. In another publication, Sagan calculated that it would take 30 million years for a comet in the vicinity of Jupiter to impact Earth.[162]

If the Internet provides access to strange and startling ideas, it also offers reasonably easy access to valuable contradictory evidence which would be difficult to find elsewhere. Among the many websites with information refuting the theories of Velikovsky are:

- "Top Ten Reasons Why Velikovsky is Wrong," by Leroy Ellenberger <http://abob.libs.uga.edu/bobk/vdtopten.html> [Accessed 15 Nov. 2000]. Along with his "An Antidote to Velikovskian Delusions" <http://abob.libs.uga.edu/bobk/velidelu.html>[163] [Accessed 15 Nov. 2000], Ellenberger, an astronomer, cites numerous negative quotes from scientists regarding Velikovsky's low comprehension of physics and astronomy. To cite but one example: Where is the physical evidence of debris

either on the ocean floor or in the polar ice caps deposited from Venus' near collision with Earth? In fact, the lack of physical evidence in the geological, archaeological, and paleontological record for Velikovsky and his supporters can be counted as one of their more egregious errors. As another author has pointed out, if the world was covered in darkness for decades as a result of this near collision between Venus and the Earth, how did bristlecone pines, more than four thousand years old, survive?[164]

• "Immanuel Velikovsky's Worlds in Collision" <http://skepdic.com/velikov. html>, from Robert Todd Carroll's online *Skeptic's Dictionary*, also provides a useful summary of the arguments [Accessed 15 Nov. 2000].

Today, Velikovsky's theories are no more tenable to the scientific establishment than they were 50 years ago. While his suggestions for interdisciplinary connections in future studies is considered positive by some critics, Velikovsky's refusal to adhere to the scientific method reduces his argument to no more than interesting science fiction. When the evidence did not fit into Velikovsky's hypothesis, he ignored it. His complete lack of understanding of cuneiform writing became apparent during a confrontation with Egyptologist Abraham Sachs during a conference in1965.[165] There is no question of the sincerity of Velikovsky's supporters, but until that day arrives when reasonable sounding assumptions replace the objective tests laid out by the scientific community, the preponderance of credulity must remain with the scientific method.

BIBLIOGRAPHIC INSTRUCTION ASPECTS

As the World Wide Web continues to expand, and as more and more students begin to rely on it for research for homework and term papers, B.I. librarians have incorporated lessons on "using the Internet" into their Information Literacy classes. The present authors have stressed throughout this paper that misinformation, disinformation, hoaxes, and fabrications freely intermingle on the Web with reliable information, and that students (as well as *all* users of the Internet) must learn how to recognize them. Teaching students how to critically evaluate *all* information should be a paramount objective in any B.I. class, and it is hoped that the websites discussed in this article will be of use to librarians and educators as they demonstrate how misinformation and fabrications can come in various packages, both print and electronic. Just as a library patron might not realize that a book is unreliable or out-of-date,[166] so too might they not realize that the professional and authoritative looking website accessed via the library's Web terminal is unreliable or out-of-date.[167] After all, not every hate site has a swastika on it.

NOTES

1. Norman Oder, "Web Estimated at Seven Million Sites," *Library Journal* 125 (15 Nov. 2000): 16, 18.

2. Carol Caruso, "Before You Cite a Site," *Educational Leadership* 55 (Nov. 1997): 24.

3. Ed Ayres, "Blinded," *World Watch* 13 (Jan./Feb. 2000): 3.

4. Gordon Stein, *Encyclopedia of Hoaxes* (Detroit: Gale Research, 1993): 72-76. Although McGraw-Hill canceled publication of the book in 1972 and both Irving and his wife were convicted and served time in prison, the book was finally published as *The Autobiography of Howard Hughes* (Santa Fe, NM: terrificbooks.com, 1999).

5. Ironically, a recent literary hoax also presented misleading historical information: *The Hand that Signed the Paper* (St. Leonards, N.S.W., Australia: Allen & Unwin, 1994), by Helen Demidenko, purported to be a novel about an Australian student (said to be loosely based on the author's own family) who discovers that her Ukrainian father and uncle were active participants in the Holocaust. The book won several Australian literary awards before it was discovered that Ukrainian "Helen Demidenko" was really Australian Helen Darville. Many writers condemned the book for being anti-Semitic and presenting a skewed version of history (e.g., Darville approvingly presents the view that the Jews "got what they deserved," claiming that the Jews had previously persecuted the Ukrainians and had caused the famine of the 1930s). See Robert Manne, *The Culture of Forgetting: Helen Demidenko and the Holocaust* (Melbourne, Vic., Australia: Text Pub. Co., 1996), and Andrew Riemer, *The Demidenko Debate* (St. Leonards, N.S.W., Australia: Allen & Unwin, 1996).

6. George-Town [D.C.]: Printed for the Author by Green & English, 1800.

7. Ronald W. Howard, "Mason Locke Weems," in *Dictionary of Literary Biography*, Vol. XXX: *American Historians, 1607-1865*, ed. Clyde N. Wilson (Detroit: Gale Research, 1984), 333-340.

8. New York: D. Appleton and Company, 7 vols., 1887-1900.

9. See Margaret Castle Schindler, "Fictitious Biography," *American Historical Review* 42 (1937): 680-690; Allan Nevins, "The Case of the Cheating Documents: False Authority and the Problem of Surmise," in Robin W. Winks (ed.), *The Historian as Detective: Essays on Evidence* (New York: Harper & Row, 1968), 192-212; Steven W. Sowards, "Historical Fabrications in Library Collections," *Collection Management* 10, no. 3/4 (1988): 81-88; and John Blythe Dobson, "The Spurious Articles in Appleton's Cyclopædia of American Biography–Some New Discoveries and Considerations," *Biography* 16 (1993): 388-408.

10. See Dobson's article cited above in note 9.

11. Nevins, 202.

12. Scottsdale, PA: Published for the Greene County Historical Society by The Herald Press, 3 vols., 1945.

13. See Arthur Pierce Middleton and Douglass Adair, "The Mystery of the Horn Papers," *William and Mary Quarterly*, 3rd ser., 4 (1947): 409-445; repr. (as "The Case of the Men Who Weren't There: Problems of Local Pride") in *The Historian as Detective: Essays on Evidence*, 142-177.

14. Stein, *Encyclopedia of Hoaxes*, 262-263.

15. London: Camden Pub. Co., 1836.

16. See Stein, *Encyclopedia of Hoaxes*, 224-226; Ray Allen Billington, "Monk, Maria," in *Notable American Women 1607-1950: A Biographical Dictionary*, Vol. II,

ed. Edward T. James (Cambridge: The Belknap Press of Harvard University Press, 1971), 560-561; and Ira M. Leonard and Robert D. Parmet, *American Nativism, 1830-1860* (New York: Van Nostrand Reinhold, 1971), 57-59, 127-128.

17. Good introductions to Holocaust-denial are: Marc Caplan, *Hitler's Apologists: The Anti-Semitic Propaganda of Holocaust "Revisionism"* (New York: Anti-Defamation League of B'nai B'rith, 1993); Deborah E. Lipstadt, *Denying the Holocaust: The Growing Assault on Truth and Memory* (New York: Free Press, 1993); Michael Shermer and Alex Grobman, *Denying History: Who Says the Holocaust Never Happened and Why Do They Say It?* (Berkeley: University of California Press, 2000); Kenneth S. Stern, *Holocaust Denial* (New York: American Jewish Committee, 1993); and Pierre Vidal-Naquet, *Assassins of Memory: Essays on the Denial of the Holocaust,* trans. Jeffrey Mehlman (New York: Columbia University Press, 1992).

18. Torrance, CA: Institute for Historical Review, 1976.

19. Austin J. App, *The Six Million Swindle: Blackmailing the German People for Hard Marks with Fabricated Corpses* (Takoma Park, MD: Boniface Press, 1974).

20. Paul Rassinier, *Debunking the Genocide Myth* (Torrance, CA: Institute for Historical Review, 1978). Reprinted as *The Holocaust Story and the Lies of Ulysses.*

21. Wilhelm Staglich, *The Auschwitz Myth: A Judge Looks at the Evidence,* trans. Thomas Francis (Torrance, CA: Institute for Historical Review), 1986.

22. Michael A. Hoffman II, *Tales of the Holohoax,* Vol. 1, no. 1 (Temecula, CA: Wiswell/Ruffin House, 1989), art by A. W. Mann.

23. Robert Faurisson, *Mémoire en défense contre ceux qui m'accusent de falsifier l'histoire: La question des chambres a gaz* (Paris: La Vieille Taupe, 1980).

24. For more information on this subject, see: John A. Drobnicki, Carol R. Goldman, Trina R. Knight, and Johanna V. Thomas, "Holocaust-Denial Literature in Public Libraries: An Investigation of Public Librarians' Attitudes Regarding Acquisition and Access," *Public & Access Services Quarterly* 1 (1995): 5-40; Stephen L. Hupp, "Collecting Extremist Political Materials: The Example of Holocaust Denial Publications," *Collection Management* 14, no. 3/4 (1991): 163-173; Suzanne M. Stauffer, "Selected Issues in Holocaust Denial Literature and Reference Work," *The Reference Librarian,* no. 61-62 (1998): 189-193; and Kathleen Nietzke Wolkoff, "The Problem of Holocaust Denial Literature in Libraries," *Library Trends* 45 (1996): 87-96.

25. New York: Schocken Books, 1996; trans. Carol Brown Janeway.

26. Walter Goodman, "Trying to Find What is Real in the Past of an Enigma," *New York Times,* 29 Dec. 1999, p. E5; Catherine Lockerbie, "Holocaust Book Withdrawn as Questions Mount Over its Truth," *The Scotsman,* 12 Nov. 1999, p. 9; "Publisher Drops Holocaust Book," *New York Times,* 3 Nov. 1999, p. E4; Renata Salecl, "Why One Would Pretend to be a Victim of the Holocaust," *Other Voices,* 2 (Feb. 2000), available online at *http://dept.english.upenn.edu/~ov/2.1/salecl/wilkomirski.html* [Accessed 13 Nov. 2000].

27. Lincoln, NE: University of Nebraska Press, 1999; trans. Dick Gerdes.

28. Kenneth Freed, "Holocaust Book Tied Up by Threat of Litigation," *Omaha World-Herald,* 6 Sept. 1998, p. 1A.

29. Gerald Early, "Understanding Afrocentrism: Why Blacks Dream of a World Without Whites," *Civilization: The Magazine of the Library of Congress* 2 (July/Aug. 1995): 32.

30. New York: Philosophical Library, 1954. Later editions have a different subtitle: *Stolen Legacy: Greek Philosophy is Stolen Egyptian Philosophy* (Newport News, VA: United Brothers Communications Systems, 1989).

31. John G. Jackson, *Ethiopia and the Origin of Civilization: A Critical Review of the Evidence of Archaeology, Anthropology, History and Comparative Religion, According to the Most Reliable Sources and Authorities* (New York: Blyden Society, 1939), quoted in Michael Shermer, comp., "Afrocentric Pseudoscience & Pseudohistory," *Skeptic* 2, no. 4 (1994): 71. For a good brief summary of Afrocentric arguments, see Mary R. Lefkowitz, "Ancient History, Modern Myths," in Mary R. Lefkowitz and Guy MacLean Rogers, eds., *Black Athena Revisited* (Chapel Hill: University of North Carolina Press, 1996), 3-23.

32. Martin Bernal, *Black Athena: The Afroasiatic Roots of Classical Civilization*, 2 vols. (New Brunswick, NJ: Rutgers University Press, 1987-1991). Owned by over 1,300 libraries, according to OCLC.

33. Molefi Kete Asante, *Afrocentricity, the Theory of Social Change* (Buffalo, NY: Amulefi Pub. Co., 1980; new rev. ed., Trenton, NJ: Africa World Press, 1988). Owned by over 700 libraries, according to OCLC.

34. Cheikh Anta Diop, *The African Origin of Civilization: Myth or Reality,* trans. Mercer Cook (New York: L. Hill, 1974); owned by over 1,000 libraries, according to OCLC. Cheikh Anta Diop, *Civilization or Barbarism: An Authentic Anthropology,* trans. Yaa-Lengi Meema Ngemi, ed. Harold J. Salemson and Marjolijn de Jager (Brooklyn: Lawrence Hill Books, 1991). Owned by over 700 libraries, according to OCLC.

35. Chancellor Williams, *The Destruction of Black Civilization: Great Issues of a Race from 4500 B.C. to 2000 A.D.* (Dubuque, Iowa: Kendall/Hunt Pub. Co., 1971; 3rd ed., Chicago: Third World Press, 1987). Owned by over 1,000 libraries, according to OCLC.

36. Yosef ben-Jochannan, *Black Man of the Nile: Contributions to European Civilization and Thought* (New York: Alkebu-Lan Books, 1970). The revised and enlarged edition is *Black Man of the Nile and His Family: African Foundations of European Civilization and Thought* (New York: Alkebu-Lan Books, 1972). Owned by approximately 350 libraries, according to OCLC.

37. Among the many works criticizing Afrocentrist writings are Mary Lefkowitz, *Not Out of Africa: How Afrocentrism Became an Excuse to Teach Myth as History* (New York: BasicBooks, 1996); Mary R. Lefkowitz and Guy MacLean Rogers, eds., *Black Athena Revisited* (Chapel Hill: University of North Carolina Press, 1996); John J. Miller, ed., *Alternatives to Afrocentrism* (Washington, DC: Center for the New American Community, Manhattan Institute, 1994); and Stephen Howe, *Afrocentrism: Mythical Pasts and Imagined Homes* (London: Verso, 1998).

38. See Fred Nesta and Henry Blanke, "Warning: Propaganda!" *Library Journal* 116 (15 May 1991): 41-43; and Louise S. Robbins, "Segregating Propaganda in American Libraries: Ralph Ulveling Confronts the Intellectual Freedom Committee," *Library Quarterly* 63 (1993): 143-165.

39. Mark Pendergrast, "In Praise of Labeling; or, When Shalt Thou Break Commandments?" *Library Journal* 113 (1 June 1988): 83-85.

40. American Library Association, Office of Intellectual Freedom, "Statement on Labeling: An Interpretation of the *Library Bill of Rights*" (Adopted July 13, 1951. Amended June 25, 1971; July 1, 1981; June 26, 1990, by the ALA Council). Available online at *http://www.ala.org/alaorg/oif/labeling.html* [Accessed 19 Sept. 2000].

41. Caruso, 25.

42. See American Library Association, Intellectual Freedom Committee, "Statement on Internet Filtering," July 1, 1997. Available online at *http://www.ala.org/*

alaorg/oif/filt_stm.html; and American Library Association, "Resolution on the Use of Filtering Software in Libraries" (Adopted by the ALA Council, July 2, 1997), available online at *http://www.ala.org/alaorg/oif/filt_res.html* [Both accessed 19 Sept. 2000].

43. The American Library Association maintains a page of links to relevant court decisions on filtering on their website at *http://www.ala.org/alaorg/oif/courtcases.html* [Accessed 19 Sept. 2000].

44. Center for Media Education, *Youth Access to Alcohol and Tobacco Web Marketing: The Filtering and Rating Debate* (Washington, DC: Center for Media Education, 1999), 11, available online at *http://www.cme.org/publications/scrnfltr/report_1104. pdf* [Accessed 11 Nov. 2000].

45. "Filters Falter," *Pressure Point: Newsletter of the Intellectual Freedom Round Table of the New York Library Association* 16 (Fall 2000): 10.

46. "Filter Contest Winners Named," *Library Journal* 125 (1 Nov. 2000): 20.

47. For a good overview, see Teri Greene, "Don't Believe Those Wild Net Rumors," *USA Today,* 7 Aug. 2000; available online at *http://www.usatoday.com/life/ cyber/tech/cti354.htm* [Accessed 13 Sept. 2000].

48. For example, see *http://www.vmyths.com*, *http://www.urbanlegends.com*, and *http://HoaxBusters.ciac.org* [All accessed 18 Aug. 2000].

49. Luciano Floridi, "Brave.Net.World: The Internet as a Disinformation Superhighway?" *Electronic Library* 14 (1996): 509-514.

50. Mary Ann Fitzgerald, "Misinformation on the Internet: Applying Evaluation Skills to Online Information," *Emergency Librarian* 24 (Jan.-Feb. 1997): 9-14.

51. Philip J. Calvert, "Web-Based Misinformation in the Context of Higher Education," *Asian Libraries* 8 (1999): 61-69.

52. Ann Scholz-Crane, "Evaluating the Future: A Preliminary Study of the Process of How Undergraduate Students Evaluate Web Sources," *Reference Services Review* 26 (Fall/Winter 1998): 53-60.

53. Tschera Harkness Connell and Jennifer E. Tipple, "Testing the Accuracy of Information on the World Wide Web Using the AltaVista Search Engine," *Reference & User Services Quarterly* 38 (1999): 360-368.

54. LaJean Humphries, "Teaching Users to Evaluate Internet Sites: Sources on Sources," *Searcher* 8 (May 2000): 69.

55. Ibid.

56. Much of what follows is based on excellent suggestions in Alison Cooke, *Neal-Schuman Authoritative Guide to Evaluating Information on the Internet* (New York: Neal-Schuman, 1999); Mary Ann Fitzgerald, "Misinformation on the Internet: Applying Evaluation Skills to Online Information," *Emergency Librarian* 24 (Jan.-Feb. 1997): 9-14; Donald T. Hawkins, "What is Credible Information?" *Online* 23 (Sept./Oct. 1999): 86-89, available online at *http://www.onlineinc.com/onlinemag/OL1999/technomonitor9.html* [Accessed 17 Oct. 2000]; and Genie Tyburski, "Honest Mistakes, Deceptive Facts: Judging Information on the World Wide Web," *Legal Assistant Today* (Mar./Apr. 2000): 54-60.

57. Hawkins, 89.

58. For an interesting study of Internet dynamics and political control in a quasi-authoritarian society, see Garry Rodan, "The Internet and Political Control in Singapore," *Political Science Quarterly* 113 (Spring 1998): 63-89.

59. See Carol J. Williams, "Cyber-Hate Panelists Duel Over Line Between Free Speech, Racism: Germany," *Los Angeles Times,* 27 June 2000, p. 8; and Mylene

Mangalindan and Kevin Delaney, "Yahoo! Ordered to Bar the French From Nazi Items," *Wall Street Journal*, 21 Nov. 2000, p. B1.

60. *Public-Access Computer Systems Review* 8, no. 3 (1997), available online at *http://info.lib.uh.edu/pr/v8/n3/smit8n3.html* [Accessed 4 Sept. 2000].

61. Janet E. Alexander and Marsha Ann Tate, *Web Wisdom: How to Evaluate and Create Information Quality on the Web* (Mahwah, NJ: Lawrence Erlbaum Associates, 1999).

62. "About the Virtual Library," available online at *http://vlib.org/AboutVL.html* [Accessed 17 Aug. 2000].

63. Paul S. Piper, "Better Read That Again: Web Hoaxes and Misinformation," *Searcher* 8 (Sept. 2000): 40-49; available online at *http://www.infotoday.com/searcher/sep00/piper.htm* [Accessed 5 Sept. 2000].

64. Irwin Suall and David Lowe, *The 1989 IHR Conference: White-Washing Genocide "Scientifically"* (New York: ADL, n.d.), 1; Alison B. Carb and Alan M. Schwartz, *Holocaust "Revisionism": A Denial of History–An Update* (New York: ADL, 1986), 13-14.

65. See Alan M. Schwartz (ed.), *Embattled Bigots: A Split in the Ranks of the Holocaust Denial Movement* (New York: ADL, 1994).

66. Shermer and Grobman, 79.

67. "Willis A. Carto: Fabricating History," available online at *http://www.adl.org/holocaust/carto.html* [Accessed 12 June 2000].

68. "Institute for Historical Review: Outlet for Denial Propaganda," available online at *http://www.adl.org/holocaust/ihr.html* [Accessed 12 June 2000].

69. "Liberty Lobby, Inc., v. Dow Jones & Company, Inc. et al." 838 F.2d 1287 (1988).

70. "Ingrid Rimland: Co-webmaster of the Zundelsite," available online from HateWatch at *http://hatewatch.org/who/rimland.html* [Accessed 12 June 2000].

71. "Ernst Zundel, Co-webmaster of The Zundelsite," available online from Hate-Watch at *http://hatewatch.org/who/zundel.html* [Accessed 12 June 2000].

72. Lipstadt, 159-160; Stern, 46-47; Judith Bolton, *Holocaust "Revisionism": Reinventing the Big Lie* (New York: ADL, 1989).

73. Frank Miele, "Giving the Devil His Due: Holocaust Revisionism as a Test Case for Free Speech and the Skeptical Ethic," *Skeptic* 2, no. 4 (1994): 58-70; available online at *http://www.skeptic.com/02.4.miele-holocaust.html* [Accessed 22 July 2000].

74. Prideaux, 36, available online at *http://www.nizkor.org/hweb/people/p/prideaux-gary/zundelsite-analysis-summary.html* [Accessed 22 June 2000].

75. Roger Smith, "Denials of the Armenian Genocide," in Israel W. Charny, ed., *Encyclopedia of Genocide*, Vol. I (Santa Barbara: ABC-CLIO, 1999), 162.

76. Roger W. Smith, Erik Markusen, and Robert Jay Lifton, "Professional Ethics and the Denial of Armenian Genocide," *Holocaust and Genocide Studies* 9 (Spring 1995): 2-3; available online at *http://www.diaspora-net.org/ucla/Holocaust_Studies_Lowry.html* [Accessed 22 Nov. 2000].

77. Peter Balakian, "Combatting Denials of the Armenian Genocide in Academia," in *Encyclopedia of Genocide*, Vol. I, 163.

78. For facsimiles of the memoranda, see the article by Smith et al. cited above in note 76, pp. 1-22.

79. Andrew Gumbel, "Briton Sued for Genocide Denial," *Guardian*, 8 Mar. 1994, p. 13; Patrick Marnham, "Sued Over a History Lesson," *Evening Standard*, 23 May

1995, p. 28; "Professor Bernard Lewis Found Guilty of Denial of Armenian Genocide," in *Encyclopedia of Genocide*, Vol. I, 177.

80. Richard G. Hovannisian, ed., *The Armenian Genocide in Perspective* (New Brunswick, NJ: Transaction Books, 1986).

81. Donald E. Miller and Lorna Touryan Miller, *Survivors: An Oral History of the Armenian Genocide* (Berkeley: University of California Press, 1993).

82. Vahakn N. Dadrian, *The History of the Armenian Genocide: Ethnic Conflict from the Balkans to Anatolia to the Caucasus* (Providence, RI: Berghahn Books, 1995); see also Vahakn N. Dadrian, *Warrant for Genocide: Key Elements of Turko-Armenian Conflict* (New Brunswick, NJ: Transaction Publishers, 1998), and Vahakn N. Dadrian, *The Key Elements in the Turkish Denial of the Armenian Genocide: A Case Study of Distortion and Falsification* (Toronto: Zoryan Institute, 1999).

83. Ara Sarafian, comp., *United States Official Documents on the Armenian Genocide*, 3 vols. (Watertown, MA: Armenian Review, 1993-1995).

84. Robert F. Melson, "The Armenian Genocide as Precursor and Prototype of Twentieth-Century Genocide," in Alan S. Rosenbaum, ed., *Is the Holocaust Unique? Perspectives on Comparative Genocide* (Boulder: Westview Press, 1996), 89-90.

85. See *http://www.northstarcompass.org/* and *http://www.northstarcompass.org/nsc9912/indx9912.htm* [Accessed 18 Aug. 2000].

86. See *http://www.plp.org/pl_magazine/pl_index.html* [Accessed 13 Nov. 2000].

87. United States, Commission on the Ukraine Famine, *Investigation of the Ukrainian Famine 1932-1933: Report to Congress* (Washington, DC: Government Printing Office, 1988). See also James E. Mace and Leonid Heretz, eds., *Investigation of the Ukrainian Famine, 1932-1933: Oral History Project of the Commission on the Ukraine Famine* (Washington, DC: GPO, 3 vols., 1990).

88. Douglas Tottle, *Fraud, Famine and Fascism: The Ukrainian Genocide Myth from Hitler to Harvard* (Toronto: Progress Books, 1987). A search of OCLC's Worldcat shows that Progress Books is a publisher of many Communist- and Socialist-oriented materials.

89. See Robert Conquest, *The Harvest of Sorrow: Soviet Collectivization and the Terror-Famine* (New York: Oxford University Press, 1986); see also his letter to the editor, *Slavic Review* 51 (Spring 1992): 192-193.

90. Robert Conquest, Letter to the Editor, *Slavic Review* 53 (Spring 1994): 318.

91. Mark B. Tauger, "The 1932 Harvest and the Famine of 1933," *Slavic Review* 50 (Spring 1991): 70-89; see also Tauger's replies to two letters to the editor by Robert Conquest, in *Slavic Review* 51 (Spring 1992): 193-194, and *Slavic Review* 53 (Spring 1994): 319.

92. R. W. Davies, M. B. Tauger, and S. G. Wheatcroft, "Stalin, Grain Stocks and the Famine of 1932-1933," *Slavic Review* 54 (Fall 1995): 642-657.

93. Barbara B. Green, "Stalinist Terror and the Question of Genocide: The Great Famine," in *Is the Holocaust Unique?*, 137-161.

94. Toronto, Ont.: The Institute, 1984.

95. Joji Sakurai, "Revisionist Japanese Academics Contest Best Seller 'Rape of Nanking,'" Associated Press wire article, 12 June 1998.

96. Masato Kishimoto, "Japanese Envoy Denounces Book on Nanking Massacre," *Mainichi Daily News*, 23 Apr. 1998.

97. Akira Suzuki, *Nankin daigyakusatsu no maboroshi* (Tokyo: Bungei Shunju, 1973), revised ed. published as *Shin "Nankin daigyakusatsu" no maboroshi* (Tokyo:

Asuka Shinsha, 1999); see also Michael Hoffman, "Wartime History in the Pen of the Author," *Mainichi Daily News*, 15 July 1999.

98. See *http://www.jiyuu-shikan.org/e/about.html* [Accessed 7 Sept. 2000].

99. See *http://members.tripod.com/~funkytomoya/massacre/conclusion.htm* [Accessed 7 Sept. 2000].

100. James Yin and Shi Young, *The Rape of Nanking: An Undeniable History in Photographs*, 2nd ed. (Chicago: Innovative Publishing Group, 1997).

101. Erwin Wickert, ed., *The Good German of Nanking: The Diaries of John Rabe*, trans. John E. Woods (London: Little, Brown and Company, 1998).

102. Peter Li, "The Nanking Holocaust: Tragedy, Trauma and Reconciliation," *Society* 37 (Jan./Feb. 2000): 57.

103. Jeff Kingston, "Yes, There Was a Nanjing Massacre," *Japan Times*, 18 Aug. 1999.

104. Sonni Efron, "War Again is Raging Over Japan's Role in 'Nanking,'" *Los Angeles Times*, 6 June 1999, p. A32.

105. Available on videocassette as *Magee's Testament*, directed by Peter Wang (Flushing, NY: Alliance in Memory of Victims of the Nanjing Massacre, 1995), and as part of *In the Name of the Emperor*, directed by Nancy Tong (New York: Filmmakers Library, Inc., 1996).

106. See the opening page at *http://www.blacksandjews.com/* [Accessed 9 Sept. 2000].

107. Historical Research Department of the Nation of Islam, *The Secret Relationship Between Blacks and Jews* (Chicago: Latimer Associates, 1991).

108. See the section on "Jews and Slavery in the Old South" at *http://www.blacksandjews.com/Jews_and_Slavery.html* [Accessed 9 Sept. 2000].

109. Although there is debate among scholars over the size of the slave trade to the Americas, there is no dispute that it reached its peak in the eighteenth century, when Jewish participation was minimal. See Philip D. Curtin, *The Atlantic Slave Trade: A Census* (Madison: University of Wisconsin Press, 1969), 5 (Table 1) for the numbers of slaves per century shipped to the Americas; for participation of Jews in the Atlantic slave trade see "Historical Facts vs. Antisemitic Fictions: The Truth About Jews, Blacks, Slavery, Racism, and Civil Rights," available online at *http://www.wiesenthal.org/resource/slavery.htm* [Accessed 13 Sept. 2000].

110. See Korn's quote at *http://www.blacksandjews.com/ Quotes_and_Facts.html#anchor22425* [Accessed 9 Sept. 2000]. A more revealing quote from Korn is in Harold Brackman's article, "The Not So Secret Relationship Between Jews and the Slave Trade: The Polemical Dimension" (available online at *http://www.wiesenthal.org/resource/confer.htm*): "none of the major slavetraders was Jewish" [Accessed 13 Sept. 2000].

111. See "Jews and the Black Holocaust" (under paragraph heading "Jewish Racism"), available online at *http://www.blacksandjews.com/Jews_and_Slavery.html* [Accessed 9 Sept. 2000].

112. Ibid.

113. Richard Cohen, "Farrakhan 101 at Wellesley," *Washington Post*, 11 Feb. 1994, p. A25.

114. David Streitfeld, "Experts Say Few Jews Held Slaves: Claims of Larger Role Labeled Antisemitic," *Washington Post*, 15 Feb 1995, p. D1.

115. David Brion Davis, "The Slave Trade and the Jews," *New York Review of Books*, 22 Dec. 1994, pp. 14-16.

116. Seymour Drescher, "The Role of Jews in the Transatlantic Slave Trade," *Immigrants and Minorities* 12 (July 1993): 113-125.

117. See *http://www.wiesenthal.org/resource/index.html* for several online articles [Accessed 13 Sept. 2000].

118. Marc Caplan, *Jew-Hatred as History: An Analysis of the Nation of Islam's "The Secret Relationship Between Blacks and Jews"* (New York: ADL, 1994), available online at *http://www.adl.org/frames/front_jew_hatred.html* [Accessed 15 Sept. 2000].

119. Harold Brackman, *Ministry of Lies: The Truth Behind the Nation of Islam's "The Secret Relationship Between Blacks and Jews"* (New York: Four Walls Eight Windows, 1994).

120. Saul S. Friedman, *Jews and the American Slave Trade* (New Brunswick, NJ: Transaction Publishers, 1998).

121. See *http://www.swagga.com/libation.htm* [Accessed 10 Oct. 2000]. According to WHOIS, the site is registered to Everton Elliott.

122. "Great African Kings," available at *http://www.swagga.com/king.htm*, and "Great African Queens," available at *http://www.swagga.com/queen.htm* [Both accessed 10 Oct. 2000].

123. "Ancient Black Inventors," available at *http://www.swagga.com/ancient_inventors.htm* [Accessed 10 Oct. 2000].

124. Joseph Nathan Kane, Steven Anzovin, and Janet Podell, *Famous First Facts* (New York: H. W. Wilson, 1997).

125. Ibid., 296 (entry no. 4402).

126. C. R. Gibbs, *Black Inventors From Africa to America: Two Million Years of Invention and Innovation* (Silver Spring, MD: Three Dimensional Pub., 1995).

127. Ibid., 178.

128. *Famous First Facts*, 607 (entry no. 7916).

129. Ibid., 97 (entry no. 2103).

130. Ibid., 292 (entry no. 4345).

131. Frank M. Snowden, Jr., "Bernal's 'Blacks' and the Afrocentrists," in Mary R. Lefkowitz and Guy MacLean Rogers, eds., *Black Athena Revisited* (Chapel Hill: University of North Carolina Press, 1996), 112-128.

132. Frank J. Yurco, "Were the Ancient Egyptians 'Black' or 'White'?" *Biblical Archaeology Review* 15 (Sept.-Oct. 1989): 25-29, 58.

133. "King Family Statement on the Justice Department 'Limited Investigation' on the MLK Assassination," June 9, 2000, available online at *http://www.thekingcenter.com/06-09-2000.htm* [Accessed 24 Sept. 2000].

134. Jim Douglass, "The Martin Luther King Conspiracy Exposed in Memphis," *Probe* 7 (May-June 2000), available online at *http://www.webcom.com/~ctka/pr500-king.html* [Accessed 24 Sept. 2000].

135. See *http://www.parascope.com/mx/luther1.htm* [Accessed 1 Oct. 2000].

136. Gerald Posner, *Killing the Dream* (New York: Random House, 1998; repr. San Diego: Harcourt, Brace, & Co., 1998), 19-20, footnote 3 (page reference is to reprint edition).

137. Ibid., 24-25, unnumbered footnote.

138. "Justice Department: King Assassination Was Not a Conspiracy. Report Follows 18-Month Investigation," available online at *http://www.cnn.com/2000/US/06/09/king.investigation.01/* [Accessed 1 Oct. 2000].

139. Frances Katz, "Bogus Newspaper Web Sites Linked to Supremacist Page," *Atlanta Journal and Constitution*, 10 Oct. 1998, p. 2E.

140. Yigal Schleifer, "Taming the Wild Web," *Jerusalem Report*, 31 Jan. 2000, p. 36; Mark Ward, "Anti-Fascists Buy Internet 'Hate' Names," *Daily Telegraph*, 20 Dec. 1999, p. 7.

141. See *http://arbiter.wipo.int/domains/* [Accessed 30 Nov. 2000].

142. "WIPO Rules Against Cyber-Squatting," available online at *http://cipherwar.com/news/00/madonna_dot_com.htm* [Accessed 30 Nov. 2000].

143. Piper, 43.

144. See *http://rtmark.com/faq.html* [Accessed 6 Oct. 2000].

145. Alissa Quart, "Cultural Sabotage Waged in Cyberspace," *New York Times*, 17 Aug. 2000, p. 10.

146. Gatt.org press release, 1 Dec. 1999, available online at *http://www.gatt.org/gattpr.html* [Accessed 7 Oct. 2000].

147. For the status and summary of this legislation, see *http://thomas.loc.gov/cgi-bin/bdquery/z?d106:h.r.03028:* and *http://thomas.loc.gov/cgi-bin/bdquery/z?d106:S.1255:* [Both accessed 4 Dec. 2000]. Also, consult the Electronic Frontier Foundation's "Cybersquatting and Internet Address & Domain Name Disputes" Archive at *http://www.eff.org/pub/Spam_cybersquatting_abuse/Cybersquatting/* [Accessed 4 Dec. 2000].

148. Lee Hubbard, "Dissing the King," *Salon*, 24 Jan. 2000; available online at *http://www.salon.com/news/feature/2000/01/24/mlk/index.html* [Accessed 2 Nov. 2000].

149. Associated Press, "Boston U. Panel Finds Plagiarism by Dr. King," *New York Times*, 11 Oct. 1991, p. A15.

150. Hubbard.

151. See, for example, Ralph T. King, Jr. and Andrew Fraser, "Hackers Post Phony Merger, Duping Traders," *Wall Street Journal*, 18 Feb. 2000, p. C1; and Josh Meyer, "Investor Indicted in Emulex Stock Market Hoax," *Los Angeles Times*, 29 Sept. 2000, p. 1. For more discussions of various types of financial- and investor-related fraud on the Web, see Carol Ebbinghouse's various columns in *Searcher* (part of the "Dangerous Data Ahead" series): "Deliberate Misinformation on the Internet!? Tell Me It Ain't So!" *Searcher* 8 (May 2000): 63-67; "Avoiding Charity Fraud and Misinformation from Non-Profits on the Internet," *Searcher* 8 (July/Aug. 2000): 58-66; "Medical and Legal Misinformation on the Internet," *Searcher* 8 (Oct. 2000): 18-35.

152. See *http://www.mcspotlight.org/help.html* [Accessed 30 Sept. 2000].

153. Jim McCartney, "Firms Buy Disparaging Addresses for Protection," *Houston Chronicle*, 17 Sept. 2000, p. 4.

154. "Hacking and Hate: Virtual Attacks with Real Consequences," 14 Aug. 2000; available online at *http://www.hatewatch.org/reports/hackingandhate.html* [Accessed 8 Dec. 2000].

155. Donna Ladd, "Living in Terror: Targets of Racist Web Sites Find Nowhere to Hide," *Village Voice*, 17-23 May 2000, available online at *http://www.villagevoice.com/issues/0020/ladd.shtml* [Accessed 30 Nov. 2000].

156. See *http://www.deeswatch.com/compound.html* [Accessed 13 June 2000].

157. Immanuel Velikovsky, *Worlds in Collision* (New York: Macmillan, 1950). After protests and threats of a boycott from some in the scientific community, Macmillan withdrew the book and it was published by its (then-) subsidiary, Doubleday.

158. See also his *Ages in Chaos*, 5 vols. (Garden City, NY: Doubleday, 1952-1977)–Vol. I: *From the Exodus to King Akhnaton*; Vol. II: *The Dark Age of Greece*; Vol. III: *The Assyrian Conquest*; Vol. IV: *Ramses II and His Time*; Vol. V: *Peoples of the Sea*; and his *Earth in Upheaval* (Garden City, NY: Doubleday, 1955).

159. Henry H. Bauer, *Beyond Velikovsky: The History of a Public Controversy* (Urbana: University of Illinois Press, 1984), 67.

160. Isaac Asimov, "Worlds in Confusion," *Magazine of Fantasy and Science Fiction* (Oct. 1969), quoted in Bauer, 51.

161. Ithaca, NY: Cornell University Press, 1977.

162. Carl Sagan, *Boca's Brain* (New York: Random House, 1979), 99.

163. First published in *Skeptic*, Vol. 3, no. 4 (1995): 49-51.

164. Sean Mewhinney, "Tree Rings," available online at *http://www.pibburns.com/smtrerng.htm* [Accessed 15 Nov. 2000].

165. The text of Sachs' 1965 speech, along with information regarding Velikovsky's response, is available online at *http://abob.libs.uga.edu/bobk/vsachs.html* [Accessed 15 Nov. 2000].

166. Marvin Scilken, publisher of *The U*N*A*B*A*S*H*E*D Librarian,* used to distribute stickers which he advocated placing on old reference books that stated (in capital letters), "Caution: Information in this book may be out of date. *Ask a Librarian.*" Copy of sticker in possession of John A. Drobnicki.

167. A recent random telephone survey of 3,097 adults conducted by the Urban Libraries Council found that 75.2% of Internet users also used the library, and that 60.3% of library users also used the Internet. For those respondents who reported using both the library and the Internet, libraries received higher ratings for (among other characteristics) *accuracy of information*: In response to the statement "I trust information to be accurate"–on a scale of 1 (very strongly disagree) to 10 (very strongly agree)–library use received a mean score of 8.5, while Internet use received a mean score of 7.3. The entire report (*The Impacts of the Internet on Public Library Use*) is available online at *http://www.urbanlibraries.org/pdfs/finalulc.pdf*, and a brief summary fact sheet is at *http://www.urbanlibraries.org/Internet%20Study%20Fact%20Sheet.html* [Accessed 14 Dec. 2000].

Government Information on the Web

Robert Machalow

SUMMARY. Government information is abundant on the World Wide Web, but finding that information is often difficult. The usual routine of utilizing search engines or directories does not work well, unless an individual is interested in a specific government agency. Instead, the savvy librarian will be well advised to check the prominent journals and newspapers for announcements of new sites and utilize the homepage of the Library of Congress. With some education and experience, a user can quickly find information using the Library of Congress' homepage, the Librarian's Index to the Internet, and Beaucoup. *[Article copies available for a fee from The Haworth Document Delivery Service: 1-800-342-9678. E-mail address: <getinfo@haworthpressinc.com> Website: <http://www.HaworthPress.com> © 2001 by The Haworth Press, Inc. All rights reserved.]*

KEYWORDS. Government information, World Wide Web, Internet, Library of Congress, search engines, Web sites, Beaucoup

INTRODUCTION

The World Wide Web is a vast resource filled with information. Unfortunately, the information found one day may or may not be readily available an-

Robert Machalow is Chief Librarian, York College Library, York College, The City University of New York, 94-20 Guy Brewer Boulevard, Jamaica, NY 11451 (E-mail: machalow@york.cuny.edu).

[Haworth co-indexing entry note]: "Government Information on the Web." Machalow, Robert. Co-published simultaneously in *The Reference Librarian* (The Haworth Information Press, an imprint of The Haworth Press, Inc.) No. 74, 2001, pp. 165-175; and: *Evolution in Reference and Information Services: The Impact of the Internet* (ed: Di Su) The Haworth Information Press, an imprint of The Haworth Press, Inc., 2001, pp. 165-175. Single or multiple copies of this article are available for a fee from The Haworth Document Delivery Service [1-800-342-9678, 9:00 a.m. - 5:00 p.m. (EST). E-mail address: getinfo@haworthpressinc.com].

other day. In addition, anyone can post information on the Web, and there is presently no authority to verify or referee the information posted. Web addresses that contain a .com can usually be considered commercially related, and thus a person might want to weigh sales and marketing aspects into considering information on sites like that. A .edu site is education-related, but one must consider that the site might be hosted by an educational institution, but the institution is not responsible for what the faculty, staff and/or students post on these Web pages. Organizations have a .org in their addresses, but once again, the basis of the organization should be taken into account when looking at the research value of the information posted on one of these pages.

One of the other Web address clues is .gov, which means that the site is government-related in some way. Governmental agency sites can be viewed with cautions of their own, but the information on a government-related Web site might be more trusted, more "factual," than the information posted elsewhere on the Web.

It should be noted that though the Web pages referred to here are all government pages, there is no consistency in their design. A user will have to study each agency's page to find any documents or links that are in it.

As of the writing of this article, three innovative Federal government Web sites had been recently announced:

a. On June 24, 2000, President Clinton addressed the United States and stated that there were more than 20,000 Federal Web pages. At this conference, the President announced the creation of a Federal Web site that will allow individuals to search *all* online resources offered by the Federal government from a single Web site. This Web site, which was unveiled in the Fall of 2000, is *firstgov.gov*. The site will also offer one stop access to billion of dollars in grants and procurement opportunities. The site offers individuals the opportunity to compete for a $50,000 prize for the next innovative idea to advance e-government. A user can get to this site, incidentally, using the above Web address (*firstgov.gov*) or either *www.firstgov.com* or *www.firstgov.org*. On this page are links to the branches of the Federal government, as well as links to local government Web pages.

b. During the summer of 2000, the Federal government announced the development of a site to be available in October of 2000: *www.pay.gov*. This site permits individuals to conduct electronic transactions with the Federal government. This site enables users to make payments to the government, including taxes, fees, and licenses using credit cards or electronic transfers.

c. At *students.gov*, the student gateway to the U.S. government, a user can find a great deal of information as well as links to a wealth of U.S. government sites.

In this article, I will look at various government-related Web sites that are currently available. As with all Web addresses, they are current at the time of the writing of this article. The addresses and/or contents of any of the sites may change at any time. As with all Web resources, they may be discontinued or modified significantly before or after this article goes to press.

LIBRARY OF CONGRESS

Librarians often like to begin their search for information in a Library. The most useful Library to begin searching for information on World Wide Web resources related to the government is the Library of Congress. The Web address for the Library of Congress is *www.loc.gov*. From this Web site a user can find links to countless government-related Web sites. Unfortunately, finding these links is not intuitively obvious.

The Library of Congress homepage has various links, including "Using the Library" which includes links to the catalog, "American Memory," which includes links to various textual, oral and video memories of the United States, and "Thomas, Congress at Work." It is within Thomas that one can find various Web links, including Legislative (bill summary and status, bill text, major legislation, public laws by number, and roll call votes), Congressional Record (including the text and index to the Congressional Record), and Committee Information (including committee reports, and House and Senate Committee homepages). If a person looks closely, there are also links to the Executive, Legislative, and Judicial branches under "Library of Congress Web Links."

From these Web links a user can find information on the committees of the three branches of the Federal government.

FEDERAL GOVERNMENT WEB SITES OF THE EXECUTIVE BRANCH

Most Federal Executive government agencies have their own Web sites. Links to many of these Federal government department and agency Web sites can be found at lcweb (*loc.gov/global/executive/fed.html*). There is a list of sites related to the Office of the President, Executive Agencies, and Independent Agencies. Also included are links to Boards, Commissions, and Committees as well as to Quasi-Official Agencies.

The White House (*www.whitehouse.gov*) is one site that can be visited. From the point of view of an interested individual, a user might want to obtain a White House tour or historical information. In addition, there is currently a children's section of the site which helps youngsters become more active and

informed. From a reference point of view, there is a virtual Library that includes an extensive archive of White House documents.

There are links to other agencies of the Executive branch of the government, but they are not obvious. At the present time, you can click on the "Interactive Citizens' Handbook" section, which will lead you to the chance to browse wherein you will be able to find White House offices and agencies, etc. In addition, you will be able to find links to the President's Cabinet here. On this page are links to departments including the Department of Commerce, Department of Defense, and the Department of Education. Also on this page are links to the Legislative and Judicial branches.

Each department and agency has created its own Web site, and as such, information from each is accessed in a different manner. For example, there are three links listed under the Department of Education in the Library of Congress links page, but when you access the Department of Education directly, there are many other links. To find the three links listed on the Library of Congress links page within the Department of Education page is a trial. One way is to use the "search" feature on the top of the page and put in the specific agency name indicated. Or, you can use the "Topics A-Z" feature to look for the particular agency. In either case, the process is time consuming and not at all intuitively obvious.

The Department of Health and Human Services homepage is a bit easier to navigate. On its homepage, there is a choice to click on HHS Agencies, and this link will lead you to a list of agencies of this Department. The agencies listed on the Library of Congress page are listed here, but not all of them have the exact same names in both places. Within this site, though, are several additional agencies that are not listed on the Library of Congress page.

There are also several non-agency links (Executive Offices of the President) on the Library of Congress' page. These change on occasion. When this article was first drafted, there was a link to the Council of Economic Advisors. At that time, this page had very little information, other than the Council's staff and the Economic Report of the President. There were not any direct links to economic information, though a user might have expected to find these on this page. This link was removed before this article's final draft.

FEDERAL GOVERNMENT WEB SITES OF THE LEGISLATIVE BRANCH

Links to Federal legislative branch Web sites can be found at lcweb (*loc.gov/global/legislative*). Included are links to members of Congress, committees of Congress and a history of Congress. Also included are links to legislation (including a summary of the status and text of bills, public laws by

number, and roll call votes on various bills). The text and index of the Congressional Record are linked here as well.

The Library of Congress page of links to Web sites of the Federal Legislative branch can be searched in two main ways: A user can search, using either a keyword or phrase, or the user can browse Legislative branch pages.

When the user browses the Legislative branch pages, a link that could be useful is "About the U.S. Congress." Following this link, a user can find a description of the differences between the two houses of Congress. It should be noted that some of the links on this page are to non-governmental Web pages.

On this page is also a link to Congressional Internet Services. This page includes links to the House of Representatives and the Senate. Legislative Branch Support Agencies (including the Library of Congress, the Government Printing Office, and the General Accounting Office), Miscellaneous Congressional Services (including the Medicare Payment Advisory Commission) and links to government publications of interest to legislative researchers (such as the Congressional Directory, Federal Register and Code of Federal Regulations) are linked from this page.

Links to the members of Congress are available. After several links, a user is able to find out about particular legislators, and even send e-mail to the particular legislators.

There are links to several committees of Congress. The House Committee information page includes links to House committee membership, Congressional committees and subcommittees, House committee schedules and recent actions, House committee hearings, and House committee reports. Links to House committee votes, rules, and Web pages are included.

FEDERAL GOVERNMENT WEB SITES OF THE JUDICIAL BRANCH

Links to Federal Judicial Web sites can be found at lcweb (*loc.gov/global/ judiciary.html*). Sections on the constitution, statutes, regulations, judicial opinions, and court rules can be found here. Included here are also a few links to law journal Internet sites that may provide indexing, abstracting and/or full text. Furthermore, there are several links to law-related Internet sites.

There are several links to Constitution-related sites available. Some of these are to sites maintained by the United States government, while others are not. For example, one link utilizes GPO Access, while another relies on an educational institution. Each of these has an advantage: The GPO-user can search, download, and browse; the one using the educational institution has a more developed search engine and has links to Supreme Court opinions. Other useful links to information related to the Constitution are included via a link to the General Services Administration.

A user can gain access to searching the U.S. Code in several ways. One is using the GPO Access, while another is using a link to an educational institution. The GPO Access version notes any amending of the law. There is a link in this section to hints for searching the U.S. Code. These hints are on a page maintained by an educational institution.

It is also possible to browse the U.S. Code. The browsing can be done by title via either GPO Access or an educational institution.

Updates to public laws are available on the Web. GPO Gate allows access by the number of the Congress (104th, 105th, or 106th at the present time). In addition, an index to public laws is available, as are tables of the popular names of laws and classification tables of laws. Also available are links to State Statutes.

Federal regulations are available on the Web. The Federal Register is updated daily. There is a cumulated daily table of contents and a cumulative index. Also included are hints for searching the Federal Register. These hints are provided in a link to an educational institution. The Code of Federal Regulations can also be found on the Web. The Code can be browsed or searched.

Judicial opinions are linked from the Judicial Web page. The judicial opinions include Federal Court opinions, Supreme Court of the United States opinions (both current and historic are available), Circuit Court of Appeals opinions, and State Court opinions. Rules of some of the courts can also be accessed. These include Federal Rules of Civil Procedures, Federal Rules of Evidence, and Rules of the Supreme Court.

Also included on the Federal Judicial Web page are links to some, but not all, Executive branch materials, and links to various law journals. These links are to various educational institutions, and the law journals that are available at those particular institutions. There are also links to law-related Internet sites on the Federal Judicial Web page.

MISCELLANEOUS FEDERAL WEB SITES

The Federal government has a great number of Web sites, some of which are more useful than others. For example, there are links from the Library of Congress page to the GPO (Government Printing Office). The Government Printing Office gives the user access to various Federal government publications (Congressional publications, as well as House and Senate publications). In addition, the user has access to the Government Information Locator Service. The Government Information Locator Service is an effort to identify, locate, and describe Federal government information that is publicly available. This includes electronic information resources. On this site, a user can search for information by keywords. Furthermore, on the Government Printing Office

homepage, there are links to databases such as the Federal Register, the Congressional Record, the Code of Federal Regulations, and the U.S. Code.

Other Federal government Web pages are probably not as useful. For example, The Official U.S. Time page at *www.time.gov* allows the user to find the exact time anywhere in the country. On this page there are various links to non-government Web sites devoted to time.

In addition to all the other sites that are linked on the Library of Congress' Thomas site, there is a link to Historical Documents. Using this link, a user can search early Congressional documents (including the Declaration of Independence, the Constitution, and the Federalist papers) by keyword or phrase. In addition, the user can browse individual documents and collections. Furthermore, the user can follow links to find out about the documents that are linked here. There is also a link to Congressional Documents and Debates, through which the user can find electronically reproduced documents from 1774-1873.

STATE GOVERNMENT WEB SITES

On the Library of Congress homepage, there is a link to State and Local governments. When this link is followed, there are links to State and Local government information. This includes links to the following:

  a. State Statutes (not hosted by a government agency; on this site, full-text State Statutes and legislation are indicated with bold type),
  b. National City Government Resource Link (which does not easily lead to individual cities),
  c. National Association of Counties, and
  d. U.S. State and Local Government Gateway, which is a Federal Interagency Project.

In addition, there are links to the Web sites of each of the fifty States of the United States, as well as the District of Columbia. When these links are followed, some have links to the state government and its agencies, as well as links to local government pages. Others do not have these links. Many conclude with links to:

  a. The Library of Congress State and Local Governments page
  b. A page of resources to browse the Library of Congress Subject Guides to Internet Resources
  c. The Library of Congress Explore the Internet page
  d. The Library of Congress homepage.

OTHER GOVERNMENT WEB RESOURCES

As with many things on the World Wide Web, with diligence, information on almost any subject can be found. Among the useful sites of the Federal government are:

a. *www.pueblo.gsa.gov*, which is the online version of the government's catalog of useful information for consumers
b. *www.fedstats.gov*, which permits access to 40 Federal statistical programs through one access point
c. *www.nlm.nih.gov*, which is the homepage of the National Institutes of Health which has links to its institutes, agencies and offices, including the National Library of Medicine
d. When an emergency situation is seen to exist, an agency of the government will often sponsor a Web site that sometimes does not have .gov in its Web address. For example, when a shortage of teachers was seen, the U.S. Department of Education sponsored The National Teacher Recruitment Clearinghouse (*www.recruitingteachers.org*) to help individuals learn the qualifications to teach throughout the country.
e. Office of Governmental Policy (*www.policyworks.gov*)
f. Fed World (*www.fedworld.gov*)
g. U.S. Info (*www.usinfo.state.gov*)

OTHER WAYS TO GOVERNMENT INFORMATION ON THE WEB

Rather than using the Library of Congress' homepage, one can use a search engine or a directory. Unfortunately, these are often more difficult to use, and the results are not uniformly useful.

Using Yahoo! (*www.yahoo.com*), a user could perform a basic search or an advanced search using the term *.gov. This search results in nearly 14,000 Web pages. Some of these are Federal government Web pages; some are state government Web pages. On the other hand, a user could use the Yahoo! directory, clicking Government, then Countries, and choosing the United States. Using this approach, the user can find links to the pages of Agencies, Documents, Embassies and Consulates, Foreign Policy, National Symbols and Songs, Local Governments, State Governments, Statistics, etc. There are also separate links for each of the three branches of the Federal government.

Using a search engine like Hotbot (*www.hotbot.com*), the results are very different. Using the basic search of *.gov, fewer than 30 matches were found. On the other hand, using the Hotbot directory, clicking on Society and then United States gives the user an opportunity to find Web pages on Agencies,

Documents, each of the three branches of the Federal government, State government, statistics, etc.

Using the Google (*www.google.com*) search engine with the basic search of *.gov gives the user well over 860,000 matching Web pages. This is clearly more than either of the other search engines, but the results are so huge that they cannot be considered unusable.

Considering the results a user would get when using a search engine or a directory, the Librarian would probably want to steer the user to the Library of Congress homepage. It seems to be well-organized and relatively easy to use.

There are a few resources that a Librarian should consider using, though, other than the Library of Congress. These resources include the Librarian's Index to the Internet and Beaucoup.

LIBRARIAN'S INDEX TO THE INTERNET

One Web site that should be consulted in a search for government (as well as most other types of) information is the Librarian's Index to the Internet (*www.lii.org*). This site is a searchable, annotated subject directory to the resources of the World Wide Web. These sources have been selected and evaluated by Librarians. It is one of the Berkeley Digital Library Sites.

One of the subject guides is "Government: Federal, International, more." Among the topics within this subject, one can find links to information on: constitutions, elections, intelligence services, international government information, law, local governments, speeches, taxes, and vital statistics. In addition, one can find Federal government information.

Federal Government information includes census information, diplomatic and consular service, emigration and immigration service, forms, impeachment information, the branches of the Federal government, taxes, and voting records.

This is a site maintained by Librarians, and thus it is a site in which many Librarians would likely be interested.

BEAUCOUP

A Web resource worth consulting in the search for government information is Beaucoup (*www.beaucoup.com*). Beaucoup is a listing of subject specific search engines with information that is without charge. The search engines listed through Beaucoup are searchable in one way or another.

Within Beaucoup, one of the choices is Society, within which are two choices: Activism and Law, Politics and Government. Choosing the latter, one is confronted with over thirty options. These include a general Government

Info option, which places the user in Infomine's Government Information database. Within this resource, the user can search in several ways:

a. alphabetically through the Table of Contents
b. alphabetically by subject
c. alphabetically by keyword
d. alphabetically by title

Furthermore, there are several "Featured Resources" that can be searched.

Beaucoup also allows the user to gain access to information on the following subjects: the IRS, The White House, the Census Bureau, Laws (U.S. Code, U.S. Laws, Find Law, and Federal Regulations as well as tools to find laws through the Internet Legal Resource Guide), information on bills, social security, the U.S. Constitution, the U.S. Department of Defense, the U.S. Air Force, the Federal Emergency Management Agency, the U.S. Intelligence Community, the Small Business Administration, HUD (Housing and Urban Development) and Embassy World (to find an embassy or consulate).

Beaucoup's Law, Politics and Government information page also gives the user access to several government related search tools, including:

1. Government Information Locator, which is an effort to "identify, locate, and describe publicly available Federal information resources . . ." Individual agencies can be searched, or all records on the GILS site can be searched.
2. GPO Access, which allows a multiple database search for information. The databases in this search include the budget of the Federal government, the Congressional Record, Economic Indicators, the Federal Register, the Government Manual, Public Laws, the United States Code, and the Weekly Compilation of Presidential Documents.
3. FDA, which includes access to the databases of the Food and Drug Administration.
4. Infospace Government, which lists databases of government agencies and third party searchers.

Other search engines that can be accessed through this Beaucoup Web page which are related to the government, but not maintained by the government, include:

1. United Nations, which permits the user to search United Nations organization
2. ACLU, which gives the user access to the American Civil Liberties Union's resources

3. Counsel Quest, which is billed as a "legal research web tool"
4. Intellectual Property Network, which includes patent documents from the United States, Europe and Japan
5. Political Action Committees, which lists campaign contributions, including who gave what and to whom
6. World Bank
7. Federalist Search, which enables the user to search the Federalist Papers
8. ABA: The American Bar Association
9. C-Span
10. Law and Politics
11. ALSO: American Law Sources Online
12. LawOffice, which includes information on more than 400 law topics
13. National Fair Housing Advocate
14. LawGuru.com, which leads to access to over 400 law search engines
15. A few non-United States government search engines:
    a. Lexplore: Canada's online law resources
    b. SINO: Australian legal research

When confronted with a request for government information, the Librarian should remember three basic starting points: the Library of Congress, the Librarian's Index to the Internet, and Beaucoup.

Finding and Evaluating
Health Sources on the Internet:
An Overview

David Garnes
Carolyn Mills

SUMMARY. Librarians and patrons searching for reliable health information are fortunate in that this subject area is one for which many reliable, in-depth sites exist. Government, education, and organization sites are, in particular, good sources of information and provide links to other Web pages. It is important, however, for both librarians and their clients to know how to access this information and, especially, how to evaluate the worthiness and usefulness of the information contained therein. *[Article copies available for a fee from The Haworth Document Delivery Service: 1-800-342-9678. E-mail address: <getinfo@haworthpressinc.com> Website: <http://www.HaworthPress.com> © 2001 by The Haworth Press, Inc. All rights reserved.]*

KEYWORDS. Internet, Web-based health sources, government health sites, Internet health directories, evaluating Web sites

The sea change that has occurred over the past few years in the way we as reference librarians deliver service to our clients shows no sign of ebbing.

David Garnes is a reference librarian specializing in the health sciences, University of Connecticut, Storrs, CT 06269 (E-mail: david.garnes@uconn.edu). Carolyn Mills is Biological Sciences Librarian, University of Connecticut, Storrs, CT 06269 (E-mail: carolyn.mills@uconn.edu).

[Haworth co-indexing entry note]: "Finding and Evaluating Health Sources on the Internet: An Overview." Garnes, David and Carolyn Mills. Co-published simultaneously in *The Reference Librarian* (The Haworth Information Press, an imprint of The Haworth Press, Inc.), No. 74, 2001, pp. 177-186; and: *Evolution in Reference and Information Services: The Impact of the Internet* (ed: Di Su) The Haworth Information Press, an imprint of The Haworth Press, Inc., 2001, pp. 177-186. Single or multiple copies of this article are available for a fee from The Haworth Document Delivery Service [1-800-342-9678, 9:00 a.m. - 5:00 p.m. (EST). E-mail address: getinfo@haworthpressinc.com].

Rather, we are faced on a daily basis with the challenges of an ever-evolving electronic world of information sources and information retrieval. At the same time, we are interacting with an equally evolving clientele in terms of expectations, computer literacy, and the ability to access both local and remote sources without the direct intervention of the librarian.

Nowhere are these challenges more evident than in the area of health and medicine. Reliable electronic sources of information in these fields were among the earliest to emerge in the beginning days of Web-based information on the Internet. This trend has produced, and continues to generate, not only an impressive base of dependable sites but also an astute consumer clientele expecting to find answers to both common and esoteric medical questions.

In this article we will discuss ways in which the reference librarian uses the Internet at the reference desk for health-related questions, especially in terms of guiding end-users to worthwhile sources. Although our particular venue is a large academic library, we will focus on issues helpful to librarians and clientele in all libraries. Our intention is not to create yet another guide *per se* to health and medical information, although we will refer to several sources from a variety of sites, especially those that serve as directories and provide a gateway to further sources. Additionally, we will speak at some length on ways in which librarians and others interested in Web-based health information can best evaluate sites.

In an early article in *FDA Consumer* entitled "Health Information On-Line," Marilynn Larkin writes of the "unprecedented popularity that the Internet is enjoying in business and professional communities, and in homes across America."[1] She cites statistics reflecting subscription access to the Internet by upwards of 12 million people, with this figure expected to increase with the then-recent advent of the World Wide Web. The fact that this article was written only five years ago is a dramatic indication of how rapidly access has evolved and increased: It is now estimated that over 70 million people searched more than 20,000 health-related Web sites alone during the year 2000.[2]

What sites are they searching, and what can we as information providers do to ensure that they are reaching the best and most reliable information?

As has been true from the beginning, a wide range of providers–governments, medical associations, academic institutions, and health advocacy groups–have provided both good primary content and links to reliable sources of information. Consumer ("dot.com") sources have proliferated in recent years, and while they can be extremely helpful as well, they are perhaps best approached with a careful initial perusal of the site. We will discuss this caveat further on.

The federal government continues to provide excellent gateways to both citation and full-text material. From the early days of access of the MED-

LINE and journal articles via Grateful Med and Lonesome Doc, the National Library of Medicine (*http://www.nlm.nih.gov/*) has operated with an ever-expanding "documents to the people" mission. The provision of free access to MEDLINE in 1997 was the beginning of a new and ongoing effort in this direction. Currently, the comprehensive and well-designed MEDLINEplus (*http://www.nlm.nih.gov/medlineplus/*) offers full-text consumer health information, while the relatively new NLM Gateway (*http://gateway.nlm.nih. gov/gw/Cmd*) allows users to search in multiple retrieval systems, including MEDLINE/PubMed, OLDMEDLINE, LOCATORplus, AIDS Meetings, HSR Meetings, HSRProj, MEDLINEplus and DIRLINE.

Beyond the National Library of Medicine, other government agencies provide easy access to a wealth of health information. The much-publicized FIRSTGOV (*http://www.firstgov.gov/*) provides a gateway to a wide variety of data and full-text material under the broad link rubrics of Healthy People, Health, Insurance, and Disease. The umbrella U.S. Department of Health and Human Services (*http://www.os.dhhs.gov/*) provides direct access to any number of government-sponsored health sites, including individual agencies such as the Centers for Disease Control and the National Institutes of Health, themselves rich sources of further hypertext links.

Librarians should also become familiar with more regional governmental/publicly funded sources. In Connecticut, for example, Healthnet: Connecticut Consumer Health Information Network (*http://library.uchc.edu/departm/hnet*) was initiated by the library of the University of Connecticut Health Center in January 1985. The purpose of Healthnet is to help make consumer health information available to Connecticut's residents through their local public libraries. Healthnet is a librarian-to-librarian outreach program, with services designed to assist in the development of local public libraries as primary access points for consumer health information.

These programs make use of the resources and efforts of a variety of public institutions and libraries working together to educate an eventual end-user clientele. In so doing, they exemplify what is perhaps the emerging key role of the librarian in giving access to this kind of information: the librarian as teacher and guide rather than as direct provider. MEDLINEplus provides a current listing by state of Consumer Health Libraries with these kinds of Web sites (*http://www.nlm.nih.gov/medlineplus/libraries.html*).

Public libraries have also linked from their homepages a variety of helpful annotated bibliographies of both book and electronic sources. "CHOICES in health information: The New York Public Library Consumer Health Reference List" (*http://www.nypl.org/branch/health/reference.html*) is a good example of an outreach effort to its clientele. As part of its mission, CHOICES states on its homepage a promise "to assure that all branch libraries have open access to current and accurate sources of health information."

While the focus of Web-based information available from academic institutions is primarily in support of student and faculty needs (with some information actually being restricted to users in the local domain), there is nonetheless a wealth of consumer-oriented information available. Most academic library sites now include a "virtual reference desk" link, invariably with a further link to some basic sources of health information. Other institutions with formal academic liaison programs between the library and the academic schools and departments have developed a wide variety of subject pages specific to the discipline. At the University of Connecticut Libraries, for example, it is the responsibility of each liaison librarian to maintain a subject-based page (see *http://www.lib.uconn.edu/subjectareas/heal.htm* as an example of a page tailored to health-related programs at the Storrs campus that at the same time offers links to a wide variety of relevant and reliable sites on the World Wide Web).

Perusing the sites of various library organizations also provides guidance to Web-based information. The Association of College & Research Libraries (ACRL), for example, has established a link to an informative article by Caryl Gray, "Medical resources information for the consumer: Helping you make informed decisions," that appeared in the December 2000 issue of its *College & Research Libraries* (*http://www.ala.org/acrl/resdec00.html*). Although one might well have seen this article when it originally appeared in journal form, access to it is also possible via a well-worded search on a good Internet tool such as Google. (Using the terms "Internet resources" and "medical" and "consumer" produced this document as the fourth-listed of retrieved sites.)

The Medical Library Association (MLA) is another impressive source of full-text and bibliographic information. Again, while the primary mission of the site is to support MLA members and member institutions, the MLA homepage provides a valuable link, "For Health Consumers" (*http://www.mlanet.org/resources/consumr_index.html*). Two particularly relevant sites linked from this page are sponsored by the MLA's Consumer and Patient Health Information Section (CAPHIS): "Web Sites You Can Trust" (*http://caphis.njc.org/caphisconsumer.html*) and, particularly for the reference librarian, "The Librarian's Role in the Provision of Consumer Health Information and Patient Education" (*http://caphis.njc.org/caphis_statement.html*).

In the fall of 2000, CAPHIS issued a list of the "Top Ten" Most Useful Websites (*http://www.mlanet.org/resources/medspeak/topten.html*). The sites were evaluated by a team of medical librarians based on the following criteria: credibility, sponsorship/authorship, content, audience, currency, disclosure, purpose, links, design, interactivity, and disclaimers. As Rosalind Dudden, health sciences librarian at the National Jewish Medical and Research Center in Denver and a member of the review team, says: "Health is the No. 1 thing people look for on the Web."[3] Dudden further explains that popular commer-

cial medical sites, such as WebMD/Health, were not included because of the advertising; instead, the group favored academic and governmental sites.

The sites chosen (listed in alphabetical, not ranked, order) are:

- Centers for Disease Control and Prevention (CDC) (*http://www.cdc.gov/*)
- healthfinder® (*http://www.healthfinder.gov/*)
- HealthWeb (*http://www.healthweb.org/*)
- HIV InSite (*http://hivinsite.ucsf.edu/*)
- Mayo Clinic Health Oasis (*http://www.mayohealth.org/*)
- MEDEM: an information partnership of medical societies (*http://medem.com/ MedLB/medlib_entry.cfm*)
- MEDLINEplus: (*http://www.nlm.nih.gov/medlineplus/*)
- National Women's Health Information Center (NWHIC) (*http://www. 4women.gov/*)
- NOAH: New York Online Access to Health: (*http://www.noah-health.org/*)
- Oncolink: A University of Pennsylvania Cancer Center Resource: (*http://www.oncolink.upenn.edu/*)

Some of these sites are subject-specific. Others are general, all-purpose consumer sites with much full-text information. Finally, several are directories, about which we will say more later on in the article.

Advocacy groups form another source of Web-based health information, with the American Association of Retired Persons (AARP) in the forefront of Web development and outreach. The AARP "health and wellness" page (*http://www.aarp.org/healthguide/*) provides links on a wide range of health topics, including much full-text material on medical insurance and legislation.

The AARP site does contain advertisements, and the locations they suggest from a Web Resources link (*http://www.aarp.org/healthguide/healthlinks.html*) do represent a number of commercial sites. Both librarians and their clientele need to be aware of the differences in the domain suffixes of a particular address (the universal research locator or URL). Many "dot.com sites" do contain a wealth of objective information, and a number of them bear in their URL the name of a respected individual, company, or organization (cf. the beleaguered *www.koop.com* and also *www.DrSpock.com* to name two). It is important to distinguish at these sites what pertains directly to the commercial entity sponsoring it, and what is being provided as unbiased information.

With the great wealth of information now on the Web, there is little difficulty finding health-related Web sites. The real problem with so much "out there" is that it can be difficult to find what patrons specifically need. Important tools for providing targeted information are medically oriented search directories. Extensive lists of medical directories and guides are available from

Looksmart (*www.looksmart.com*) and Yahoo! (*www.yahoo.com*) as well as from other general Internet directories.

Librarians and others interested in health information made a concerted effort early in the development of the Web to organize and categorize health information. The result is a series of good quality directories and guides to medical and health information resources, more developed and more helpful, in fact, than those available for many other subjects.

These collections of health information directory Web sites have been researched and evaluated by authoritative professionals and made available to librarians and their patrons in logical and helpful ways. Again, governments and educational organizations, or some combination of the two, provide some of the best sites. Frequently, medical practitioners or non-profit health-oriented groups provide trustworthy, authoritative resources as well. Some commercial sites are also good sources for organized health information access, though again, careful evaluation of commercial sites is important. Following is a sampling of several high quality health information search tools, in alphabetical order.

Achoo (*http://www.achoo.com/main.asp*)

A broad directory covering all aspects of healthcare, Achoo is owned and managed by MNI Systems Corporation, a team of individuals specializing in a variety of Internet and healthcare areas in Ontario, Canada. Their goal is to provide comprehensive access to healthcare information.

Hardin Meta Directory (*http://www.lib.uiowa.edu/hardin/md/*)

A product of the Hardin Library for Health Sciences at the University of Iowa, this directory's purpose is to provide easy access to comprehensive resource lists in health-related subjects. It includes subject listings in large "one-stop-shopping" sites, such as MedWeb and Yahoo!, and also independent discipline-specific lists.

Health Web (*http://www.healthweb.org/*)

A collaborative project of the health sciences libraries of the Greater Midwest Region (GMR) of the National Network of Libraries of Medicine (NN/LM) and those of the Committee for Institutional Cooperation, a group of 12 educational institutions, Health Web was developed in 1994 to provide an interface to evaluated non-commercial, health-related, Internet-accessible resources.

Healthfinder (*http://www.healthfinder.gov/default.htm*)

Healthfinder is a gateway to reliable consumer health information developed by the U.S. Department of Health and Human Services. Launched in 1997, Healthfinder provides access to selected online publications, clearinghouses, databases, Web sites, and support and self-help groups, as well as the government agencies and not-for-profit organizations that produce reliable information for the public.

Health on the Net (*http://www.hon.ch/home.html*)

The Health On the Net Foundation (HON), created in 1995, is a not-for-profit International Swiss Organization. HON's mission is to guide lay persons or non-medical users, as well as medical practitioners, to useful and reliable online medical and health information. HON provides leadership in setting ethical standards for Web site developers.

Martindale's Health Science Guide
(*http://www-sci.lib.uci.edu/HSG/HSGuide.html*)

This site is the brainchild of Jim Martindale, an individual with great interest and skill in providing easy access to a broad range of medical and other health information. The University of California at Irvine hosts the site.

The above sites can be assumed to be reliable in terms of the links they have provided. Knowing and using good directories such as these, however, is not intuitive and will become part of a librarian's or client's routine only after experience or formal instruction.

There are also many general search tools to direct patrons to informative, valuable Web sites. Most users are already availing themselves of these increasingly "high profile" engines whose names are becoming part of our everyday vocabulary.

An essential skill for any Web searcher, and especially for those looking for medical information, therefore, is knowing how to evaluate sites and the information found on them. Most librarians already have some knowledge about how to evaluate Web sites, but many of our patrons do not. It is important, especially when users are looking for health information, for librarians to offer guidance on weeding out the quality information from the chaff. Offering on-site instruction is always helpful, with available written or Web-based guides (for remote users) providing further assistance.

The three major areas to consider in evaluating a Web site are the content of the site, the authority of the author, and technical considerations involving the

site and the subsequent ability of the patron to use it successfully. Some questions to ask when evaluating a site might be:

* Who is the audience for which the site is intended?
* What is the purpose of the site? Why was it created and what does the author hope to achieve with it?
* How current is the information?
* Who created the site? What experience does this person have?
* Could the person or group who created and maintains the site have a possible bias or hidden agenda?
* Does the site use multi media methods of presentations, such as video or audio clips? Does it offer high-resolution images? Does the patron or the library have the hardware and software to load and view these media?

The audience for whom the Web site is intended absolutely affects the type of information offered and the way it is presented. For instance, if a Web site is designed for clinical researchers, information will probably be very detailed and specific with little effort made to explain medical terminology. If college undergraduate students are the audience, the site may be oriented towards academic requirements of the course or institution rather than to a broader view of medical issues, diseases, drugs or whatever the subject of the site might be.

Answers to this question of intended audience can often be found in a "welcome" or "who we are" statement or link from the homepage. Often these sections will also have information about the purpose of the site, which may be to educate its user–or to sway opinions or sell goods and services.

Currency of information is certainly another concern for those seeking medical information. If a site is not updated regularly, there may be a question as to its usefulness, particularly for medical issues involving current or evolving research. Information indicating when the site was last updated is often located at the very bottom of the homepage.

The authority of the person producing and maintaining the site is crucial to the value of a site. Does the author have substantial education or experience in the subject matter? Most quality sites will give some information about the author's background, or it will be clear from the sponsoring organization that the site is reliable. If the professional credentials are not apparent or little professional expertise is in evidence on the part of an individual author, the searcher should treat the site with caution.

Information about any possible bias on the part of the creator must usually be gleaned from between the lines, so to speak, but it is important to recognize whether any extenuating factors exist before evaluating the usefulness of the information at the site. One way to scout out potential bias is to look at the site's URL. If the URL has a ".com" ending, look the site over carefully: It is a

commercial site. There are certainly many commercial sites that are valuable and worthwhile, but this key characteristic increases the potential for a non-educational bias.

Technical considerations of both the Web site and the patron's access method are also important to evaluate. Many Web sites now offer multi-media clips to provide further information. Viewing these clips generally requires specific equipment or software to load and play. Other health related sites have impressive but demanding high-resolution images or extensive graphics that can be time-intensive to load. And even more basically, the computer must have the capability of handling intensive demands on storage space and memory. Sometimes complex Web sites will provide a text-only version of a page for those viewers who are "hardware-challenged."

Most quality Web sites will have at least some of this information readily available. But few sites have everything, and some high quality sites provide very little background information to the viewer. There is no standardization for Web formats or authors. Librarians need to continually help patrons consider how to evaluate Web sites and the information they contain in this "searcher beware" environment.

Nevertheless, however well- or ill-informed they may be, consumers are indeed integrating the Internet more and more into their daily lives. For example, Dr. David Leffell, a professor of dermatology and associate dean for clinical affairs at Yale Medical School, has actually begun to correspond with his patients via e-mail, reporting that e-mail saves time, is accurate–because it's written–and provides a written record of the communication that he puts in the patient's chart. He also tells patients up front that it's not confidential (a potential problem relating to patient privacy issues) and not for emergencies.[4] Although most doctor-patient relationships have not yet expanded to include this kind of interaction, this use heralds the ever-expanding uses of the Web.

The tremendous increase in the numbers of post-baby boomers using the Internet from home or from their local libraries can only signify a concomitant increase in the use of Web resources to find information of particular interest to them. According to Sam Karp, CIO of the California HealthCare Foundation, "Doctors say that, more and more, patients are bringing information from the Internet with them. They find the quality of information is mixed, but it does allow them to have more in-depth conversations with their patients."[5]

Encounters at the reference desk may not be as frequent as before because of the ability of so many clients to access the Web from places other than the library. Web-based instruction and clear homepages will certainly help instruct our users to use World Wide Web intelligently and efficiently. But whatever our means of communication with them, we as reference librarians have a responsibility as never before to guide our students, faculty, commercial users and private consumers to the best information. It's there, and we need to show the way.

NOTES

1. Marilyn Larkin, "Health Information On-Line," *FDA Consumer* 30, June 1996, 21-24.

2. Jim Ritter, "Medical Librarians List Top Web Sites," *Chicago Sun-Times*, 10/23/00, 19.

3. Jenny Deam, "What's Best Way to Find Medical Info on the Web? Librarians Compile a List of Top Sites," *Denver Post*, 1/28/01, E-7.

4. "Trends & Timelines–Ehealth: Internet Health Information Becomes the 'Rule,'" *American Health Line*, 2/28/01, 2.

5. Garret Condon, "What's Up, E-Doc? How the Internet Is Changing Doctor-Patient Relationships," *Hartford Courant*, 12/05/00, D3.

INFORMATION TECHNOLOGY (IT) MANAGEMENT

The Impact of "Scholar's Workstations" in an Undergraduate Academic Library: Would a Holistic Approach Work?

Tina C. Fu

Kim Bartosz

Guy LaHaie

SUMMARY. The Eastern Connecticut State University library planned, with the new facility, a new configuration for user computers to be one-stop-shopping "Scholar's Workstations." The impact on reference services was dramatic, resulting in modifications in staffing, poli-

Tina C. Fu is Director of Library Services (E-mail: fut@easternct.edu), Kim Bartosz is Assistant Librarian, Technical Services (E-mail: bartoszk@easternct.edu), and Guy LaHaie is Library Computer Specialist (E-mail: Lahaieg@easternct.edu), all at J. Eugene Smith Library, Eastern Connecticut State University, 83 Windham Street, Willimantic, CT 06226-2295 (http://www.easternct.edu/library).

[Haworth co-indexing entry note]: "The Impact of 'Scholar's Workstations' in an Undergraduate Academic Library: Would a Holistic Approach Work?" Fu, Tina C., Kim Bartosz, and Guy LaHaie. Co-published simultaneously in *The Reference Librarian* (The Haworth Information Press, an imprint of The Haworth Press, Inc.) No. 74, 2001, pp. 187-205; and: *Evolution in Reference and Information Services: The Impact of the Internet* (ed: Di Su) The Haworth Information Press, an imprint of The Haworth Press, Inc., 2001, pp. 187-205. Single or multiple copies of this article are available for a fee from The Haworth Document Delivery Service [1-800-342-9678, 9:00 a.m. - 5:00 p.m. (EST). E-mail address: getinfo@haworthpressinc.com].

cies/procedures, printing practices, user orientation and education, etc. Moreover, the reference librarians were troubled by their perceptions of how these workstations were utilized, challenging us to conduct a user survey to determine the validity of these perceptions. In this article, we will describe (1) how we conceived this new configuration and its impact, (2) modifications made, and (3) an analysis of the user survey. *[Article copies available for a fee from The Haworth Document Delivery Service: 1-800-342-9678. E-mail address: <getinfo@haworthpressinc.com> Website: <http://www.HaworthPress.com> © 2001 by The Haworth Press, Inc. All rights reserved.]*

KEYWORDS. Reference, e-mail, Internet, research, public workstations, scholar's workstations, community users, use patterns, user surveys, reference staffing, Web filtering, reference policies, recreational use, academic use, undergraduate students

PLANNING AND BACKGROUND

The J. Eugene Smith Library at Eastern Connecticut State University provides over 90 computers to our users. We have configured the majority of these workstations (all but 11) to be "Scholar's Workstations." These Scholar's Workstations are loaded with not only the traditional library electronic resources (OPAC, library databases including full-text, Internet access) but also the full suite of MS software (i.e., Access, Word, Excel, and PowerPoint) and the university's mail utility Outlook 2000. These workstations require a university computing account with the account owner's password to access. We also provide six non-passworded workstations for community users, and these are the traditional library types (OPAC, library databases including full-text, and Internet access). The remaining five computers are "quick search stations," all stand-ups loaded with only our OPAC: No passwords are required. In this article, we will describe how the library staff came to consensus in providing these Scholar's Workstations to our student and faculty users, and further, how they have impacted the reference librarians' work, policies and procedures at the reference desk, and the staffing pattern of the desk. An analysis of a user survey is conducted to provide a vignette of how these Scholar's Workstations are actually used by our students. Some observations are made at the end by the authors regarding lessons learned and future directions.

The library staff at the J. Eugene Smith Library had the unique opportunity in planning a new library building, three times the size of the original one, in 1992-5. The building program planning started in 1992, with the actual design

of the building being completed in 1995. The foci during those three years were not only to plan a flexible and expandable physical space, but also an infrastructure that could accommodate existing and emerging information technologies. In January, 1996, however, planning in more detailed form regarding the specifics in preparing for the move commenced in earnest with the library's First Retreat from Jan. 4 to Jan. 5, 1996. The "move," in the view of the library staff, was not only moving physically the hundreds of thousands of volumes, but also a gigantic leap in information technology, taking full advantage of a completely new infrastructure and the building equipment budget to achieve the dreams of a high-tech library.

The library staff during the 1996 Retreat identified seven topics of concern, and seven Focus Groups were formed to tackle each topic. Among them is a very popular Systems Focus Group. In the reading packet for the 1996 Library Retreat, the Library Director included two chapters from *Academic Libraries as High-tech Gateways: A Guide to Design and Space Decisions.*[1] (The two chapters are: "The Library Becomes a Teaching Instrument," and "Academic Libraries at the Millennium.") In these chapters, the idea of multi-purpose workstations in the library and reference librarians' new approach to "Electronic Research Skills" (ERS) were topics discussed in the Systems Focus Group. Since the teaching of ERS aims "to produce university graduates who are familiar with online systems, who use computers to research and write assignments . . ."[2] library staff asked of themselves the question of what kind of workstations we should provide to our users. Should we provide, as the authors (Richard Bazillion and Connie Brown) suggested, a Scholar's Workstation where students can retrieve, evaluate, organize, and *manipulate* information, or should we provide a traditional library workstation which has the OPAC, the electronic resources including library database and the Internet? Should we load the Microsoft suite so that students can use what they just get from library research to fashion a PowerPoint presentation, to write a research paper, or to do a spreadsheet? Should we also load the campus e-mail software so that after all is done, they can e-mail it to their professor after having saved it on disk or the campus server? What challenges would the reference librarians encounter with these Scholar's Workstations? What do we do with the workstations for the community users whom Eastern Connecticut State University, as a state institution, is obliged to serve as an information resource center?

During the subsequent two years (1996-98), many discussions occurred in both the Systems Focus Group and the library professional staff meetings. By January, 1998, when the Third Library Retreat occurred, the consensus among the library professional group leaned toward having the workstations in the new building configured as the Scholar's Workstations. Although some librarians were very concerned about the impact of these workstations on the refer-

ence librarians' workload and their expertise level of non-library technical packages such as Access, they all agreed that for students' convenience, this holistic approach would encourage student library use rather than discourage it. Moreover, the library has already enabled full-text and Web-based databases so that in regular computer labs and dorm labs, students could access the virtual library time and distance free. If the library took the piecemeal and conservative approach, not enabling students to do MS suite and e-mail, we might end up with a fairly large and empty new library! If we would provide them with a convenient, one-stop-shopping Scholar's Workstation, with the added value of reference librarians' friendly and expert help, they should find the new building and computers very enticing. In the meantime, we might lead them to a few good books, or they very well might find a few themselves serendipitously on locale.

The new building was slated to be completed in October 1998. It was planned that we would place furniture and equipment such as the specially designed computer carrels and computers in the new building, and moving day would be December 1998 and January 1999, during the Christmas/New Year intercession. In September 1998, a one-day Mini-retreat was conducted in preparation for the upcoming move. It was then that the types of configuration for the new computers were decided upon. We would configure the computers into three categories: (1) some with library and Internet resources only, for the community and visitors, (2) some with the addition of the MS Suite, and (3) the rest with the MS Suite and the university e-mail package. It was also decided that for the last two categories, a University computer account and password would be required to gain access. By this time, the Systems Focus Group had also completed their research and investigation of a charge-for-printing setup and recommended that the library charge for printing. This is a new practice, which caused a few reference librarians to have philosophical qualms about the library charging for what we had been giving away free for many years.

IMPLEMENTATION

When the computers were configured in January 1999 after we were in the new building, our computer specialist found that it was not practical to configure them into three categories. Two were recommended and accepted–that we only would give community and visiting users the traditional library and Internet resources, and we would configure faculty and student workstations to be all Scholar's Workstations, requiring a university computer account and password to access.

MODIFICATIONS

During the last two years, we believe that this holistic approach has been successful. Library and its computer uses were phenomenal. Our highest gate count used to top at 121,044 per year in the old building: Our first year in the new one more than doubled at over 242,586 in 1999. The 1999 computer logons were 238,175 times. Moreover, it is a pleasure for us to report that we have stemmed the tide for further slide in the book circulation rate with a small increase (16%) in 1999 over 1998. The library's Web page use has been 17% to 18% of all University Web logons. However, the impact of these Scholar's Workstations on the reference department was indeed great, and the following modifications had to be made during 1999/2000:

1. Staffing the Reference Desk

With the onset of technical questions (e.g., how do I log on, how do I save my research paper in my server space, how do I print, etc.), the reference librarians were extremely busy, to the dangerous point that they might not be able to devote their full attention to content. Our computer specialist suggested that he could train a few Systems students who would staff the reference desk, assisting the reference librarians in answering technical questions. This double staffing not only helped the Main Reference Desk but also the Curriculum Center Desk and the unstaffed workstation users on the third floor, since these student assistants are free to circulate and answer calls for help. It also seems that student users are now accustomed to the Scholar's Workstation concept and once trained, seemed to be on their way working independently. It is not usual for librarians to rejoice in the drop in use statistics, but in this instance we were very happy about it. Please note the "Equipment" category of the Reference log: This category was added to gauge the technical questions that are directly answered by the reference librarians:

	Oct. 99	Oct. 00	Nov. 99	Nov. 00
Equipment	288	184	263	90

2. Modification in the Library's Approach to Freshmen Orientation

In the Summer of 2000, the Associate Director for Student Affairs contacted the library with an invitation to participate in the planning of a day-long Freshman Orientation in August. In the past, the librarians felt that very little could be achieved during the orientation sessions in terms of content, but felt that our participation was necessary, if just for showing the new students that there were friendly and helpful staff in the library. In the old building, we used to have a "table" in the exhibit hall with colorful brochures and freebies, and

volunteers from staff would wear the library t-shirts and interact with whomever stopped by. With the new building, we changed to touring the students in an Open House setup. However, the approaches we took in the 2000 Freshman Orientation had an additional element: We trained the student freshman orientation counselors in not only giving a good tour of the library, but also provided them with a check list of things a freshman should have in order to make full use of the Scholar's Workstations. In the checklist, for example, is the strong suggestion that they should obtain a computer account from the Data Center with a password already configured before coming to use the library. Tips on printing are also provided. When the semester opened in late August 2000, there was a marked drop in the computer account/password confusion among freshmen. Frustration level among these freshman users was reduced; thus, all could start their initial library experience on the right foot.

3. Additions of "Quick Search Stations"

After a few months in the new building, the Circulation staff and reference librarians recommended that we add a few standup OPAC only computers, two by the Reserves Desk, one by the Reference Desk, one by the Curriculum Center Desk, and one on the unstaffed Third Floor. This was done, and they became very useful and popular for users who just want to do quick checks of the OPAC, since our Scholar's Workstations have become very popular on campus with the students and are always highly occupied. These are walk-up, no password required machines: We recycled some of the older pentiums for this use. These new additions have become very popular and alleviate pressure from the busy Scholar's Workstations.

4. Community/Visitors Workstations

Our library is mandated to abide by the Connecticut State University System Board of Trustees Resolution 88-49 which resulted in the "Connecticut State University Policy on Sharing of Library Resources."[3] In this policy, it is stated: "Another form of sharing of library resources arises when individual citizens of Connecticut (who are not CSU students or faculty or students of other units of the state system of public higher education) demonstrate to CSU library staff a legitimate need for access to a University library." Since our University has always prided itself for "service" (for example, all our students have to earn mandated service credits with community service), we feel that with library computer access to the OPAC, the electronic library and Internet, we are expected to provide community users with computers. We at first provided them with twenty-one (21) computers and required no age limit, no time limit. This proved to be a disaster. Children in large and small groups flooded

to the building to play games or surf the Web. They were at times noisy and unruly, seriously upsetting our academic atmosphere the librarians were trying hard to create in the new building. One of the reference librarians called and wrote to neighboring schools for their computer use policies and reported that we were providing much more liberal access to them than they could get from their own schools. Since the librarians have abided by the code of intellectual freedom in providing unfiltered Internet access, we felt that allowing unrestricted access to children might lead us into undesirable ground. So the following policies were quickly put into practice:

1. Reducing the public/visitor workstations from twenty-one (21) to six (6), and all six were right beside the reference desk for easy supervision.
2. Implementing a sign-up sheet to limit time (each sign-up block is two hours), and limiting the age for computer access. Unless accompanied by a parent, guardian, or teacher, who can present an ID with photograph, children under 18 cannot gain access to the library computers. They can use the Quick Search OPAC computers, however. These changes have proven to be very successful, and we were able to restore the serious academic atmosphere in the library while fulfilling our mandate from the Board of Trustees. Furthermore, as one librarian puts it, we do not have to play the role of cyber-police any more!
3. Posting a code of conduct for computer use on the library's Web was done quickly, thus ensuring that if misconduct occurs, we can limit the abusers' access to library computers. Since we have already posted the no-filtering guidelines by the Connecticut Library Association, we have taken steps for the University Senate to rectify the Association of College & Research Libraries "Intellectual Freedom Principles for Academic Libraries." After the Senate motion is passed, we will also post it on the Web for public record.

5. Printing and Charge for Printing

One of the major topics that the Systems Focus Group was asked to investigate and research was charge for printing. With the Scholar's Workstations, it was anticipated before the library building's opening that students would print an enormous volume. If we would keep the free printing setup, impact on the library's Operational Expense budget could be huge. The Focus Group, after having visited some libraries to learn about the various printing charge technologies, did a survey of academic libraries on their printing charge practices. In both the full Library Retreat in January of 1998 and the Mini-Retreat in September, the Focus Group recommended that we should charge for printing.

A charge for printing Proposal was submitted to the University Administration in March 1999, two months after the library's Grand Opening. In the meantime, the library had been working with the Card Services staff in the Auxiliary Services to see whether the library's printing, copier, and library fines could be on the University's universal card system. The technology for charging was UniPrint, and Card Services made sure that it was compatible with the universal card (also the university ID card). A "bucket" was created by Card Services to receive the card money from the library printers, copiers, etc., ensuring that the library would get the money in its income funds. Also, the library had the foresight when purchasing equipment for the new building that a cash-to-money machine was installed by the Circulation Desk. Decisions were made that the six public workstations would not be on the UniPrint system, but on a coin-op system to take cash. While all the technical discussions and arrangements went on, the University Administration, at the request of student leaders, put their approval of the Proposal on hold until students had a chance to review the whole picture.

Subsequent to this, two hearing sessions with student leaders were scheduled in the Fall semester, 1999. Both times the Library Director went before the leaders to defend the Proposal, which outlined a five cents (5 cents) per page charge for students and ten cents (10 cents) for community users. A detailed cost analysis was conducted based on half a year's expenditure and the results shared with students: The cost for paper and printer cassettes turned out to be 3.72 cents per page. Not included were printer replacement costs, and in 1999, because of the heavy use, four printers had to be replaced. The Director reported that 410,000 pages were printed between July to December 1999, costing the library $15,252, literally breaking the bank! Also reported was the wastage: Reams of printouts were left behind in waste paper bins, with the average wastage rate estimated to be 20 to 25 percent. Students would print out several drafts of research papers or unwanted Web pages. The library presented the charge for printing proposal not as a charge, but as a cost recovery measure. Fortunately, in the Spring of 2000, all levels supported the charge for printing: Community users were charged beginning in May 2000, with students beginning in August 2000.

Since then we feel that things are working much better: Students and community users are more careful in requesting printing, and the money accumulated would enable the library to regularly replace printers with high volume ones without incurring any downtime. Printing service has actually improved. Since there is practically no wastage, long printing queues and equipment breakdowns are things of the past. Only one minor adjustment was made for student convenience: We enabled all Scholar's Workstations to route printing requests to the coin-op printer, in case the students forget to bring their ID card.

SURVEY

Queries

After establishing the Scholar's Workstations in J. Eugene Smith Library in January 2000, it was observed that usage of the library increased. However, concern arose as to how the patrons were using the workstations. Additionally, through turnstile counts, it was determined that following the installation of Scholar's Workstations, the count rose. In 1998, the turnstile count totaled 121,044 and increased to 242,586 in 1999.[4] With free unfiltered access to email, popular Web sites and gaming, the library staff informally observed students using the library computers for recreation rather than for research. To determine if the main use of the Scholar's Workstations was in fact for recreation, a survey was commissioned to track how the library workstations were used and by whom. Originally, the main goal of the survey was to discover how the Eastern Connecticut State University (ECSU) students were using the library computers, but further broadened to include all types of users (such as the general public, faculty and staff, etc.). Questions addressed by the survey were: Was the use of library computers for recreation high? Did students come to the library just to use the computers? What length of time did students use the library workstations and who utilized the Scholar's Workstations most? Finally, in 1999, the J. Eugene Smith Library was equipped with more powerful and advanced computers than anywhere else on campus. This study would discover if upgrades in the campus computer lab before the spring semester would affect library computer usage, and in turn, affect library usage as a whole.

Process

Survey questions were created to reflect concerns of the library staff and were reviewed and revised by all participating members. The survey (see the appendix for survey sample) asked users to identify themselves and to describe their use of the library computers. Specifically, the survey requested users to note their affiliation to ECSU, whether student, faculty, staff, or a member of the general public. Users then reported how they used the computers primarily at the time the survey was taken, with choices of research (using the library's online catalog CONSULS, CD-ROM or other databases) or academic purposes (writing papers, spread sheets, working on resumes or conducting academic email correspondence or Web research) or recreation (social email, game playing, chat rooms, or visiting non-academic Web sites) or performing all the above tasks. Further questioning followed usage patterns among library patrons, asking how often they came to the library to use the computers, was the

visit to the library solely for computer use, how many hours per week and day did they use the computers, and to list other computers to which they had access.

Surveys were taken during the academic year 1999-2000. Implementation of the surveys and their tabulation were as follows: The week prior to implementing the survey, the entire staff was reminded through email of the process and their participation. Survey forms were distributed to the various departments (who generously volunteered their students), including the circulation department, the systems department, government documents, and technical services. Student workers would be scheduled in advance for the times they were responsible for dispensing the forms. Starting on Sunday, students would give a form to each person at a library computer on the second floor, informing the users that the forms would be collected in the next fifteen minutes or could be dropped off at the reference desk. This was done three times a day, except on Fridays and Saturdays when the library had retracted hours and surveys were collected twice. At the end of the week, all the forms were collected, bundled by day and time and sent to the systems department. The systems staff designed a Microsoft Access database and students entered the data from each form. For each month of the survey, this process was repeated, different colored paper used to differentiate the times the survey was taken. Finally, the database was copied into Excel, enabling the tabulation of the results.

Limiting the survey to the Scholar's Workstations in the reference area on the second floor of the library created a sample of general computer use throughout the library. This area was chosen as the sample because forty-six of the over ninety library computers, or about 50% of all the library's computers, were in the reference section and are subject to high volume. In addition, the reference section is in close proximity to the systems office, which allowed for easy access for student workers.

Questions existed as to whether computer use reflected student use of the library. To track time of usage, the surveys were taken during the two middle months of the semester. The first month of the semester would not accurately reflect true student computer usage because of few assignments at the beginning of the semester, and in the last month of the semester, students might not tolerate being disturbed in the midst of their studies. Forms were distributed every day for one week, three times a day. The times of day were chosen based on typical times for students to be in the library and staff considerations. Mornings at 10 a.m., afternoons at 2 p.m. and evenings at 8 p.m. did not conflict with the opening or closing of the library or the lunch periods of students and staff. Daily statistics of questions asked at the reference desk were used to determine periods of high use. The highest number of reference questions in three of the four months of the survey was at 2 p.m. The reference area saw somewhat lower rates of business at 10 a.m. and 8 p.m.

A priority for the surveys was to achieve the highest return rate possible. Thusly, the forms were designed to be short and consist of pre-determined responses for the students to choose. Instead of mailing the forms to the student body, the forms were to be administered at the library while the students were at the computers. There were two benefits to this approach. The survey instructed students to describe how they were using the computers at the time the survey was taken. It can be assumed that this will be more accurate than the traditional "mail in" survey which requires the recipient to remember past usage. Also, the close monitoring and quick retrieval of completed surveys prevented forms being lost or ignored.

After the first survey in October 1999 was reviewed, changes to the form were made. In November 1999, spaces were added for students to specify their major and the day of the week that the survey was taken. These changes were made after preliminary results were presented to the library professional staff. The staff also held interest in ascertaining which students, grouped by major, used the library computers heavily for research or academic purposes and which days use was highest. The former would assist collection development and the latter would help the systems department with student staffing at the reference desk. Surveys were taken the weeks of October 10th-16th 1999, November 14th-20th 1999, March 5th-11th 2000, April 2nd-8th and the week of May 1st 2000. However, the May 2000 survey was not included in the final results because only Sunday and Monday were collected. With its proximity to the end of the semester, few student workers were available to minister the surveys the first week of May, resulting in only having completed surveys for Sunday and Monday of that week. Additionally, by May 2000, the student workers tired of distributing and collecting the forms. Scholar's Workstation users disliked disturbances while conducting research or writing and informed the student workers verbally, increasing their distaste of this task.

Results

A total of 1,011 forms comprised this survey, with 292 forms collected in October 1999, 273 in November 1999, 247 in March 2000, and 197 forms in April 2000. Not every form was filled out completely, requiring an additional category for blank, of which two forms didn't have the month designated. Successful computer login rates (library logins only, does not include remote logins or on campus logins) mirror this drop. In October 1999, 32,980 users successfully logged onto the library computers and November 1999 had 33,650, while March 2000 dropped to 22,680 logins, and April 2000 saw 23,695 logins. ECSU's campus computer lab finished updating their hardware by Fall 2000. This data reinforces the hypothesis that library computer usage would decline once the campus computer center updated its hardware. Also, these

numbers reflect an increase of out of library/off campus use of the CONSULS online catalog and J. Eugene Smith Library's database array.

Users of the J. Eugene Smith Library included not only members of the Eastern Connecticut State University community (students, staff, and faculty), but members of the general public. ECSU historically has encouraged ties to Windham and surrounding municipalities. The library offers the general public community borrowers' cards, enabling them to borrow books and to access a limited number of computer workstations in the library. These general public workstations are not Scholar's Workstations because they are not loaded with the Microsoft Office suite or the campus email utility Outlook. They have full access to the CONSULS online catalog, the library's CD-ROM and online databases, and the World Wide Web and a basic word processing program. General public users can conduct academic work, but not to the extent the ECSU student, faculty and staff are able.

Each form for this survey requested users to identify their relationship to Eastern. By far the majority of library computer users were ECSU students. Nine hundred twenty-four (924) out of 1,011 forms were from students. The highest rate of usage was noted in the senior population at 30% of the total, followed by the usage rate of juniors at 24.3%, freshmen with 24.1%, sophomores with 12% and graduate students at 2%. Enrollment numbers partially explain these numbers. There were 4,987 students enrolled at Eastern Connecticut State University in Fall 1999, with 1,865 (40%) freshmen, 854 (17%) sophomores, 922 (18%) juniors, 1032 (21%) seniors, and 314 (6%) graduate students.[5]

The additional categories of computer users were ECSU faculty and staff, the general public and others. Faculty and staff had the lowest rate of usage with .20% (2 out of 1,011 users). This survey only tracked onsite library computer usage. The low rate may be because faculty and staff have access to the online catalogs and databases from their offices and departments as well as email and word processing software and thus do not need to be physically in the library. The general public made up 4% (44) of the computer users with access to only 6 out of 46 of the library workstations. This number may not accurately reflect the use rate of the general public. Since users determined their own category of identification, interpretation of these groupings could not be easily defined. The lines between general public and other users could have blurred. "Others" made up 2% (21 users). Users identifying themselves as "other" were asked to specify their affiliation and few did. Since "others" had to write in their affiliation, this would explain the low number of responses. Some others who made further comments were from sister Connecticut State Universities or from the University of Connecticut.

ECSU is a liberal arts institution with strong professional programs such as business, education and communications. The professional programs had the

largest full time enrollments (FTEs). The School of Education and Professional Studies comprised 37.7% of the credit hours offered at ECSU. The strength of the professional programs was parallel in computer usage. Business and accounting majors had the highest rate of usage with 103 users (10%), followed by psychology (68 users, 6.7%) and education and physical education (68 users, 6.7%), communications (38 users, 4%), and sports management (12 users, 1%). Of the forms with a major specified, 218 of the 571 students (38%) were from the professional studies. ECSU's master's degrees also were from the professional programs, accounting, education, and organizational management. Of the 571 users reported, 222 were humanities majors.

One of the main questions to prove or disprove was the perception that students mainly used the library computers solely for recreation. The results verified the opposite was true. Thirty-seven percent (378 users) utilized the computers for academic purposes, which included writing papers, preparing spreadsheets or electronic presentations, searching academic content on the Web or conducting academic correspondence via email. Twenty-seven percent (275 users) employed computers for searching the CONSULS online catalog or the CD-ROM/online databases. Twenty-one percent (213 users) used the library computers for gaming, personal email, or for searching non-academic Web sites. Significantly, 14% (141 users) were multi-tasked, conducting all three functions at once.

The previous discussion chronicled general results from the user survey. When responses from the questions were compared to one another, several usage trends were found. Broken down by the months of the survey, a decrease in usage rates were found from October to April in each category, although the numbers stayed constant with the trend set by the overall findings. Academic usage remained the top function of use for the Scholar's Workstations, followed by research, recreation, and conducting all three at a time (Table 1). Usage was also followed to determine what time of week was highest. Usage peaked in all categories early in the week, Monday through Wednesday, and fell off by Friday and Saturday. Saturday was consistently the lowest day for usage and Monday the highest in all categories (Table 2). Type of user and type of use were compared together (Table 3), and seniors led academic (126 users, 33%) and research computer usage (92 users, 33%), while freshmen were found to have the highest recreational use (72 users, 34%). The category academic purpose possessed the highest rate of usage among all categories except for the general public category. The general public mainly utilized the library computers for recreation, not surprisingly due to their lack of access to office software. The research category was a strong second in usage (except for sophomores, but the number remained close), refuting the library staff's impression that the majority of students spent the bulk of their time at recreation.

TABLE 1. Type of Computer Usage by Month

Month	Academic purposes		Research		Recreational		All the above	
	number	percentage	number	percentage	number	percentage	number	percentage
October	102	27%	87	32%	59	28%	44	31%
November	103	27%	76	27%	48	22%	46	33%
March	92	24%	68	25%	61	29%	25	18%
April	81	22%	44	16%	45	21%	26	18%
Totals	378	100%	275	100%	213	100%	141	100%

TABLE 2. Type of Computer Usage by Day of the Week

Day of Week	Academic purposes		Research		Recreational		All the above	
	number	percentage	number	percentage	number	percentage	number	percentage
Sunday	46	12%	29	10%	17	8%	15	10%
Monday	61	16%	39	14%	55	26%	29	20%
Tuesday	49	13%	40	15%	26	12%	17	12%
Wednesday	36	10%	39	14%	19	9%	14	10%
Thursday	49	13%	19	7%	18	8%	14	10%
Friday	27	7%	17	6%	14	7%	7	5%
Saturday	7	2%	5	2%	4	2%	3	2%
(blank)	103	27%	87	32%	60	28%	44	31%
Totals	378	100%	275	100%	213	100%	141	100%

Another question the library staff asked was whether library computer users came to the library solely to use the computers (in any capacity). With the opening of the new facility, staff hoped to attract new patrons, and the turnstile counts confirmed an increase in library traffic. Did the users expand their library usage beyond the Scholar's Workstations? Overall numbers did not bear out the assumption that most patrons only used the computers. Forty-six percent (471 users) compared to 53% (537 users) came to the library just for computer access. Over the four months of the survey, computer only library use steadily rose. In October the difference was 55 in favor of non-computer only library use, in November the difference dropped to 9 users, and then to 4 users in March. By April, 2 more users were only visiting the library to use the computers than not (Table 4). When comparing use of the computers to use of the library, those who conducted either academic work (203 over 174), research (162 over 112) or multi-tasked (73 over 68) came to the library for more than

TABLE 3. Type of Computer Usage by Category of User

User category	Academic purposes		Research		Recreational		All the above	
	number	percentage	number	percentage	number	percentage	number	percentage
Freshmen	88	23%	51	19%	72	34%	32	23%
Sophomore	46	12%	27	10%	31	14%	20	14%
Junior	93	25%	78	28%	44	21%	30	21%
Senior	126	33%	92	33%	41	19%	45	32%
Graduate student	8	2%	7	2.5%	3	1%	5	4%
Faculty/staff	2	.5%	0	0%	0	0%	0	0%
General public	9	2%	13	5%	16	8%	6	4%
Other	6	0%	6	2%	6	3%	2	1%
(blank)	0	0%	1	.5%	0	0%	1	1%
Totals	378	100%	275	100%	213	100%	141	100%

TABLE 4. Use of Library for Computer Use Only by Month

Month	Yes		No		Difference
	number	percentage	number	percentage	
October	118	25%	173	32.5%	55
November	132	28%	141	26%	9
March	121	25.5%	125	23%	4
April	99	21%	97	18%	− 2
(blank)	1	.5%	1	.5%	
Totals	471	100%	537	100%	

the computers. Recreational users only used the library mostly for computer access (116 over 97). Comparing class standing to computer library use, only freshmen used the library solely for the computers–193 freshmen users versus 104 just used the library computers. All other classes had lower usage rates for computer only library usage. Fourteen more sophomores (55 yes to computer only library use, 69 no computers part of library use), 37 juniors (103 yes, 142 no), and 48 seniors (128 yes, 176 no) cited computer use as a component of library use.

Users were asked how often they came to the library to use the computers. Of the 1,011 responses, 1% said never, 1.8% said once a semester, and 8% said monthly. Then the numbers jumped to 42% for weekly and 46% for daily use. The majority of library computer use was consistently steady. Steady computer users had the highest usage rates of academic computer use with 185 of

470 daily users, 160 of 426 weekly users, 24 of 80 monthly users and 5 out of 19 once a semester users. The percentage of academic use remained consistent, ranging from 30%-39%.

The final subject in question was how long were students using the computers. Fifty percent (507 users) were at the computers 0-5 hours a week, 33% (333 users) utilized the library 6-10 hours per week, 11% (13 users) used the computers 16-19 hours per week, and 4% (38 users) made use of the computers more than 20 hours per week (three users left this question blank). Examination of library computers for daily usage found 24% (245 users) used the computer less than one hour per day, 19% used the computers for an hour per day (199 users), 37% spent between one and two hours per day at the computers, 14% (142 users) used the computers two to three hours per day, and 4% (42 users) spent more than four hours daily using the library computers.

Themes of Usage Findings

Usage of the library computer for any function was assumed high. While this theory bore out considering the numbers from October 1999, each month afterwards usage has slipped. Some of the high usage in October 1999 corresponds to freshmen usage. These students were new to the campus and found free and open access to computers and printing in an inviting atmosphere. At the time of the last survey in April, the library had begun to move to charging for printing, possibly bringing down computer usage. While turnstile counts and survey results illustrated that library and computer usage is higher than in the past, usage of the library and its computers began to level off.

The work the students performed while at the library computers also did not mirror preconceptions. Members of the general public had higher usage rates of recreation, but all classes of students, undergraduate or graduate, were found to be performing academic work. The rates of research usage exceeded recreation as well. The Scholar's Workstations have provided ECSU students "one stop shopping" for the research, writing, and sending (submitting) of assignments. J. Eugene Smith Library provides the equipment and environment to allow students to remain in one location to conduct these tasks instead of having students move from building to building. The statistics from the surveys illustrate that the students have reacted favorably to the new functions of the library computers.

One of the more interesting findings from the survey was the discovery of students multi-tasking. A steady percentage, between 10%-16%, of each month of the survey found students performing research, recreation and academic all at the same time.

CONCLUDING OBSERVATIONS

At this point, we feel that we are pretty unique in that the library has been very proactive in meeting students' needs, taking advantage of the new building. Moreover, we think that the flexibility of the reference and Systems staff have really contributed to the acceptance and success of the Scholar's Workstations. Below are our observations based on our two-year experience and the use survey we conducted:

1. We strongly recommend that libraries should involve staff when planning changes in the library, including information technologies. This will result in a problem solving approach, teamwork, flexibility, and an atmosphere for growth.
2. Library staff in general, and reference librarians specifically, should not worry about students coming to the library just to use the computers, or to use the computers just for recreational purposes. In the use survey, while we witnessed an increase in "coming to the library just for computers," we also experienced an increase in their use for academic and research work. These academic and research users are consistent users of the library. Oftentimes, it is the inconsistent users that use us for recreational purposes.
3. In our use survey, we detected a rise in academic and research use as the students progress through the grades. Freshmen tend to use library computers more for recreational purposes. We feel that this is a good "lure" to get the freshman in the library doors, and once they feel comfortable, they eventually use the library for academic and research purposes. We also feel that the library Scholar's Workstations have contributed greatly to the information literacy of students, especially with adult learners.
4. We observe that libraries have always for ages been used by students in a multi-purpose manner, e.g., doing research, meeting friends in the library, using library typewriters to fill out income tax forms, writing letters, taking a nap, using the phone, recreational reading, etc. Library staff should not feel uncomfortable when library computers are used in a multi-purpose manner. Moreover, when faculty have begun to load courseware on the campus network, the library should be right in step with the computer center and classroom faculty in these innovative approaches and making sure our computers can support these new student needs.

In conclusion, our experiences and survey study bear out the fact that while it is the librarians' wish to have a library full of users pursuing academic and/or research activities, the trend of the future should point to a more flexible and

holistic environment where the emphasis is on meeting students' ever changing needs. With the growth of the virtual or electronic library and new trends in online courseware (including electronic reserves), we believe that an open and holistic approach in the library's information technology programming will fare far better than a restrictive and piecemeal one.

NOTES

1. Richard J. Bazillion and Connie Braun. *Academic Libraries as the High-tech Gateways: A Guide to Design and Space Decisions.* (Chicago: American Library Association, 1995).

2. Richard J. Bazillion and Connie Braun, "Academic Library Design: Building a 'Teaching Instrument,'" *Computers in Libraries* 14 (February 1994): 12.

3. Connecticut State University System. 1988. Board of Trustee's Resolution 88-49. *Connecticut State University Policy on Sharing of Library Resources.*

4. J. Eugene Smith Library. *Eastern Connecticut State University Library Turnstile Counts and Circulation Counts 1998-2000, 2000,* Eastern Connecticut State University, Willimantic, Connecticut.

5. Eastern Connecticut State University. *Planning and Institutional Research Enrollment Statistics 1995-1999,* 10/5/99, Eastern Connecticut State University, Willimantic, Connecticut.

APPENDIX

Date: Time:

COMPUTER USE SURVEY
J. Eugene Smith Library
Eastern Connecticut State University

1. You are (choose 1)
ECSU student
Major
__ Freshman
__ Sophomore
__ Junior
__ Senior
__ Graduate student
__ ECSU faculty/staff
__ General public
__ Other (please specify)

_____

2. What are you using the computer primarily for right now?
(choose 1)
__ **Research** (ex. using CONSULS, electronic indexes, or Web to find materials or information)
___ CONSULS
___ CD-ROM databases
___ other databases
__ **Academic purposes** (ex. writing papers, working on resume, academic e-mail)
__ **Recreational** (ex. social e-mail, using chat rooms, playing games, visiting non-academic Web sites)

3. How often do you come to the library to use the computers? (pick one that best describes your use)
__ Once a semester
__ Monthly
__ Weekly
__ Daily
__ Never

4. Do you usually come to the library just to use the computers?
__ yes
__ no

5. How many hours a **WEEK** do you use the computers?
__ 0-5
__ 6-10
__ 11-15
__ 16-19
__ 20 or more

6. How many hours a **DAY** do you use the library computers?
__ 1 hour
__ 1-2 hours
__ 2-3 hours
__ 4 hours or more

7. Other computers I use (check all that apply)
__ computer I own
__ computer in residence hall
__ campus computer lab
__ other (computers from work, other libraries, etc.)

Libraries to Labs:
Managing Public Access Computer Labs in an Academic Library Environment

Sheryl Moore

SUMMARY. The contemporary academic library increasingly provides one or more public access computer labs. Students use these labs for word processing, Internet browsing, creating spreadsheets, and other related applications. Providing these types of computer labs in academic libraries is a relatively new development and requires effective management techniques. The purpose of this article is to examine some of the current management concepts, including background, funding, design and implementation, staffing, equipment, software, security and control, and patron relations. Effective management relies on a combination of physical and internal measures as well as a knowledgeable support staff. With the advancement of the Internet and other emerging technologies, the library must strive to maintain its position as a leader in the university environment. Providing computer labs is a valid response to the increasing demand by patrons for electronic resources. *[Article copies available for a fee from The Haworth Document Delivery Service: 1-800-342-9678. E-mail address: <getinfo@haworthpressinc.com> Website: <http://www.HaworthPress.com>* © 2001 by The Haworth Press, Inc. All rights reserved.]

Sheryl Moore is Head of Internet Access Services, Edith Garland Dupre Library, University of Louisiana at Lafayette, 302 East St. Mary Boulevard, Lafayette, LA 70504 (E-mail: sherry@louisiana.edu).

[Haworth co-indexing entry note]: "Libraries to Labs: Managing Public Access Computer Labs in an Academic Library Environment." Moore, Sheryl. Co-published simultaneously in *The Reference Librarian* (The Haworth Information Press, an imprint of The Haworth Press, Inc.) No. 74, 2001, pp. 207-220; and: *Evolution in Reference and Information Services: The Impact of the Internet* (ed: Di Su) The Haworth Information Press, an imprint of The Haworth Press, Inc., 2001, pp. 207-220. Single or multiple copies of this article are available for a fee from The Haworth Document Delivery Service [1-800-342-9678, 9:00 a.m. - 5:00 p.m. (EST). E-mail address: getinfo@haworthpressinc.com].

KEYWORDS. Computer labs, PC labs, academic library labs, public access workstations

How many of us veteran librarians remember the prehistoric days when there was only one public access computer workstation in the library standing conspicuously in the corner of the Reference Department? It was usually accompanied by a tractor-fed printer that typed out results from *ERIC*, the only online database we offered. Relying on our imagination, we anticipated the big day when we could install one or two more databases–on the same workstation. For most of us, however, our vision was perhaps too limited. Today it is common to enter an academic library and find two or three computer labs and several electronic classrooms well-equipped with computers and other technology. At Wayne State's David Adamany Undergraduate Library, there are 700 computer workstations available to students. This new library, which opened in fall 1997, features several different models of computers, some of which are located in a 24-hour study area (*http://www.wayne.edu/imp_profile.html*).

The purpose of my article is to examine some of the current concepts in the management of public access computer labs in an academic library environment. I do not intend to discuss the more detailed technical aspects of the hardware and software, as there are some extremely helpful journal articles, books, listservs, and web sites which serve that purpose. Instead, my contributions are from personal experiences as a lab supervisor for two semesters at Edith Garland Dupre Library, UL Lafayette, and from a survey of the literature on library computer lab management. Topics include background, funding, design and implementation, staffing, equipment, software, security and control, and patron relations.

BACKGROUND

Managing computer labs in academic libraries is a fairly recent topic of discussion despite prolonged deliberations on the library's relevance in the digital age. Dozens of publications have emerged about electronic texts, digitized collections, and the fate of the physical book. Some feared that the Internet would replace us librarians, and that the computing center staff would evict the library staff and take control. All quite relevant concerns, indeed, but during the discussions few contributors seemed to recognize or even celebrate the fact that one way libraries were responding to the call of the Information Highway was by establishing public access Internet labs in small increments. When Dupre Library's first Internet lab was installed in the mid-1990s, my literature search at the time turned up very few articles on the subject. Today, a review of

the literature reveals not only in-depth articles and Web sites but comprehensive books as well (Barclay 2000).

Contemporary high school and college students are born with *intel inside*. Therefore, they expect their campus support services to provide them widespread access to computers. Dorms, student unions, computing centers, academic departments and libraries have responded to their demands. As services develop, academic libraries and the university's computing center have formed unique alliances. Historically, the computing staff was the backbone of the first computer labs in libraries, and often still is today. A recent survey of electronic resources in academic libraries reports that many libraries are still without adequate technical staff support. Twenty percent of the responses revealed that when technical problems arose, the person responding to them was "anyone who is able" (Shaw 1999, 24). They either attempt to troubleshoot on their own, or they rely on the computing center. Thus, until an adequate in-house systems staff is available or some of us achieve computer-guru status from our ordeals, it is essential that we continue to sustain a positive working relationship with the computing center.

FUNDING

Establishing a computer lab obviously requires a healthy amount of funding. Priority must be given to budget planning because of the high cost of equipment, installation and staffing. Maintenance contracts may seem expensive at the time but they will undoubtedly pay for themselves over time. At Dupre Library one of our most troublesome printers was constantly going to the repair shop. It was always a relief to know that we were covered by such an agreement.

Today, funding can originate from several sources. Student technology enhancement fees assessed by academic institutions are a fairly new but significant source of funding. What is a more appropriate use of technology funding than a library computer lab? Dupre Library was fortunate to receive a technology grant which first established and later expanded its Internet computer lab. Technology fee grants were also allocated to several electronic classrooms across campus. Academic libraries should be more aware of the benefits of technology fee resources (see Photo 1).

University administration remains a key participant in funding of computer labs. When collaborative agreements with other university departments are made in the establishment of a lab, the administration may be more generous than usual. That being said, the library must be cautious in maintaining a good balance between funding for computer labs and other important services and collections. Supplemental resources may also be secured through grants, friends of the library organizations, and other external funding. Finally, ob-

PHOTO 1. The Dupre Library STEP Lab, Funded by the Student Technology Enhancement Program

taining educational licensing agreements for software and discounts for equipment are appropriate measures which can significantly reduce original costs.

DESIGN AND IMPLEMENTATION

Integrating computer labs into existing buildings can be a challenge. A little creative thinking is essential. Many older buildings lack the necessary wiring for incorporating technology. Finding space is another challenge. Stacks often need shifting, index tables removed, and walls constructed in order to make room for a new lab. Some other considerations include:

- Keep the needs of the user in mind. In addition to lab workstations, consider distributing workstations with Internet access and the library's catalog throughout the building. Many libraries are applying the concept of an *information commons,* integrating key service desks and computer labs in one area.
- Encourage collaborative learning by providing students large areas for group projects. Some library labs have set aside computers and work tables for this purpose.

- Plan for adequate lighting and wiring. There can never be enough acti-vated data lines in the building. Pay attention to minor details, such as ar-ranging for recycle bins in the lab.
- Security, security, security. Expensive equipment should be protected so that it won't be tampered with or stolen. Locking devices, security sys-tems installed at exits, and software security are standard measures that need to be taken (see Figures 1 and 2).
- Multimedia. Most labs forbid game playing, which typically uses sound. However, sometimes sound is necessary, such as speaking devices for the visually impaired. If so, consider proper placement of multimedia equipment so that others are not disturbed, or purchase headphones or other accessories.
- ADA requirements. Assistive and adaptive technology fortunately now exist for disabled patrons. We need to encourage and provide access to them. Information is available on the Web and in print (Mates 2000).

FIGURE 1. Cables Hooked to Adhesive Plates Mounted to Equipment Pre-vents Theft and Accidents

Tufnut Security Devices (http://www.tufnut.com)
Reprinted with permission.

FIGURE 2. Cable Anchors and Adaptors Lock Components Together

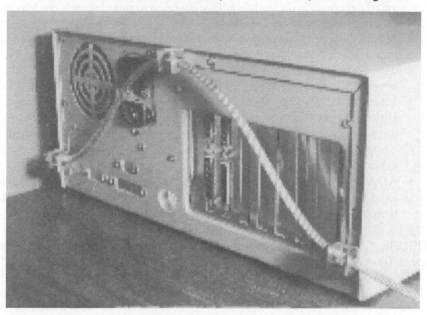

Tufnut Security Devices (http://www.tufnut.com)
Reprinted with permission.

There are many other factors related to lab design. Privacy, number of workstations, systems equipment storage and work room location, community access areas and proximity to service desks are just a few.

STAFFING

Student Assistants

Many of the computer lab battlefields are staffed by undergraduate and graduate students. This provides a good combination of youthful enthusiasm, innovation and expertise. While they can call on their supervisor(s) for backup assistance, the students provide immediate support for printing, hardware and software troubleshooting, user support and other areas.

At Dupre Library, positions in the computer lab are very much in demand. Students are attracted to the high pay, the flexible working hours, and the opportunity to work with computers. After taking applications and resumes, we frequently wind up with students majoring in engineering and computer sci-

ence. Employment in the lab gives them a chance to get their feet wet before they move on, several semesters later, to graduate assistantships or other positions within their major department.

While working with computers is the main attraction to potential student assistants, they need to be conscious that they are employees in a public environment. During the hiring period, supervisors must emphasize that they are expected to be professional, friendly, dependable and articulate. They will be required to maintain a working knowledge of computer applications, lab policies and procedures. As always, they should not be exempt from any of the lab's policies. Most student employees are valuable assets to library computer labs. They are generally friendly, fun, responsible, and bright. As fellow workers, they deserve our respect and support. Who knows–one of our students may be the next Bill Gates.

Professional Staffing

Although student assistants are a precious commodity, smaller labs such as reference centers may not be able to depend on them or on computing center support. If so, library staff should maintain a familiarity with all features of the lab. Not only should we know the contents of the programs or databases, we should also be able to prepare them for access, promote them, and protect them. Responsibilities in this type of lab environment are "mechanical as well as intellectual" (McDermott 2000, 17).

Much has been eloquently written about how we have changed our roles to adapt to our evolving environment. I will only stress that if our libraries are going to provide computers in every aisle, we must learn to be technologically self-sufficient. As the Purdue University Libraries Strategic Plan states, we must be "approachable, knowledgeable, and technically skillful" (Purdue 2000).

EQUIPMENT

It would appear that we have reached the limits of what it is possible to achieve with computer technology, although one should be careful with such statements, as they tend to sound pretty silly in 5 years.

–John von Neumann (1949)

Von Neumann, a prominent mathematician and early computer scientist, was very perceptive. It seems as if the more computers we install in our labs, the faster they are destined to become dinosaurs. Unfortunately, we do not have the luxury of waiting for the next level of Pentium to arrive before we

send our equipment request list to the Purchasing Division. Points for consideration include:

- PC or Macintosh? PC computers dominate in libraries, but Macs and other types are there as well. Each has its own merits and purposes, but there is generally more help available to library PC users. In addition, if you do provide more than PCs, your staff will need to be trained to support both systems.
- Provide support equipment such as printers, scanners, uninterruptible power supply (UPS), and video monitors in strategic places.
- Again, be sure there is adequate wiring, lighting and security.
- Pay-for-printing is becoming a trend in libraries, due to rising costs of printer paper and ink. As the electronic resources survey reveals, "charging for printing of online search results appears to be necessary for many libraries to recoup rising costs of paper and toner" (Shaw 1999, 25).
- As universities move towards a cash-free environment, smart/swipe cards are gaining in popularity. A number of libraries are already using smart cards in their computer labs for login and pay-for-printing purposes. The allocation of smart cards has raised questions: How does the library provide access to the non-affiliated public who do not have smart cards? If smart cards are sold to the public, will the price be any different than student cards? Should designated workstations and printers be set aside? More discussion is needed on this concern.
- Workstations for disabled users should be purchased or modified to comply with ADA requirements. All furniture should have an ergonomic style.
- Consider the computer disk drive options. Should you provide CD- ROM, DVD, floppy, zip, or temporary drives? One unpopular option is to forbid downloading to computer drives. An unconventional alternative for users is downloading to virtual drive file storage on the Web. *DriveBackup.com* offers information on various providers of this service *(http://www.drivebackup.com/).*
- Be sure to include maintenance contracts and warranties when acquiring equipment. Also try to purchase computers with minimal software. As one lab supervisor stated in a personal interview at Dupre Library, "Computers with built-in programs are way too loaded for our requirements. All we need are the library catalog, the Internet, and a few applications" (Lance Chance 12 Jan. 2001). It is cheaper and more efficient to buy them with modest built-ins and add software later. However, don't sacrifice on details. Compiling a list of specific requirements takes time. If you are given funding with a very short deadline, it is best to be ready with an already prepared list.

MAINTENANCE

Failure to perform routine maintenance on computer equipment and accessories could result in undesirable consequences. For example, printers are especially prone to breakdowns if they are not cleaned and sent for regular service. The other usual preventive measures apply, including emptying the cache and temporary drives, cleaning the mouse tracking balls, using compressed air on the keyboard, and other steps. Backup devices including UPS or surge suppressors should be included in the equipment list. A systems workroom is recommended for day-to-day operations. Student assistants and lab supervisors should have a private area to work on problems, install software, repair equipment, and schedule lab hours.

SOFTWARE

Program applications and software for security and control are abundant. Those involved in computer lab administration should investigate what other libraries are offering. From a review of the library literature and informal polling, the most common application software provided include word processing, spreadsheets, library catalogs and databases, publishing software, the two standard Web browsers, and plug- ins such as Adobe Acrobat, Real Player, and Shockwave. Standard accessories including WordPad, telnet, and FTP are usually provided.

The needs of the user should be regarded when contemplating software. Offering a program that nobody seems to want or use is a waste of time and effort. On the other hand, providing email and games is asking for trouble if the lab is designated for educational purposes. Eric Schnell points out that limiting personal email and other services on public access workstations creates

> more opportunities for patrons wishing to access instructional and research resources. . . . With less people spending hours reading email or playing chess, more patrons had access to online resources. (Schnell 2000)

Installing more than one computer lab in the library also deters students from using a lab for non-designated purposes. At Dupre Library, our students and public users are considerate about utilizing the Reference Lab for online research (see Photo 2). They take advantage of the other larger lab for Internet browsing and other functions. In addition, they are able to access the Internet and the library's catalog from workstations scattered throughout the library. Recent advances in remote patron authentication, wireless technology, and further developments may also provide users with alternative methods of re-

PHOTO 2. The Edith Garland Dupre Library Reference Online Research Center

motely accessing the library's electronic resources. Wireless technology is a significant development which has led to a debate on its limitations in academic institutions. It can be expensive, and older wireless networks tend to operate at slow speeds (Young 2000).

Since academic library computer labs are intended to support the educational mission of the institution, lab administrators should consider allowing students to load their own educational software onto designated workstations. Plugins for unique instructional functions such as *HyperChem Web Viewer,* a free helper application that allows 3-D molecule viewing, may be required as well. Electronic resources in CD-ROM and DVD format are still widely used. Alternative solutions to providing access to these tools include designating several standalone workstations, creating a small LAN, or providing access over a server. For more information, see Chapter Five, "CD-ROM," of Barclay's *Managing Public-Access Computers* (Barclay 2000, 77-87).

SECURITY AND CONTROL

Security and control are essential to the management of library computer labs. Sixty-five percent of libraries surveyed recently claimed to use some type of desktop security on their computer workstations (Shaw 1999, 22). Access to specified applications is effectively supported through the use of a networked

server, such as *Windows NT Server*. Advantages include tighter security and the ease of loading software applications to some or all of the workstations in the network. The University of Texas at Austin has gone even further by developing their own client-server based software. The *UT-LabMan Win 95/98/NT Client Software* is used to login users, load applications, enforce time limits, control workstation access, administer waiting lists, and perform several other functions (*http://www.utexas.edu/cc/ds/labman/about/specs.htm*). One distinct feature is the LabMan web site, which allows a user to view specific details on the status of a lab and its workstations. The user has the option of signing up on a waiting list for a specified station. Wayne State's undergraduate library has recently acquired the LabMan software. Accounts are only available for students and WSU affiliates and must be activated for login.

Implementing a server is desirable but does have its disadvantages. Among them are that software applications generally require a networking license for loading onto a server. Also, programs and queue printing may take longer to run (Barclay 2000, 75). Furthermore, server maintenance is not for the uninitiated.

Good security and control are equivalent to a strong health insurance policy. Peace of mind and a strategy for backup and repairs are as essential as undergoing regular medical checkups. At a minimum, the administrator should implement the computer operating system's security attributes. For instance, the NT Server Policy Editor can be initiated; two levels of administrative passwords can be incorporated in the CMOS Setup parameters (for more information, go to InfoPeople Project/Bill Moseley's web site on *Public Access Computer Security for Windows 95/98* at *http://www.infopeople.org/Security*). Other minimal security solutions include requiring user login, running Netscape in Kiosk mode, which disables many toolbar functions, using the disable functions of the Internet Explorer Administration Kit (*http://www.microsoft.com/windows/ieak/*), locking in web addresses by fake proxy, and several additional techniques. Of course, old-fashioned monitoring by the lab assistants works quite well, too.

Maximum security and control are best achieved with a combination of these minimum methods and standard commercial security and control packages. An effective package may provide virus defense, hard disk protection, file deletion, access control, system setting management, and a host of other features. *Fortres 101 (http://www.fortres.com), WinSelect/KIOSK 5.0 (http://www.winselect.com), LibraryGuardian (http://www.libraryguardian.com),* and *Bardon's WinU (http://www.bardon.com/winn.htm)* are popular programs that are worth the cost.

WinSelect, for example, provides lab administrators several functions: configuration options, browser control, short-cut key disable, boot security, opening, saving, and printing options (see Graphic 1). It and other programs run discretely in the background, alerting the lab supervisor of any problems.

GRAPHIC 1. WinSelect Windows NT/2000 Options

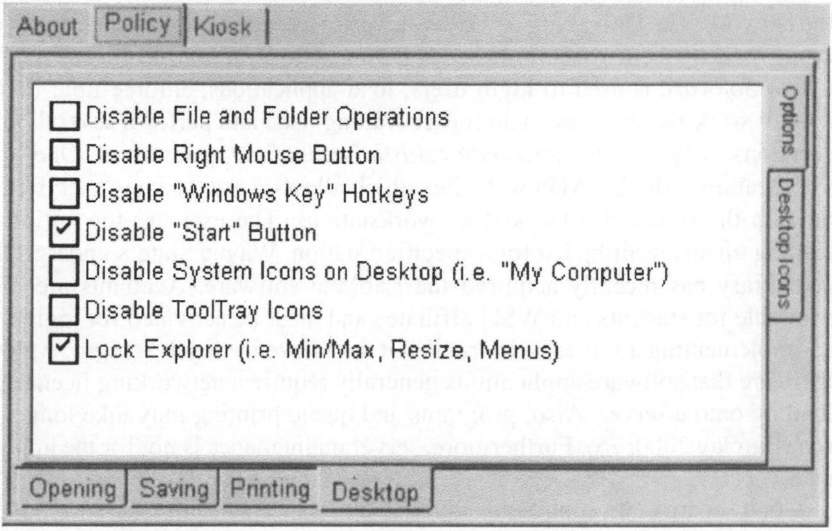

About | Policy | Kiosk |

☐ Disable File and Folder Operations
☐ Disable Right Mouse Button
☐ Disable "Windows Key" Hotkeys
☑ Disable "Start" Button
☐ Disable System Icons on Desktop (i.e. "My Computer")
☐ Disable ToolTray Icons
☑ Lock Explorer (i.e. Min/Max, Resize, Menus)

Options Desktop Icons

Opening | Saving | Printing | Desktop

Reprinted with permission.

Since no strategy is foolproof, administrators should have additional backup resources for effective security and control. These range from providing 15 minute express workstations to possessing a software utility specifically designed for hard drive backup (such as *Norton Ghost 2000, http://www.symantec.com*). Written policies, physical security, and privacy protection are other essential management strategies. For valuable guidance, the *PACS-L* and *Web4LIB* listservs frequently discuss library computer lab management issues *(PACS-L* information available at *http://info.lib.uh.edu/pacsl.html* and *Web4LIB* information available at *http://sunsite.berkeley.edu/Web4Lib/*). A web resource guide, "The Library Web Manager's Reference Center: Public Access Measures," available at *http://sunsite.berkeley.edu/Web4Lib/RefCenter/lwmrcpublic.html* and Barclay's book chapters on software and security are also indispensable (Barclay 2000, 61-76; 115-135).

PATRON RELATIONS

Establishing a computer lab and an effective management strategy are really just the beginning. The fun part is the development of patron relations, including workstation assistance and patron education. Although we can draw on our previous experiences with library-patron relations, we must prepare ourselves–and our lab assistants–for the heavy demands which our computer

users will cast upon us. These interactions inspire several questions and comments:

- If you build it, they will come. This is a tired old cliche, but it's true. Whether or not we publicize our labs, our students will be irresistibly drawn to them like moths to a lightbulb. As Jennifer Cargill and Ronald D. Hay confirm, their "laboratories function at nearly 100 percent capacity most hours of operation" (Cargill and Hay 1995, 150).
- As electronic resources multiply, our users will also require some form of initial instruction in their application. Will we librarians continue our responsibility for instruction, or will we leave it up to their fellow students? While trained student assistants can provide some instruction, there are limits to what they can perform, especially if it involves the explanation of online databases.
- In a related question, how do we help users when they are accessing our resources from the dorm room or their apartment? Email, telephone, and feedback forms on the Web are some current methods. Although remote patron assistance is beyond the scope of this article, it is a very important development in the changing roles of librarians.
- How much assistance and workstation access do we provide to the public user? Libraries like Wayne State are already providing restricted access to community users. This is partly due to the increasing demand for lab resources from our paying students. Fortunately, public libraries are now also providing computer lab resources for the community.
- We need more librarians with technological skills. Who has not observed the abundance of position announcements for systems librarians? It can take up to two years to find and hire a qualified candidate as a result of the high demand. Library schools need to be attentive to the demand for library graduates who are trained in systems administration. In turn, university administrators should realize that it may take a higher salary to attract a qualified candidate.

CONCLUSION

To maintain our position as leaders in the university environment, we must continue to respond to the user's increasing demand for electronic resources. Although funding may be limited, access is essential. Supplying space for these resources is a priority, and may require a creative solution such as converting study carrels into mini-computer labs. Providing public access computers also requires security and control. Effective management relies on a combination of physical and internal measures and a high quality support staff.

The library continues to adapt to the phenomenon of the Internet and other emerging technologies. Ten years ago, who would have expected that we would depend on resources named *Google* and *Yahoo!*? This transformation has been costly but beneficial. The library has reached beyond its walls to attract more users, both academic and public. It remains to be seen what innovative computer resources will debut in the future. The library should anticipate, examine and then, most probably, welcome the opportunities these resources will provide.

REFERENCES

Barclay, Donald A. 2000. *Managing Public-Access Computers: A How-to-do-it Manual for Librarians.* New York: Neal-Schumann Publishers, Inc.

Cargill, Jennifer and Ronald D. Hay. 2000. Beneficial Collaboration: Meeting Information Delivery Needs. In *Books, Bytes, and Bridges: Libraries and Computer Centers in Academic Institutions.* Chicago: American Library Association.

Mates, Barbara T. 2000. *Adaptive Technology for the Internet: Making Electronic Resources Accessible to All.* Chicago: American Library Association.

McDermott, Irene E. 2000. Digital Grease Monkeys: Librarians Who Dare to Repair. *Searcher,* 8: 10-17.

Purdue University Libraries. 2000. Strategic Directions and Goals: User-Centered Services. In *Plan 2004: A Framework for Action. http://www.lib.purdue.edu/plan2004/strategic_directions_and_goals.html.* Accessed 1/15/01.

Schnell, Eric H. *Limiting Email (and other such services) on Public Access Workstations. http://bones.med.ohio-state.edu/eric/email.html.* Accessed 1/12/01.

Shaw, Beth Hansen. 1999. *Managing Electronic Resources: A Survey of Current Practices in Academic Libraries.* ERIC ED 434 658.

Young, Jeffrey R. 1999. Are Wireless Networks the Wave of the Future? *The Chronicle of Higher Education,* 5 February, sec. A.

Index

Abbate, J., 12
Abels, E.G., 115,120
Achoo site, 182
ACRL (Association of College and
    Research Libraries),
    20,34,180
Active learning, 23-26
ADA (Americans with Disabilities
    Act), 211
Adams, M., 91-101
Adobe Acrobat, 215
Afrocentric sites, evaluation of,
    141-144
ALA (American Library Association),
    106-109,125,157
Allen, G., 28,36
AltaVista, 77
Analysis processes. *See* Evaluation and
    analysis processes
Andereesen, M., 8
AOL (America Online), 50
Ardis, S.B., 75-89
Argus Clearinghouse, 129
ARL (Association of Research
    Libraries), 15-16,46,
    104-105,113-118
Armenian genocide-denial sites,
    evaluation of, 135-137
Arms, W.Y., 119
Arnold, E.S., 11
Arnold, S.E., 11
ARPANET, 8
Asaro, R., 121-164
AskERIC, 110-111
AskJeeves, 39
Assurance, 116

Badics, J., 24-25,35
Barclay, D.A., 209,220
Bartosz, K., 187-204
Bates, M.E., 34
Bates-Stacy, K.K., 101
Bazillion, R.J., 189,204
Beaucoup site, 173-175
Benchmarks, 110-111
Berners-Lee, T., 131
Bibliographic Instruction. *See*
    Teaching and training
Bicknell-Holmes, T., 35
Bina, E., 8
Blanke, H., 157
Blythe, B., 120
Borgman, C.L., 47
Brandt, D.S., 37-47
Braun, C., 204
Breivik, P., 30,35-36
Bristow, A., 118
Brown, C., 189
BRS, 4-5
Bryant, E., 16,34
Buckland, M., 10
Bunge, C., 22,35,104-105,111,119
Burke, M., 12
Bush, V., 2-3,11
Bushallow-Wilbur, G.D., 118

California HealthCare Foundation, 185
Calvert, P.J., 158
Campbell, F., 118
Cargill, J., 219-220
Carr, D.W., 21,35
Caruso, C., 155